THE
MEANING *of*
MARRIAGE

REDEEMER

THE
MEANING *of*
MARRIAGE

Facing the Complexities
of Commitment with the
Wisdom of God

TIMOTHY KELLER

WITH KATHY KELLER

DUTTON

DUTTON
Published by Penguin Group (USA) Inc.
375 Hudson Street, New York, New York 10014, U.S.A.
Penguin Group (Canada), 90 Eglinton Avenue East, Suite 700, Toronto, Ontario M4P 2Y3,
Canada (a division of Pearson Penguin Canada Inc.); Penguin Books Ltd, 80 Strand, London
WC2R 0RL, England; Penguin Ireland, 25 St Stephen's Green, Dublin 2, Ireland (a division
of Penguin Books Ltd); Penguin Group (Australia), 250 Camberwell Road, Camberwell,
Victoria 3124, Australia (a division of Pearson Australia Group Pty Ltd); Penguin Books
India Pvt Ltd, 11 Community Centre, Panchsheel Park, New Delhi—110 017, India;
Penguin Group (NZ), 67 Apollo Drive, Rosedale, Auckland 0632, New Zealand
(a division of Pearson New Zealand Ltd); Penguin Books (South Africa) (Pty) Ltd,
24 Sturdee Avenue, Rosebank, Johannesburg 2196, South Africa

Penguin Books Ltd, Registered Offices: 80 Strand, London WC2R 0RL, England

Published by Dutton, a member of Penguin Group (USA) Inc.

First printing, November 2011
10

REGISTERED TRADEMARK—MARCA REGISTRADA

LIBRARY OF CONGRESS CATALOGING-IN-PUBLICATION DATA
Keller, Timothy J., 1950–
The meaning of marriage : facing the complexities of commitment with the wisdom
of God / Timothy Keller with Kathy Keller.—1st ed.
p. cm
Includes bibliographical references and index.
ISBN 978-0-525-95247-3 (alk. paper)
1. Marriage—Religious aspects—Christianity. I. Keller, Kathy (Kathy Louise)
II. Title III. Title: Facing the complexities of commitment with the wisdom of God.
BV835. K455 2011
248.8' 44—dc23
2011032434

Printed in the United States of America
Set in ITC Galliard Std.
Designed by Leonard Telesca

To Our Friends for Four Decades

Our journeys have taken us to different places
but never away from one another,
or from each other,
or from our First Love

Adele and Doug Calhoun

Jane and Wayne Frazier

Louise and David Midwood

Gayle and Gary Somers

Cindy and Jim Widmer

CONTENTS

INTRODUCTION

God, the best maker of all marriages,
Combine your hearts in one.

—William Shakespeare, *Henry V*

A Book for Married People

Think of this book as a tree supplied by three deep roots. The first is my thirty-seven-year marriage to my wife, Kathy.[1] She helped me write this book, and she herself wrote chapter 6, Embracing the Other. In chapter 1, I caution readers about the way contemporary culture defines "soul mate" as "a perfectly compatible match." Nevertheless, when we first began to spend time with each other, we each realized that the other was a rare fit for our hearts. I first met Kathy through her sister, Susan, who was a student with me at Bucknell University. Susan often spoke to Kathy about me and to me about Kathy. As a young girl, Kathy had been led toward the Christian faith by C. S. Lewis's *The Chronicles of Narnia*.[2] She urged Susan to recommend them to me. I read and was moved by the books and by other Lewis volumes that I subsequently studied. In 1972, we both enrolled at the same school, Gordon-Conwell Theological Seminary on Boston's North Shore, and there we quickly came to see that we shared the "secret thread" that Lewis says is the thing that turns people into close friends—or more.

> You may have noticed that the books you really love are bound together by a secret thread. You know very well what is the common quality that makes you love them, though you cannot put it into words:. . . . Are not all lifelong friendships born at the moment when at last you meet another human being who has some inkling . . . of that something which you were born desiring . . . ?[3]

Our friendship grew into romance and engagement, and then from a fragile new marriage into a tested and durable one. But this only happened through the "pearls before swine" speech, the Great Dirty Diaper Conflict, the "smashing the wedding china" affair, and other infamous events in our family history that will be described in this book—all mileposts on the very bumpy road to marital joy. Like most young modern couples, we found that marriage was much harder than we expected it to be. At the conclusion of our wedding ceremony, we marched out singing to the hymn "How Firm a Foundation." Little did we know how relevant some of the lines would be to the arduous and painful work of developing a strong marriage.

> When through fiery trials, thy pathway shall lie,
> My grace all-sufficient will be thy supply.
> For I will be with thee, thy troubles to bless
> And sanctify to thee thy deepest distress.[4]

This book, therefore, is for those spouses who have discovered how challenging day-to-day marriage is and who are searching for practical resources to survive the sometimes overwhelming "fiery trials" of matrimony and to grow through them. Our society's experience with marriage has given us the metaphor "the honeymoon is over." This is a book for those who have experienced this as a literal truth and may have fallen back to earth with a thud.

A Book for Unmarried People

The second source for this book is a long pastoral ministry in a city with millions (and a church with thousands) of single adults. Our congregation, Redeemer Presbyterian Church in Manhattan, is a rarity—a very large church that has been for years composed predominantly of singles. Several years ago, when we had about four thousand people in attendance, I asked a very prominent church consultant, "How many churches do you know of our size with three thousand singles?" He answered, "Your church is unique, as far as I know."

Ministering in the center of New York City in the late 1980s, Kathy and I were constantly struck by the deep ambivalence with which Western culture views marriage. It was then we began to hear all the now society-wide objections—marriage was originally about property and is now in flux, marriage crushes individual identity and has been oppressive for women, marriage stifles passion and is ill-fitted to psychological reality, marriage is "just a piece of paper" that only serves to complicate love, and so on. But beneath these philosophical objections lies a snarl of conflicted personal emotions, born out of many negative experiences with marriage and family life.

Early in our New York City ministry, in the fall of 1991, I preached a nine-week series on marriage. It has since been the most listened-to set of sermons or talks the church has ever produced. I had to begin the series by giving some justification for devoting weeks of teaching on being married to a congregation of mainly unmarried people. My main rationale was that single people today need a brutally realistic yet glorious vision of what marriage is and can be. What I said then fits single readers today, and this book is for them, too.

In preparation for writing this, I read a host of Christian books on marriage. Most of them were written to help married couples work through specific problems. This volume will be useful for that as well, but its primary goal is to give both married and unmarried people a vision for what marriage is according to the Bible. That will help married people correct mistaken views that might be harming their marriage, and it will help single people stop destructively over-desiring marriage or destructively dismissing marriage altogether. Also, a Bible-based marriage book will help each reader have a better idea of who he or she should consider as a prospective mate.

A Book about the Bible

There is a third source for the material in this book, and it is the most foundational. Though this book is rooted in my personal experience of marriage and ministry, it is even more grounded in the teachings of the Old and New Testaments. Nearly four decades ago, as theological students, Kathy and I studied the Biblical teachings on sex, gender, and marriage. Over the next fifteen years, we worked them out in our own marriage. Then, over the last twenty-two years, we have used what we learned from both Scripture and experience to guide, encourage, counsel, and instruct young urban adults with regard to sex and marriage. We offer the fruit of these three influences to you in this book.

But the foundation of it all is the Bible.

In the Bible there are three human institutions that stand

apart from all others—the family, the church, and the state. There's nothing in the Bible about how schools should be run, even though they are crucial to a flourishing society. There's nothing there about business corporations or museums or hospitals. In fact, there are all sorts of great institutions and human enterprises that the Bible doesn't address or regulate. And so we are free to invent them and operate them in line with the general principles for human life that the Bible gives us.

But marriage is different. As the Presbyterian *Book of Common Worship* says, God "established marriage for the welfare and happiness of humankind." Marriage did not evolve in the late Bronze Age as a way to determine property rights. At the climax of the Genesis account of creation we see God bringing a woman and a man together to unite them in marriage. The Bible begins with a wedding (of Adam and Eve) and ends in the book of Revelation with a wedding (of Christ and the church). Marriage is God's idea. It is certainly also a human institution, and it reflects the character of the particular human culture in which it is embedded. But the concept and roots of human marriage are in God's own action, and therefore what the Bible says about God's design for marriage is crucial.

That is why the Presbyterian service of marriage says that marriage is "instituted by God, regulated by his commandments, blessed by our Lord Jesus Christ." What God institutes he also regulates. If God invented marriage, then those who enter it should make every effort to understand and submit to his purposes for it. We do this in many other aspects of our lives. Think of buying a car: If you purchase a vehicle, a machine well beyond your own ability to create, you will certainly take up the owner's manual and abide by what the designer says the car needs by way of treatment and maintenance. To ignore it would be to court disaster.

Plenty of people who do not acknowledge God or the Bible, yet who are experiencing happy marriages, are largely abiding by God's intentions, whether they realize it or not. But it is far better if we are conscious of those intentions. And the place to discover them is in the writings of the Scripture.

What if you want to read this book and you don't share the assumption that the Bible is the authoritative revelation from God? Maybe you appreciate the Bible in some regards, but you don't trust it on the subjects of sex, love, and marriage. These topics of ancient wisdom are at great variance with contemporary Western sensibilities, and therefore the Bible has a reputation for being "regressive" on those subjects. We would urge you give this book a try anyway. Over the years both Kathy and I have taught at length on marriage, and I have spoken on marriage at innumerable weddings. There we've learned that most people who do not share our view of the Bible or even our Christian faith are often shocked by how penetrating the Biblical perspective on marriage is and how relevant it is to their own situations. So often people have told me after the ceremony, "I'm not religious at all, but that was the most helpful and practical explanation of marriage I've ever heard."

It is hard to get a good perspective on marriage. We all see it through the inevitably distorted lenses of our own experience. If you came from an unusually stable home, where your parents had a great marriage, that may have "made it look easy" to you, and so when you get to your own marriage you may be shocked by how much it takes to forge a lasting relationship. On the other hand, if you have experienced a bad marriage or a divorce, either as a child or an adult, your view of marriage may be overly wary and pessimistic. You may be *too* expectant of relationship problems and, when they appear, be too ready to say, "Yup, here it goes," and to give up. In other words, any kind of background experience of marriage may make you ill equipped for it yourself.

So where can you go for a comprehensive view of marriage? There are many good "how-to" volumes usually written by counselors that can be very helpful. In a few years, however, marriage manuals look dated. In the Bible you have teaching that has been tested by millions of people over centuries and in multiple cultures. Do we have any other resource on marriage like that?

The Plan of the Book

The substance of this book draws on St. Paul's great passage on marriage in Ephesians 5, not only because it is so rich and full in itself, but also because it connects and expounds on the other most important Biblical text on marriage, Genesis 2. In chapter 1, we put Paul's discussion into today's cultural context and lay out two of the most basic teachings by the Bible on marriage—that it has been instituted by God and that marriage was designed to be a reflection of the saving love of God for us in Jesus Christ. That is why the gospel helps us to understand marriage and marriage helps us to understand the gospel. In chapter 2, we present Paul's thesis that all married partners need the work of the Holy Spirit in their lives. The work of the Spirit makes Christ's saving work real to our hearts, giving us supernatural help against the main enemy of marriage: sinful self-centeredness. We need the fullness of the Spirit if we are to serve one another as we should.

Chapter 3 gets us into the heart of what marriage is all about—namely, love. But what is love? This chapter discusses the relationship of feelings of love to acts of love and the relationship of romantic passion to covenantal commitment. Chapter 4 addresses the question of what marriage is *for*: It is a way for two spiritual friends to help each other on their journey to become the persons

God designed them to be. Here we will see that a new and deeper kind of happiness is found on the far side of holiness. Chapter 5 lays out three basic skill sets with which we can help each other on that journey.

Chapter 6 discusses the Christian teaching that marriage is a place where the two sexes accept each other as differently gendered and learn and grow through it. Chapter 7 helps single people use the material in this book to live the single life well and to think wisely about seeking marriage themselves. Finally, chapter 8 takes on the subject of sex, why the Bible confines it to marriage, and how, if we embrace the Biblical view, it will play out in both the single life and in marriage.[5]

In this book we examine the Christian understanding of marriage. It is based, as we have said, on a straightforward reading of Biblical texts. This means we are defining marriage as a lifelong, monogamous relationship between a man and a woman. According to the Bible, God devised marriage to reflect his saving love for us in Christ, to refine our character, to create stable human community for the birth and nurture of children, and to accomplish all this by bringing the complementary sexes into an enduring whole-life union. It needs to be said, therefore, that this Christian vision for marriage is not something that can be realized by two people of the same sex. That is the unanimous view of the Biblical authors, and therefore that is the view that we assume throughout the rest of this book, even though we don't directly address the subject of homosexuality.

The Bible's teaching on marriage does not merely reflect the perspective of any one culture or time. The teachings of Scripture challenge our contemporary Western culture's narrative of individual freedom as the only way to be happy. At the same time, it critiques how traditional cultures perceive the unmarried adult to be less than a fully formed human being. The book of Genesis radically critiques the institution of polygamy, even though it was the accepted cultural practice of the time, by vividly depicting the misery and havoc it plays in family relationships, and the pain it caused, especially for women. The New Testament writers, in a way that startled the pagan world, lifted up long-term singleness as a legitimate way to live.[6] In other words, the Biblical authors' teaching constantly challenged their own cultures' beliefs—they were not simply a product of ancient mores and practices. We cannot, therefore, write off the Biblical view of marriage as one-dimensionally regressive or culturally obsolete. On the contrary, it is bristling with both practical, realistic insights and breathtaking promises about marriage. And they come not only in well-stated propositions but also through brilliant stories and moving poetry.[7] Unless you're able to look at marriage through the lens of Scripture instead of through your own fears or romanticism, through your particular experience, or through your culture's narrow perspectives, you won't be able to make intelligent decisions about your own marital future.

Ephesians 5:18–33
(New International Version—1984)

18 Do not get drunk on wine, which leads to debauchery. Instead, be filled with the Spirit. 19 Speak to one another with psalms, hymns and spiritual songs. Sing and make music in your heart to the Lord, 20 always giving thanks to God the Father for everything, in the name of our Lord Jesus Christ. 21 Submit to one another out of reverence for Christ.

22 Wives, submit to your husbands as to the Lord. 23 For the husband is the head of the wife as Christ is the head of the church, his body, of which he is the Savior. 24 Now as the church submits to Christ, so also wives should submit to their husbands in everything.

25 Husbands, love your wives, just as Christ loved the church and gave himself up for her 26 to make her holy, cleansing her by the washing with water through the word, 27 and to present her to himself as a radiant church, without stain or wrinkle or any other blemish, but holy and blameless. 28 In this same way, husbands ought to love their wives as their own bodies. He who loves his wife loves himself. 29 After all, no one ever hated his own body, but he feeds and cares for it, just as Christ does the church 30— for we are members of his body. 31 "For this reason a man will leave his father and mother and be united to his wife, and the two will become one flesh." 32 This is a profound mystery—but I am talking about Christ and the church. 33 However, each one of you also must love his wife as he loves himself, and the wife must respect her husband.

ONE

THE SECRET OF MARRIAGE

*A man shall leave his father and mother and be united
to his wife, and the two will become one flesh. This is a
profound mystery. . . .*

Ephesians 5:31–32

I'm tired of listening to sentimental talks on marriage. At weddings, in church, and in Sunday school, much of what I've heard on the subject has as much depth as a Hallmark card. While marriage is many things, it is anything *but* sentimental. Marriage is glorious but hard. It's a burning joy and strength, and yet it is also blood, sweat, and tears, humbling defeats and exhausting victories. No marriage I know more than a few weeks old could be described as a fairy tale come true. Therefore, it is not surprising that the only phrase in Paul's famous discourse on marriage in Ephesians 5 that many couples can relate to is verse 32, printed above. Sometimes you fall into bed, after a long, hard day of trying to understand each other, and you can only sigh: "This is all a profound mystery!" At times, your marriage seems to be an unsolvable puzzle, a maze in which you feel lost.

I believe all this, and yet there's no relationship between human beings that is greater or more important than marriage. In the Bible's account, God himself officiates at the first wedding

(Genesis 2:22–25). And when the man sees the woman, he breaks into poetry and exclaims, "At last!"[1] Everything in the text proclaims that marriage, next to our relationship to God, is the most profound relationship there is. And that is why, like knowing God himself, coming to know and love your spouse is difficult and painful yet rewarding and wondrous.

The most painful, the most wonderful—this is the Biblical understanding of marriage, and there has never been a more important time to lift it up and give it prominence in our culture.

The Decline of Marriage

Over the last forty years, the "leading marriage indicators"—empirical descriptions of marriage health and satisfaction in the United States—have been in steady decline.[2] The divorce rate is nearly twice the rate it was in 1960.[3] In 1970, 89 percent of all births were to married parents, but today only 60 percent are.[4] Most tellingly, over 72 percent of American adults were married in 1960, but only 50 percent were in 2008.[5]

All of this shows an increasing wariness and pessimism about marriage in our culture, and this is especially true of younger adults. They believe their chances of having a good marriage are not great, and, even if a marriage is stable, there is in their view the horrifying prospect that it will become sexually boring. As comedian Chris Rock has asked, "Do you want to be single and lonely or married and bored?" Many young adults believe that these are indeed the two main options. That is why many aim for something in the middle between marriage and mere sexual encounters—cohabitation with a sexual partner.

This practice has grown exponentially in the last three decades. Today more than half of all people live together before getting married. In 1960, virtually no one did.[6] One quarter of all unmarried women between the ages of twenty-five and thirty-nine are currently living with a partner, and by their late thirties over 60 percent will have done so.[7] Driving this practice are several widespread beliefs. One is the assumption that most marriages are unhappy. After all, the reasoning goes, 50 percent of all marriages end in divorce, and surely many of the other 50 percent must be miserable. Living together before marriage, many argue, improves your chances of making a good marriage choice. It helps you discover whether you are compatible before you take the plunge. It's a way to discover if the other person can really keep your interest, if the "chemistry" is strong enough. "Everyone I know who's gotten married quickly—and failed to live together [first]—has gotten divorced," said one man in a Gallup survey for the National Marriage Project.[8]

The problem with these beliefs and assumptions, however, is that every one of them is almost completely wrong.

The Surprising Goodness of Marriage

Despite the claim of the young man in the Gallup survey, "a substantial body of evidence indicates that those who live together before marriage are more likely to break up after marriage."[9] Cohabitation is an understandable response from those who experienced their own parents' painful divorces, but the facts indicate that the cure may be worse than the alleged disease.[10]

Other common assumptions are wrong as well. While it is true that some 45 percent of marriages end in divorce, by far the greatest percentage of divorces happen to those who marry before the age of eighteen, who have dropped out of high school, and who have had a baby together before marrying. "So if you are a reasonably well-educated person with a decent income, come from an intact family and are religious, and marry after twenty-five without having a baby first, your chances of divorce are low indeed."[11]

Many young adults argue for cohabitation because they feel they should own a home and be financially secure before they marry.[12] The assumption is that marriage is a financial drain. But studies point to what have been called "The Surprising Economic Benefits of Marriage."[13] A 1992 study of retirement data shows that individuals who were continuously married had 75 percent more wealth at retirement than those who never married or who divorced and did not remarry. Even more remarkably, married men have been shown to earn 10–40 percent more than do single men with similar education and job histories.

Why would this be? Some of this is because married people experience greater physical and mental health. Also, marriage provides a profound "shock absorber" that helps you navigate disappointments, illnesses, and other difficulties. You recover your equilibrium faster. But the increased earnings probably also come from what scholars call "marital social norms." Studies show that spouses hold one another to greater levels of personal responsibility and self-discipline than friends or other family members can. Just to give one example, single people can spend money unwisely and self-indulgently without anyone to hold them accountable. But married people make each other practice saving, investment, and delayed gratification. Nothing can mature character like marriage.[14]

Perhaps the main reason that young adults are wary of marriage is their perception that most couples are unhappy in their marriages. Typical is a Yahoo! Forum in which a twenty-four-year-old male announced his decision to never marry. He reported that as he had shared his decision over the past few months to his married friends, everyone laughed and acted jealous. They all said to him that he was smart. He concluded that at least 70 percent of married people must be unhappy in their relationships. A young woman in a response to his post agreed with his anecdotal evidence. That fit her own assessment of her married friends. "Out of 10 married couples . . . 7 are miserable as hell," she opined, and added, "I'm getting married next year because I love my fiancé. However, if things change, I won't hesitate to divorce him."[15]

Recently the *New York Times Magazine* ran an article about a new movie called *Monogamy* by Dana Adam Shapiro.[16] In 2008, Shapiro came to realize that many of his married thirty-something friends were breaking up. In preparation for making a film about it, he decided to do an oral history of breaking up—collecting fifty in-depth interviews with people who had seen their marriages dissolve. He did no research, however, on happy, long-term marriages. When asked why he did not do that, he paraphrased Tolstoy: "All happy couples are the same. Which is to say they're just boring."[17] "So it will not be surprising," the *Times* reporter concluded, "to say that the film, in the end, takes a grim, if not entirely apocalyptic, view of relationships." The movie depicts two people who love each other very much but who simply "can't make it work." In other interviews about the movie, the filmmaker expresses his belief that it is extraordinarily hard though not completely impossible for two modern persons to love each other without stifling one another's individuality and freedom. In the reporter's words, the never-married Shapiro, though he hopes to be married someday and does not believe his film is anti-marriage, finds an "intractable difficulty" with monogamy. In this he reflects the typical view of young adults, especially in the more urban areas of the United States.

As the pastor of a church containing several thousand single people in Manhattan, I have talked to countless men and women who have the same negative perceptions about marriage. However, they underestimate the prospects for a good marriage. All surveys tell us that the number of married people who say they are "*very* happy" in their marriages is high—about 61–62 percent—and there has been little decrease in this figure during the last decade. Most striking of all, longitudinal studies demonstrate that two-thirds of those unhappy marriages out there will become happy within five years if people stay married and do not get divorced.[18] This led University of Chicago sociologist Linda J. Waite to say, "the benefits of divorce have been oversold."[19]

During the last two decades, the great preponderance of research evidence shows that people who are married consistently show much higher degrees of satisfaction with their lives than those who are single, divorced, or living with a partner.[20] It also reveals that most people are happy in their marriages, and most of those who are not and who don't get divorced eventually become happy. Also, children who grow up in married, two-parent families have two to three times more positive life outcomes than those who do not.[21] The overwhelming verdict, then, is that being married and growing up with parents who are married are enormous boosts to our well-being.

The History of Marriage

Belief in the desirability and goodness of marriage was once universal, but that is no longer true. A recent report by the University of Virginia's National Marriage Project concluded the following: "Less than a third of the [high school senior] girls and only slightly more than a third of the boys seem to believe . . . that marriage is more beneficial to individuals than the alternatives. Yet this negative attitude is contrary to the available empirical evidence, which consistently indicates the substantial personal as well as social benefits of being married compared to staying single or just living with someone."[22] The report argues that the views of most young adults not only are unsupported by the older consensus, and against the teaching of all the major religions of the world, but they are also unsupported by the accumulated evidence of the most recent social science.

So where did this pessimism come from, and why is it so out of touch with reality? Paradoxically, it may be that the pessimism comes from a new kind of unrealistic idealism about marriage, born of a significant shift in our culture's understanding of the purpose of marriage. Legal scholar John Witte, Jr., says that the earlier "ideal of marriage as a permanent contractual union designed for the sake of mutual love, procreation, and protection is slowly giving way to a new reality of marriage as a 'terminal sexual contract' designed for the gratification of the individual parties."[23]

Witte points out that in Western civilizations there have been several competing views of what the "form and function" of marriage should be.[24] The first two were the Catholic and the Protestant perspectives. Though different in many particulars, they both taught that the purpose of marriage was to create a framework for lifelong devotion and love between a husband and a wife. It was a solemn bond, designed to help each party subordinate individual impulses and interests in favor of the relationship, to be a sacrament of God's love (the Catholic emphasis) and serve the common good (the Protestant emphasis). Protestants understood marriage to be given by God not merely to Christians but to benefit the entirety of humanity. Marriage created character by bringing male and female into a binding partnership. In particular, lifelong marriage was seen as creating the only kind of social stability in which children could grow and thrive. The reason that society had a vested interest in the institution of marriage was because children could not flourish as well in any other kind of environment.[25]

However, Witte explains that a new view of marriage emerged

from the eighteenth- and nineteenth-century Enlightenment. Older cultures taught their members to find meaning in duty, by embracing their assigned social roles and carrying them out faithfully. During the Enlightenment, things began to shift. The meaning of life came to be seen as the fruit of the freedom of the individual to choose the life that most fulfills him or her personally. Instead of finding meaning through self-denial, through giving up one's freedoms, and binding oneself to the duties of marriage and family, marriage was redefined as finding emotional and sexual fulfillment and self-actualization.

Proponents of this new approach did not see the essence of marriage as located in either its divine sacramental symbolism or as a social bond given to benefit the broader human commonwealth. Rather, marriage was seen as a contract between two parties for mutual individual growth and satisfaction. In this view, married persons married for themselves, not to fulfill responsibilities to God or society. Parties should, therefore, be allowed to conduct their marriage in any way they deemed beneficial to them, and no obligation to church, tradition, or broader community should be imposed on them. In short, the Enlightenment privatized marriage, taking it out of the public sphere, and redefined its purpose as individual gratification, not any "broader good" such as reflecting God's nature, producing character, or raising children. Slowly but surely, this newer understanding of the meaning of marriage has displaced the older ones in Western culture.

This change has been a very self-conscious one. Recently, *New York Times* columnist Tara Parker-Pope wrote an article entitled "The Happy Marriage Is the 'Me' Marriage":

> The notion that the best marriages are those that bring
> satisfaction to the individual may seem counterintui-

tive. After all, isn't marriage supposed to be about putting the relationship first? Not anymore. For centuries, marriage was viewed as an economic and social institution, and the emotional and intellectual needs of the spouses were secondary to the survival of the marriage itself. But in modern relationships, people are looking for a partnership, and they want partners who make their lives more interesting . . . [who] help each of them attain valued goals.[26]

This change has been revolutionary, and Parker-Pope lays it out unashamedly. Marriage used to be a public institution for the common good, and now it is a private arrangement for the satisfaction of the individuals. Marriage used to be about *us*, but now it is about *me*.

But ironically, this newer view of marriage actually puts a crushing burden of expectation on marriage and on spouses in a way that more traditional understandings never did. And it leaves us desperately trapped between both unrealistic longings for *and* terrible fears about marriage.

The Search for a Compatible "Soul Mate"

A clear picture of this expectation can be found in a significant study from 2002 by the National Marriage Project entitled "Why Men Won't Commit," by Barbara Dafoe Whitehead and David Popenoe.[27] Men are often accused by women of being "commitment-phobic," afraid of marriage. The authors of the report respond that, indeed, "Our investigation of male attitudes indicates there is evidence to support this popular view." They go on to list the reasons that men give for why they would rather not get married, or at least not soon. Most striking, however, is how many men said they wouldn't marry until they found the "perfect soul mate," someone very "compatible." But what does that mean?

When I met my future wife, Kathy, we sensed very quickly that we shared an unusual number of books, stories, themes, ways of thinking about life, and experiences that brought us joy. We recognized in one another a true "kindred spirit" and the potential for a bond of deep friendship. But this is not what many young adults mean when they speak of a compatible soul mate. According to Whitehead and Popenoe, there were two key factors.

The first is physical attractiveness and sexual chemistry. One of the most obvious themes in Shapiro's interviews with recently divorced people was how crucial it was that they had great sex. One woman explained that she had married her husband because "I thought he was hot." But to her distress, he put on weight and stopped caring about his appearance. The honeymoon was over. And the main way she knew was sex. She made it a rule not to have sex unless she really *wanted* to, but she seldom wanted to: "We had settled into a routine where we only had sex once a week or so, maybe even less. There was no variety, and no real mental or emotional rewards. There was none of the urgency or tension that makes sex so great—that sense of wanting to impress or entice someone. . . ."[28]

In her view, sexual attraction and chemistry were foundational requirements to finding someone compatible.

However, sexual attractiveness was not the number one factor that men named when surveyed by the National Marriage Project. They said that "compatibility" above all meant someone who showed a "willingness to take them as they are and not change them."[29] "More than a few of the men expressed resentment at women who try to change them. . . . Some of the men describe marital compatibility as finding a woman who will 'fit into their life.' 'If you are truly compatible, then you don't have to change,' one man commented."[30]

Making Men Truly Masculine

This is a significant break with the past. Traditionally, men married knowing it would mean a great deal of personal alteration. Part of the traditional understanding of marriage was that it "civilized" men. Men have been perceived as being more independent and less willing and able than women to enter into relationships that require mutual communication, support, and teamwork. So one of the classic purposes of marriage was very definitely to "change" men and be a "school" in which they learned how to conduct new, more interdependent relationships.

The men in the study revealed these very attitudes that marriage was supposed to correct in the past. The researchers asked the men they were interviewing if they realized that women their age face pressures to marry and bear children before they were biologically unable. The men knew full well that their postponement of marriage made it more difficult for peer women to achieve *their* life goals—but they were unsympathetic. As one put it, "That's their issue."[31] Many of the males in the research were adamant that their relationship with a woman should not curtail their freedom at all. The report concluded, "Cohabitation gives men regular access to the domestic and sexual ministrations of a girlfriend while allowing them . . . to lead a more independent life and continue to look around for a better partner."[32]

In a *New York Times* op-ed piece, Sara Lipton drew up a list of prominent married political men who had refused to let marriage confine them sexually to their spouses: Arnold Schwarzenegger, Dominique Strauss-Kahn, Mark Sanford, John Ensign,

John Edwards, Eliot Spitzer, Newt Gingrich, Bill Clinton, and Anthony Weiner. In every case, they had resisted the traditional purposes of marriage: to change their natural instincts, to reign in passions, to learn denial of one's own desires, and to serve others.

The conventional explanation for this is that marriage simply doesn't fit the male nature. In particular, it is said, the most masculine of men do not do well in marriage. It is argued that "a need for sexual conquest, female adulation, and illicit and risky liaisons seems to go along with drive, ambition, and confidence in the 'alpha male.'" But Lipton argued that marriage was traditionally a place where males *became* truly masculine: "For most of Western history, the primary and most valued characteristic of manhood was self-mastery. . . . A man who indulged in excessive eating, drinking, sleeping or sex—who failed to 'rule himself'—was considered unfit to rule his household, much less a polity. . . ."

Lipton, a professor of history at SUNY Stony Brook, concluded, "In the face of recent revelations about the reckless and self-indulgent sexual conduct of so many of our elected officials, it may be worth recalling that sexual restraint rather than sexual prowess was once the measure of a man."[33]

It would be wrong to lay on men the full responsibility for the shift in marriage attitudes. Both men and women today want a marriage in which they can receive emotional and sexual satisfaction from someone who will simply let them "be themselves." They want a spouse who is fun, intellectually stimulating, sexually attractive, with many common interests, and who, on top of it all, is supportive of their personal goals and of the way they are living now.

And if your desire is for a spouse who will not demand a lot of change from you, then you are also looking for a spouse who is almost completely pulled together, someone very "low maintenance" without much in the way of personal problems. You are looking for someone who will not require or demand significant change. You are searching, therefore, for an ideal person—happy, healthy, interesting, content with life. Never before in history has there been a society filled with people so idealistic in what they are seeking in a spouse.

The Irony of Pessimistic Idealism

It seems almost oxymoronic to believe that this new idealism has led to a new pessimism about marriage, but that is exactly what has happened. In generations past there was far less talk about "compatibility" and finding the ideal soul mate. Today we are looking for someone who accepts us as we are and fulfills our desires, and this creates an unrealistic set of expectations that frustrates both the searchers and the searched for.

The search for a satisfying sexual partner is a problem all by itself. Another report by the National Marriage Project states:

> A pornographic media culture may [also] contribute to unrealistic expectations of what their future soul mate should look like. Influenced by the sexy images of young women on MTV, the Internet, and on the runway in televised Victoria's Secret specials, men may be putting off marriage to their current girlfriend in the hopes that they will eventually find a combination "soul mate/babe."[34]

But it would be wrong to pin the culture's change in attitude toward marriage fully on the male quest for physical beauty. Women have been just as affected by our consumer culture. Both men and women today see marriage not as a way of creating character and community but as a way to reach personal life goals. They are all looking for a marriage partner who will "fulfill their emotional, sexual, and spiritual desires."[35] And that creates an extreme idealism that in turn leads to deep pessimism that you will ever find the right person to marry. This is the reason so many put off marriage and look right past great prospective spouses that simply are "not good enough."

This is ironic. Older views of marriage are considered to be traditional and oppressive, while the newer view of the "Me-Marriage" seems so liberating. And yet it is the newer view that has led to a steep decline in marriage and to an oppressive sense of hopelessness with regard to it. To conduct a Me-Marriage requires two completely well-adjusted, happy individuals, with very little in the way of emotional neediness of their own or character flaws that need a lot of work. The problem is—there is almost no one like that out there to marry! The new conception of marriage-as-self-realization has put us in a position of wanting too much out of marriage and yet not nearly enough—at the same time.

In John Tierney's classic humor article "Picky, Picky, Picky," he tries nobly to get us to laugh at the impossible situation our culture has put us in. He recounts many of the reasons his single friends told him they had given up on their recent relationships:

"She mispronounced 'Goethe.'"

"How could I take him seriously after seeing 'The Road Less Traveled' on his bookshelf?"

"If she would just lose seven pounds."

"Sure, he's a partner, but it's not a big firm. And he wears those short black socks."

"Well, it started out great . . . beautiful face, great body, nice smile. Everything was going fine—until she turned around." He paused ominously and shook his head. ". . . she had dirty elbows."[36]

After scanning the extraordinarily unrealistic personal ads (where the kind of partners "wanted" almost never really exist), Tierney decided that young adults were increasingly afflicted with what he called the "Flaw-o-Matic." It is "an inner voice, a little whirring device inside the brain that instantly spots a fatal flaw in any potential mate." What is the purpose of the Flaw-o-Matic? One possibility he considers is that it is something developed by people "determined to get more than they deserve—and [to] reject anyone remotely like themselves." But Tierney concludes that more often than not this is a device that gives us an excuse to stay alone and therefore safe. "In their hearts they know why they need the Flaw-o-Matic. . . . It's not an easy thing to admit, especially not on Valentine's Day, but what they're really trying to say in those personal ads is, 'Wanted: To Be Alone.'"

In other words, some people in our culture want too much out of a marriage partner. They do not see marriage as two flawed people coming together to create a space of stability, love, and consolation—a "haven in a heartless world," as Christopher Lasch describes it.[37] This will indeed require a woman who is "a novelist/astronaut with a background in fashion modeling"[38] or the equivalent in a man. A marriage based not on self-denial but on self-fulfillment will require a low- or no-maintenance partner who meets your needs while making almost no claims on you. Simply put—today people are asking far too much in the marriage partner.

Others, however, do not want too much out of marriage but

rather are deeply afraid of it. Tierney believes, at least among his New York friends, that there are even more people in this category. Those dreaming of the perfect match are outnumbered by those who don't really want it at all, though perhaps they can't admit it. After all, our culture makes individual freedom, autonomy, and fulfillment the very highest values, and thoughtful people know deep down that any love relationship at all means the loss of all three. You can say, "I want someone who will accept me just as I am," but in your heart of hearts you know that you are not perfect, that there are plenty of things about you that need to be changed, and that anyone who gets to know you up close and personal will want to change them. And you also know that the other person will have needs, deep needs, and flaws. That all sounds painful, and it is, and so you don't want all that. Yet it is hard to admit to the world or to yourself that you don't want to be married. And so you put your Flaw-o-Matic on high. That will do it. That will keep marriage away.

But if you avoid marriage simply because you don't want to lose your freedom, that is one of the worst things you can do to your heart. C. S. Lewis put it vividly:

> Love anything, and your heart will certainly be wrung and possibly broken. If you want to make sure of keeping it intact, you must give your heart to no one, not even to an animal. Wrap it carefully round with hobbies and little luxuries; avoid all entanglements; lock it up safe in the casket or coffin of your selfishness. But in that casket—safe, dark, motionless, airless—it will change. It will not be broken; it will become unbreakable, impenetrable, irredeemable. The alternative to tragedy, or at least to the risk of tragedy, is damnation.[39]

So in our society we are too pessimistic about the possibility of "monogamy" *because* we are too idealistic about what we want in a marriage partner, and this all comes because we have a flawed understanding of the purpose of marriage itself.

You Never Marry the Right Person

What, then, is the solution? It is to explore what the Bible itself says about marriage. If we do, the Bible not only explains the cleft stick of our own making that our culture is in but also how to fix it.

The Bible explains why the quest for compatibility seems to be so impossible. As a pastor I have spoken to thousands of couples, some working on marriage-seeking, some working on marriage-sustaining, and some working on marriage-saving. I've heard them say over and over, "Love *shouldn't* be this hard; it should come naturally." In response, I always say something like, "Why believe that? Would someone who wants to play professional baseball say, 'It shouldn't be so hard to hit a fastball?' Would someone who wants to write the greatest American novel of her generation say, 'It shouldn't be hard to create believable characters and compelling narrative?'" The understandable retort is, "But this is not baseball or literature. This is *love*. Love should just come naturally if two people are compatible, if they are truly soul mates."

The Christian answer to this is that *no* two people are compatible. Duke University ethics professor Stanley Hauerwas has famously made this point:

> Destructive to marriage is the self-fulfillment ethic that assumes marriage and the family are primarily institutions of personal fulfillment, necessary for us to become

"whole" and happy. The assumption is that there is someone just right for us to marry and that if we look closely enough we will find the right person. This moral assumption overlooks a crucial aspect to marriage. It fails to appreciate the fact that we always marry the wrong person.

We never know whom we marry; we just think we do. Or even if we first marry the right person, just give it a while and he or she will change. For marriage, being [the enormous thing it is] means we are not the same person after we have entered it. The primary problem is . . . learning how to love and care for the stranger to whom you find yourself married.[40]

Hauerwas shows that the quest for a perfectly compatible soul mate is an impossibility. Marriage brings you into more intense proximity to another human being than any other relationship can. Therefore, the moment you marry someone, you and your spouse begin to change in profound ways, and you can't know ahead of time what those changes will be. So you don't know, you can't know, who your spouse will actually be in the future until you get there.

Many people have bristled at Hauerwas's statement, and that is to be expected, because he intentionally is looking for a head-on collision with the spirit of the age. To create this collision, he generalizes. Of course there are good reasons not to marry someone who is a great deal older or younger, or someone with whom you do not share a common language, and so on. Marriage is hard enough, so why add the burden of bridging those gaps? There are gradations, then, in Hauerwas's Law. Some people are really, *really* the wrong people to marry. But everyone else is still incompatible. All who win through to a good, long-term marriage know what Hauerwas is talking about. Over the years you will go through seasons in which you have to learn to love a person who you didn't marry, who is something of a stranger. You will have to make changes that you don't want to make, and so will your spouse. The journey may eventually take you into a strong, tender, joyful marriage. But it is not because you married the perfectly compatible person. That person doesn't exist.

The people to whom this book is dedicated are friends Kathy and I have known for nearly forty years. Through them we have received intimate views into marriages besides our own. We became close friends with these five other couples during our seminary days; that is, the women became close friends and gradually their husbands became close as well. We have spent nearly four decades writing, calling, e-mailing, visiting, vacationing, grieving, and rejoicing together. Not much about any of our marriages or our lives is hidden from each other. One of the most satisfying evenings we can have together (say, at the beach) is to laugh over our early days of courtship and marriage. How on earth did we ever choose our spouses? From the outside, it must have looked nuts.

Cindy and Jim: She was an elegant woman raised Greek Orthodox, quiet, contemplative, and GREEK. Jim was boisterous, rowdy, funny, and Baptist. Then Gayle and Gary: Besides the seven-year age disparity and serious theological differences, Gary led two-week wilderness tours for college students, while Gayle's idea of camping out was staying at the Holiday Inn. Louise and David: Louise majored in art history and English literature and was serious about her Reformed faith. David was an Assembly of God lay pastor who woke up everyone in the dorm singing praise choruses. Wayne and Jane: According to Jane, Wayne was pure, unrefined gold, hidden under a Pittsburgh exterior, while she was a self-confessed Southern snob. Then there was Doug and Adele:

Adele was a world traveler and seasoned missionary, Doug a younger Inter-Varsity Fellowship staff member. She had just had a bad breakup with another man (also named Doug). On the eve of their wedding, Adele sat on the bottom of Kathy's and my bed and wept, wondering if she was doing the right thing. She now says, "Our marriage began at the gates of doubt and hell but is now at the gates of Heaven."

And, of course, us. Kathy was Presbyterian, opinionated, and sure that she wanted to be involved in urban ministry (based on one reading of *The Cross and the Switchblade* by David Wilkerson). I had just promised the bishop of my tiny rural, non-Presbyterian denomination that I would *not* become Presbyterian, though I was attending a seminary that tilted in that direction.

Not a chance for any of us. But here we all are, happy, thriving, seeing our adult children marry and give birth, helping one another through surgeries and deaths of parents and crises of every sort.

Hauerwas gives us the first reason that no two people are compatible for marriage—namely, that marriage profoundly changes us. But there is another reason. Any two people who enter into marriage are spiritually broken by sin, which among other things means to be self-centered—living life *incurvatus in se*.[41] As author Denis de Rougemont said, "Why should neurotic, selfish, immature people suddenly become angels when they fall in love . . . ?"[42] That is why a good marriage is *more* painfully hard to achieve than athletic or artistic prowess. Raw, natural talent does not enable you to play baseball as a pro or write great literature without enduring discipline and enormous work. Why would it be easy to live lovingly and well with another human being in light of what is profoundly wrong within our human nature? Indeed, many people who have mastered athletics and art have failed miserably at marriage. So the Biblical doctrine of sin explains why marriage—more than anything else that is good and important in this fallen world—is so painful and hard.

Apocalyptic Romance

Modern people make the painfulness of marriage even greater than it has to be, because they crush it under the weight of their almost cosmically impossible expectations. Pulitzer Prize–winning author Ernest Becker believed that modern culture had produced a desire for what he called "apocalyptic romance." At one time we expected marriage and family to provide love, support, and security. But for meaning in life, hope for the future, moral compass, and self-identity we looked to God and the afterlife. Today, however, our culture has taught us to believe that no one can be sure of those things, not even whether they exist. Therefore, Becker argued, something has to fill the gap, and often that something is romantic love. We look to sex and romance to give us what we used to get from faith in God. He writes:

> The love partner becomes the divine ideal within which to fulfill one's life. All spiritual and moral needs now become focused in one individual. . . . In one word, the love object is God. . . . Man reached for a "thou" when the world-view of the great religious community overseen by God died. . . . [43] After all, what is it that we want when we elevate the love partner to the position of God? We want redemption—nothing less.[44]

As a pastor, I've listened to hundreds of plaintive accounts of difficult relationships and lost love. Typical is the case of Jeff and

Sue.[45] Jeff was tall and handsome, the kind of mate Sue had always pictured in her mind. He was talkative and she was shy and quiet in public, so she loved how he took the lead in social gatherings and directed the conversation. Sue was also decisive and future oriented, while Jeff tended to "live in the present." Their differences seemed to complement each other perfectly. Secretly Sue was shocked someone this good-looking would fall for her, while Jeff, who many women found to be too unambitious, was glad to find a girl who was so adoring. Just a year after getting married, however, Jeff's talkativeness looked to Sue like self-absorption and an inability to listen. His lack of career orientation was a bitter disappointment to her. Meanwhile, Sue's quietness looked to Jeff like a lack of transparency, and her soft-spoken shyness masked what he now saw to be a domineering personality. The marriage quickly spiraled down and ended in a speedy divorce.

Disenchantment, the "end of the honeymoon," is common and has been for centuries. It is normal, even inescapable. But the depth of the disillusionment people experience in our time is something new, as is the speed with which marriages collapse. In our day, something has intensified this natural experience and turned it toxic. It is the illusion that if we find our one true soul mate, everything wrong with us will be healed; but that makes the lover into God, and no human being can live up to that.

So why not, as many have proposed, do away with marriage as a dated cultural artifact? Contemporary people are now free and autonomous individuals. We have seen how family, religious institutions, and nation-states—all the basic human social institutions—have been instruments of oppression. Perhaps the time for marriage itself is past. Since the 1970s, there have been predictions that marriage as an institution is dying. More recently, news outlets reported the findings of a Pew Research Center survey that found that nearly 40 percent of Americans believed that marriage is becoming obsolete.[46] As one star of the film *Monogamy* put it in an interview, "In this country, we have kind of failed with marriage. We're so protective of this really sacred but failed institution. There's got to be a new model."[47]

Deep Ambivalence

But despite this popular impression that marriage is on the way out, the critics of marriage are not so sure, and they are conflicted about it. Two typical examples are Laura Kipnis's *Against Love: A Polemic* (Pantheon, 2003) and Pamela Haag's *Marriage Confidential: The Post-Romantic Age of Workhorse Wives, Royal Children, Undersexed Spouses, and Rebel Couples Who Are Rewriting the Rules* (Harper, 2011). Both authors spend a great deal of time making the case that traditional marriage is suffocating and that finding a genuinely contented long-term marriage is a near impossibility. In the end, however, they argue almost begrudgingly that we must keep marriage, though we should be very open to extramarital sexual relationships and encounters.

But Elissa Strauss, reviewing Haag's book in *Slate*, counters that the author "supplies no evidence that trailblazers in non-monogamous relationships are any better off than those in monogamous ones."[48] Indeed, the "rebel couples" Haag does report on—married people who have had affairs or engaged with others through chat rooms—found the experiences unsatisfying or even damaging to their marriages. "Ultimately," Strauss concludes, "there is something strange about Haag's loyalty to the institution of marriage . . . as she all but fully disassembles it."[49] That nicely expresses the deep ambivalence with which the cultured critics of marriage today regard the institution.

There are few if any serious, sustained arguments being made today that society can do without marriage. Even today's critics of monogamy must grant that, at least pragmatically, we can't really live without it.[50] One of the reasons for this is the growing body of empirical research to which we have been referring in this chapter.[51] Evidence continues to mount that marriage—indeed traditional, exclusively monogamous marriage—brings enormous benefits of all kinds to adults, and even more to children and society at large.

But we do not need to look to scientific research to learn that marriage is here to stay. The ubiquity of marriage speaks for itself. There has never been a culture or a century that we know of in which marriage was not central to human life.[52] And even though the number of married people has decreased in our Western culture, the percentage of people who hope to be married has not diminished at all. There is a profound longing we feel for marriage. We hear it in Adam's "At last!" cry at the sight of Eve, the indelible sense that locked within marriage is some inexpressible treasure. And that is right. The problem is not with marriage itself. According to Genesis 1 and 2, we were made for marriage, and marriage was made for us. Genesis 3 tells us that marriage, along with every other aspect of human life, has been broken because of sin.

If our views of marriage are too romantic and idealistic, we underestimate the influence of sin on human life. If they are too pessimistic and cynical, we misunderstand marriage's divine origin. If we somehow manage, as our modern culture has, to do both at once, we are doubly burdened by a distorted vision. Yet the trouble is not within the institution of marriage but within ourselves.

The Great Secret

As we noted at the beginning of this chapter, Paul declared that marriage is a "great mystery." We have recounted all the ways in which marriage is indeed a mystery to us. We cannot discard it, as it is too important, but it overwhelms us. However, the Greek word Paul used, *mysterion*, has a lexical range that also includes the idea of a "secret." In the Bible, this word is used to mean not some esoteric knowledge known only to insiders but rather some wondrous, unlooked-for truth that God is revealing through his Spirit.[53] Elsewhere, Paul uses the term to refer to other revelations of God's saving purposes in the gospel. But in Ephesians 5 he applies this rich term, surprisingly, to marriage. In verse 31 he quotes the final verse of the Genesis account of the first marriage: "A man shall leave his father and mother and be united to his wife, and the two will become one flesh." Then he says, literally, that this is a *mega-mysterion* (verse 32)—an extraordinarily great, wonderful and profound truth that can be understood only with the help of God's Spirit.

But what *is* the secret of marriage? Paul immediately adds, "I am talking about Christ and the church," referring to what he said earlier in verse 25: "Husbands, love your wives as just as Christ loved the church and gave himself up for her. . . ." In short, the "secret" is not simply the fact of marriage per se. It is the message that what husbands should do for their wives is what Jesus did to bring us into union with himself. And what was that?

Jesus *gave himself up* for us. Jesus the Son, though equal with the Father, gave up his glory and took on our human nature (Philippians 2:5ff). But further, he willingly went to the cross and paid the penalty for our sins, removing our guilt and condemnation, so that we could be united with him (Romans 6:5) and take on his nature (2 Peter 1:4). He gave up his glory and power and became a servant. He died to his own interests and looked to our needs and interests instead (Romans 15:1–3). Jesus's sacrificial service to us has brought us into a deep union with him and he with us. And *that*, Paul says, is the key not only to understanding marriage but to living it. That is why he is able to tie the original statement about marriage in Genesis 2 to Jesus and the church. As one commentator put it, "Paul saw that when God designed the original marriage, He already had Christ and the church in mind. This is one of God's great purposes in marriage: to picture the relationship between Christ and His redeemed people forever!"[54]

Here we have a powerful answer to the objection that marriage is inherently oppressive and therefore obsolete. In Philippians 2, Paul tells us that the Son of God did not exploit his equality with the Father, but his greatness was revealed in his willingness to become the Father's servant. He went to the cross, but the Father raised him from the dead.

> This shows us what God is like. . . . The Father, the Son, and the Holy Spirit do not manipulate each other for their own ends. . . . There is no conquest of unity by diversity or diversity by unity. The three are one and the one is three.[55]

But we must not stop there. In Ephesians 5, Paul shows us that even on earth Jesus did not use his power to oppress us but sacrificed everything to bring us into union with him. And this takes us beyond the philosophical to the personal and the practical. If God had the gospel of Jesus's salvation in mind when he established marriage, then marriage only "works" to the degree that approximates the pattern of God's self-giving love in Christ. What

Paul is saying not only answers the objection that marriage is oppressive and restrictive, but it also addresses the sense that the demands of marriage are overwhelming. There is so much to do that we don't know where to start. Start here, Paul says. Do for your spouse what God did for you in Jesus, and the rest will follow.

This is the secret—that the gospel of Jesus and marriage explain one another. That when God invented marriage, he already had the saving work of Jesus in mind.

No False Choices

We should rightly object to the binary choice that both traditional and contemporary marriage seem to give us. Is the purpose of marriage to deny your interests for the good of the family, or is it rather to assert your interests for the fulfillment of yourself? The Christian teaching does not offer a choice between fulfillment and sacrifice but rather mutual fulfillment through mutual sacrifice. Jesus gave himself up; he died to himself to save us and make us his. Now we give ourselves up, we die to ourselves, first when we repent and believe the gospel, and later as we submit to his will day by day. Subordinating ourselves to him, however, is radically safe, because he has already shown that he was willing to go to hell and back for us. This banishes fears that loving surrender means loss of oneself.

So, what do you need to make marriage work? You need to know the secret, the gospel, and how it gives you both the power and pattern for your marriage. On the one hand, the experience of marriage will unveil the beauty and depths of the gospel to you. It will drive you further into reliance on it. On the other hand, a greater understanding of the gospel will help you experience deeper and deeper union with each other as the years go on.

There, then, is the message of this book—that through marriage, "the mystery of the gospel is unveiled."[56] Marriage is a major vehicle for the gospel's remaking of your heart from the inside out and your life from the ground up.

The reason that marriage is so painful and yet wonderful is because it is a reflection of the gospel, which is painful and wonderful at once. The gospel is this: We are more sinful and flawed in ourselves than we ever dared believe, yet at the very same time we are more loved and accepted in Jesus Christ than we ever dared hope. This is the only kind of relationship that will really transform us. Love without truth is sentimentality; it supports and affirms us but keeps us in denial about our flaws. Truth without love is harshness; it gives us information but in such a way that we cannot really hear it. God's saving love in Christ, however, is marked by both radical truthfulness about who we are and yet also radical, unconditional commitment to us. The merciful commitment strengthens us to see the truth about ourselves and repent. The conviction and repentance moves us to cling to and rest in God's mercy and grace.

The hard times of marriage drive us to experience more of this transforming love of God. But a good marriage will also be a place where we experience more of this kind of transforming love at a human level. The gospel can fill our hearts with God's love so that you can handle it when your spouse fails to love you as he or she should. That frees us to see our spouse's sins and flaws to the bottom—and speak of them—and yet still love and accept our spouse fully. And when, by the power of the gospel, our spouse experiences that same kind of truthful yet committed love, it enables our spouses to show us that same kind of transforming love when the time comes for it.

This is the great secret! Through the gospel, we get both the power and the pattern for the journey of marriage. But there is far more to say about what that pattern is and how that power works. So we turn back to Ephesians 5 to understand this great secret more fully.

THE POWER FOR MARRIAGE

Submit to one another out of reverence for Christ.

Ephesians 5:21

Be Filled with the Spirit

The introductory statement for Paul's famous paragraph on marriage in Ephesians is verse 21: "Submit to one another out of reverence for Christ."[1] In English, this is usually rendered as a separate sentence, but that hides from readers an important point that Paul is making. In the Greek text, verse 21 is the last clause in the long previous sentence in which Paul describes several marks of a person who is "filled with the Spirit." The last mark of Spirit fullness is in this last clause: It is a loss of pride and self-will that leads a person to humbly serve others. From this Spirit-empowered submission of verse 21, Paul moves to the duties of wives and husbands.

Modern Western readers immediately focus on (and often bristle at) the word "submit," because for us it touches the controversial issue of gender roles. But to start arguing about that is a mistake that will be fatal to any true grasp of Paul's introductory point. He is declaring that everything he is about to say about marriage assumes that the parties are being filled with

God's Spirit. Only if you have learned to serve others by the power of the Holy Spirit will you have the power to face the challenges of marriage.

The first place in the New Testament that discusses the work of the Spirit at length is in the gospel of John. Jesus considered the teaching so important that he devoted much time to it on the night before he died. When we hear of "spiritual filledness," we think of inner peace and power, and that may indeed be a result. Jesus, however, spoke of the Holy Spirit primarily as the "Spirit of Truth" who will "remind you of everything I have said to you" (John 14:17, 26). The Holy Spirit "will bring glory to me by taking from what is mine and making it known to you" (John 16:14). What does this mean?

"Make known" translates a Greek word meaning a momentous announcement that rivets attention. The Holy Spirit's task, then, is to unfold the meaning of Jesus's person and work to believers in such a way that the glory of it—its infinite importance and beauty—is brought home to the mind and heart.[2] This is why earlier in the letter to the Ephesians, Paul can pray that "the eyes of your heart be enlightened" (1:18), that they might "have power . . . to grasp how wide and long and high and deep is the love of Christ . . ." (3:17–18). The Holy Spirit's ministry is to take truths about Jesus and make them clear to our minds and real to our hearts—so real that they console and empower and change us at our very center.

To be "filled with the Spirit," then, is to live a life of joy, sometimes quiet, sometimes towering. Truths about God's glory and Jesus's saving work are not just believed with the mind but create inner music (Ephesians 5:19) and an inner relish in the soul. "Sing and make music in your heart to the Lord, always giving thanks to God the Father for everything, in the name of our Lord Jesus Christ . . ." (verses 19–20). And because the object of this song is not favorable life circumstances (which can change) but rather the truth and grace of Jesus (which cannot), this heart song does not weaken in times of difficulty.

Immediately after discussing the Spirit-filled life, Paul turns to the subject of marriage, showing the tight connection between marriage and the life in the Spirit. And this connection teaches us two things.

First, the picture of marriage given here is not of two needy people, unsure of their own value and purpose, finding their significance and meaning in one another's arms. If you add two vacuums to each other, you only get a bigger and stronger vacuum, a giant sucking sound. Rather, Paul assumes that each spouse already has settled the big questions of life—why they were made by God and who they are in Christ. No one lives a life of continual joy in God, of course. It is not automatic and constant. If that were the case, Paul would not have had to start verse 18 with an imperative, exhorting them literally to "go on being filled with the Spirit!" We are often running on fumes, spiritually, but we must know where the fuel station is and, even more important, that it exists. After trying all kinds of other things, Christians have learned that the worship of God with the whole heart in the assurance of his love through the work of Jesus Christ is the thing their souls were meant to "run on." That is what gets all the heart's cylinders to fire. If this is not understood, then we will not have the resources to be good spouses. If we look to our spouses to fill up our tanks in a way that only God can do, we are demanding an impossibility.

Submit to One Another

So only if you have the ministry of the Spirit in your life will you be fully furnished to face the challenges of marriage in general.

And only if you are filled with the Spirit will you have all you need to perform the duty of serving your spouse in particular. In verses 22–24, Paul says, controversially, that wives should submit to their husbands. Immediately, however, he tells husbands to love their wives as Christ loved the church and "gave himself up for her" (25), which is, if anything, a stronger appeal to abandon self-interest than was given to the woman. As we shall see, each of these exhortations has a distinct shape—they are not identical tasks. And yet each partner is called to sacrifice for the other in far-reaching ways. Whether we are husband or wife, we are not to live for ourselves but for the other. And that is the hardest yet single most important function of being a husband or a wife in marriage.

Paul is applying to marriage a general principle about the Christian life—namely, that all Christians who really understand the gospel undergo a radical change in the way they relate to people. In Philippians 2:2–3, Paul says bluntly that Christians should "in humility consider others better than [them]selves." Notice that he doesn't say that we should unrealistically try to believe that all others are better than us in every way. That would be nonsense. Rather, we should *consider* and count the interests of others as more important than our own. Elsewhere he says that we should not "please ourselves" but rather should "please our neighbor, for his own good, to build him up. For even Christ did not please himself" (Romans 15:1–3). Paul goes so far as to tell Christians to be *douloi* of one another (Galatians 5:13)— literally bond-servants. Because Christ humbled himself and became a servant and met our needs even at the cost of his own life, now we are like servants—but to one another.

This is a radical, even distasteful image for modern people. Servant? When Paul uses this metaphor, he is not saying that we are to relate to one another in every way that literal bond-servants served their masters in ancient times. What he is saying is this: A servant puts someone else's needs ahead of his or her own. That is how all believers should live with each other. And if all believers are to serve each other in this way, how much more intentionally and intensely should husbands and wives have this attitude toward one another? This principle cannot be dismissed, however we define the husband's role. While Paul writes that the husband is "head" of his wife, whatever it means cannot negate the fact that he is also his wife's Christian brother and bond-servant, according to Galatians 5:13. Husbands and wives must serve each other, must "give themselves up" for one another. That does not destroy the exercise of authority within a human relationship, but it does radically transform it.[3]

It is hard enough in relationships with friends and associates to put their interests ahead of our own and live to please them rather than ourselves. But to practice these principles inside marriage is to practice them in the most intense way. If two spouses are spending a day together, the question of who gets each's pleasure and who gives in can present itself every few minutes. And when it does, there are three possibilities: You can offer to serve the other with joy, you can make the offer with coldness or resentment, or you can selfishly insist on your own way. Only when both partners are regularly responding to one another in the first way can the marriage thrive. But how hard that is!

Kathy and I remember a pivotal incident in our marriage that occurred during a visit to New England, where we had attended seminary. The two of us along with our three sons were staying with friends, and I had hoped very much at some point to be able to get away to the nearby seminary bookstore, just to see what was new, maybe pick up a few interesting books. But I knew that it would mean precious time taken out of the other things we were doing together as a family, and it would leave Kathy with the full burden of caring for the kids. And so I was afraid to ask for it. Instead, I hoped Kathy would guess about my desire and simply offer the time to me. But she didn't do it, and soon I found myself deeply resentful of her "failure" to read my mind. Surely she should know how much I love visiting that bookstore! I work very hard—why doesn't she propose that I take the afternoon away simply because I deserve the break? I began to imagine that she *knew* I wanted to go to the bookstore but was dead set against it.

After a long, grumpy day helping Kathy with the kids and feeling sorry for myself, I finally told her how sorry I was that I had never made it to the bookstore. She was rightfully unhappy with me, and said, "Yes, that would have been inconvenient for me, but I would have *loved* to have given you that freedom. I never get a chance to give you gifts, and you're always helping me with something. You denied me a chance to serve you!"

I immediately realized, however, that *I didn't want to be served.* I didn't want to be in a position where I had to ask for something and receive it as a gift. Kathy was deeply disappointed and insulted that I had robbed her of the opportunity to do so. We drove home in angry silence as I tried to figure out what had happened.

Finally I began to see. I wanted to serve, yes, because that made me feel in control. Then I would always have the high moral ground. But that kind of "service" isn't service at all, only manipulation. But by not giving Kathy an opportunity to serve me, I had failed to serve her. And the reason underneath it all was my pride.

It is at this very point that the Spirit of God helps us so much. In each text, Paul links a willing "servant heart" to the gospel itself. And what is that gospel? It is that you are so lost and flawed, so sinful, that Jesus had to die for you, but you are also so loved and valued that Jesus was glad to die for you. Now you are fully accepted and delighted in by the Father, not because you deserve it but only by free grace. My reluctance to let Kathy serve me was, in the end, a refusal to live my life on the basis of grace. I wanted to earn everything. I wanted no one to give me any favors. I wanted to give undeserved gifts to others—so I could have satisfaction of thinking of myself as a magnanimous person—but I did not want to receive someone else's service myself. My heart still operated like this even though my head had accepted the basic gospel thesis that through faith in Christ we live by God's grace alone.

That gospel message *should* both humble and lift the believer up at the same time. It teaches us that we are indeed self-centered sinners. It perforates our illusions about our goodness and superiority. But the gospel also fills us with more love and affirmation than we could ever imagine. It means we don't need to earn our self-worth through incessant service and work. It means also that we don't mind so much when we are deprived of some comfort, compliment, or reward. We don't have to keep records and accounts anymore. We can freely give and freely receive.

So why did I fail to allow my relationship with Kathy to be shaped by this gospel? It was because I believed the gospel with my head but it wasn't operational in my heart. The ability to serve another person requires the Holy Spirit, the Spirit of Truth, to drive this very gospel into our hearts until it changes us.

The Problem of Self-Centeredness

The main barrier to the development of a servant heart in marriage is what we touched on in the first chapter—the radical self-centeredness of the sinful human heart. Self-centeredness is a havoc-wreaking problem in many marriages, and it is the ever-present enemy of *every* marriage. It is the cancer in the center of a marriage when it begins, and it has to be dealt with. In Paul's classic description of love, in 1 Corinthians 13, he says,

> *Love is patient and kind. It does not envy, it does not boast, is not proud. It is not rude, it is not self-seeking, it is not easily angered, it keeps no record of wrongs.*

(verses 4–5)

Repeatedly Paul shows that love is the very opposite of "self-seeking," which is literally pursuing one's own welfare before those of others. Self-centeredness is easily seen in the signs Paul lists: impatience, irritability, a lack of graciousness and kindness in speech, envious brooding on the better situations of others, and holding past injuries and hurts against others. In Dana Adam Shapiro's interviews of divorced couples, it is clear that this was the heart of what led to marital disintegration. Each spouse's self-centeredness asserted itself (as it always will), but in response, the other spouse got more impatient, resentful, harsh, and cold. In other words, they responded to the self-centeredness of their partner with their own self-centeredness. Why? Self-centeredness by its very character makes you blind to your own while being hypersensitive, offended, and angered by that of others.[4] The result is always a downward spiral into self-pity, anger, and despair, as the relationship gets eaten away to nothing.

But the gospel, brought home to your heart by the Spirit, can make you happy enough to be humble, giving you an internal fullness that frees you to be generous with the other even when you are not getting the satisfaction you want out of the relationship. Without the help of the Spirit, without a continual refilling of your soul's tank with the glory and love of the Lord, such submission to the interests of the other is virtually impossible to accomplish for any length of time without becoming resentful. I call this "love economics." You can only afford to be generous if you actually have some money in the bank to give. In the same way, if your only source of love and meaning is your spouse, then anytime he or she fails you, it will not just cause grief but a psychological cataclysm. If, however, you know something of the work of the Spirit in your life, you have enough love "in the bank" to be generous to your spouse even when you are not getting much affection or kindness at the moment.

To have a marriage that sings requires a Spirit-created ability to serve, to take yourself out of the center, to put the needs of others ahead of your own. The Spirit's work of making the gospel real to the heart weakens the self-centeredness in the soul. It is impossible for us to make major headway against self-centeredness and move into a stance of service without some kind of supernatural help.[5]

The deep happiness that marriage can bring, then, lies on the far side of sacrificial service in the power of the Spirit. That is, you only discover your own happiness after each of you has put the happiness of your spouse ahead of your own, in a sustained way, in response to what Jesus has done for you. Some will ask, "If I put the happiness of my spouse ahead of my own needs— then what do *I* get out of it?" The answer is—happiness. That is what you get, but a happiness through serving others instead of using them, a happiness that won't be bad for you. It is the joy that comes from giving joy, from loving another person in a costly way. Today's culture of the "Me-Marriage" finds this very proposal—of putting the interests of your spouse ahead of your own—oppressive. But that is because it does not look deeply enough into this crucial part of Christian teaching about the nature of reality. What is that teaching?

Christianity asserts, to begin with, that God is triune—that is,

three persons within one God. And from John 17 and other passages we learn that from all eternity, each person—Father, Son,
and Holy Spirit—has glorified, honored, and loved the other
two. So there is an "other-orientation" within the very being of
God. When Jesus Christ went to the cross, he was simply acting
in character. As C. S. Lewis wrote, when Jesus sacrificed himself
for us, he did "in the wild weather of his outlying provinces" that
which from all eternity "he had done at home in glory and glad-
ness."[6]

Then the Bible says that human beings were made in God's
image. That means, among other things, that we were created to
worship and live for God's glory, not our own. We were made
to serve God and others. That means paradoxically that if we try
to put our own happiness ahead of obedience to God, we violate
our own nature and become, ultimately, miserable. Jesus restates
the principle when he says, "Whoever wants to save his life shall
lose it, but whoever loses his life *for my sake* will find it" (Matthew 16:25). He is saying, "If you seek happiness more than you
seek me, you will have neither; if you seek to serve me more than
serve happiness, you will have both."

Paul applies this principle to marriage. Seek to serve one
another rather than to be happy, and you will find a new and
deeper happiness. Many couples have discovered this wonderful,
unlooked-for reality. Why would this be true? It is because marriage is "instituted of God." It was established by the God for
whom self-giving love is an essential attribute, and therefore it
reflects his nature, particularly as it is revealed in the person and
work of Jesus Christ.

Therefore, when facing any problem in marriage, the first thing
you look for at the base of it is, in some measure, self-centeredness
and an unwillingness to serve or minister to the other. The word
"submit" that Paul uses has its origin in the military, and in Greek

it denoted a soldier submitting to an officer. Why? Because when you join the military you lose control over your schedule, over when you can take a holiday, over when you're going to eat, and even over what you eat. To be part of a whole, to become part of a greater unity, you have to surrender your independence. You must give up the right to make decisions unilaterally. Paul says that this ability to deny your own rights, to serve and put the good of the whole over your own, is not instinctive; indeed, it's unnatural, but it is the very foundation of marriage.

This sounds oppressive, but that's just the way relationships work. Indeed, it has been argued that that is how everything works. You must be willing to give something up before it can be truly yours. Fulfillment is on the far side of sustained unselfish service, not the near side. It is one of the universal principles of life:

> Even in social life, you will never make a good impression on other people until you stop thinking about what sort of impression you are making. Even in literature and art, no man who bothers about originality will ever be original: whereas if you simply try to tell the truth (without caring two pence how often it has been told before), you will, nine times out of ten, become original without having noticed it. The principle runs through life from top to bottom. Give up yourself, and you will find your real self. Lose your life and you will save it. . . . Nothing that you have not given away will be really yours. . . . [7]

The Wounds We Carry

There are many reasons that we cannot see our own self-centeredness. One of the main factors that hides it from us is our own history of mistreatment. Many people come to marriage having been seriously hurt by parents, lovers, or former spouses. I am not talking about parents who physically or sexually abuse their children. I'm talking of the more widespread experiences of cold and indifferent parents or of verbally abusive parents who know how to punish children emotionally. Then there are the dating relationships or former marriages in which the other party wronged and betrayed you. All of these experiences can make it extremely difficult to trust the other sex, while at the same time filling you with deep doubts about your own judgment and character. "Woundedness" is compounded self-doubt and guilt, resentment and disillusionment.

We come to one another in marriage with these things in our backgrounds. And when the inevitable conflicts occur, our memories can sabotage us. They can prevent us from doing the normal, day-to-day work of repentance and forgiveness and extending the grace that is so crucial to making progress in our marriages. The reason is that woundedness makes us self-absorbed.

This is not hard to see in others, of course. When you begin to talk to wounded people, it is not long before they begin talking about themselves. They're so engrossed in their own pain and problems that they don't realize what they look like to others. They are not sensitive to the needs of others. They don't pick up the cues of those who are hurting, or, if they do, they only do so in a self-involved way. That is, they do so with a view of helping to "rescue" them in order to feel better about themselves. They get involved with others in an obsessive and controlling way because they are actually meeting their own needs, though they deceive themselves about this. We are always, always the last to see our self-absorption. Our hurts and wounds can make our self-centeredness even more intractable. When you point out selfish behavior to a wounded person, he or she will say, "Well, maybe so, but you don't understand what it is like." The wounds justify the behavior.

There are two ways to diagnose and treat this condition. In our culture, there is still a widespread assumption of basic human goodness. If people are self-absorbed and messed up, it is argued, it is only because they lack healthy self-esteem. So what we should do is tell them to be good to themselves, to live for themselves, not for others. In this view of things, we give wounded people almost nothing but support, encouraging them to stop letting others run their lives, urging them to find out what their dreams are and take steps to fulfill them. That, we think, is the way to healing. But this approach assumes that self-centeredness isn't natural, that it is only the product of some kind of mistreatment. That is a very popular understanding of human nature, but it is worth observing that it is an article of faith—a religious belief, as it were. No major religion in the world actually teaches that, yet this is the popular view of many people in the West.

But this view of things simply doesn't work. A marriage relationship unavoidably entails self-denial, even in the most mundane day-to-day living. It is impossible to have a smooth-running relationship with even one person, let alone two, always feeling that his or her desires should have preeminence because of all he or she has been through in life.

The Christian approach begins with a different analysis of the situation. We believe that, as badly wounded as persons may be, the resulting self-absorption of the human heart was not caused by the mistreatment. It was only magnified and shaped by it. Their mistreatment poured gasoline on the fire, and the flame and smoke now choke them, but their self-centeredness already existed prior to their woundedness. Therefore, if you do nothing but urge people to "look out for number one," you will be setting them up for future failure in any relationship, especially marriage.

This is not to say that wounded people don't need great gentleness, tender treatment, affirmation, and patience. It is just that this is not the whole story. Both people crippled by inferiority feelings *and* those who have superiority complexes are centered on themselves, obsessed with how they look and how they are being perceived and treated. It would be easy to help someone out of an inferiority complex into a superiority complex and leave them no better furnished to live life well.

Confronting Our Self-Centeredness

Paul's description of the effect of the gospel is striking:

> *And he died for all, that those who live should no longer live for themselves but for him who died for them and was raised again.*

(2 Corinthians 5:15)

There is the essence of sin, according to the Bible—living for ourselves, rather than for God and the people around us. This is why Jesus can sum up the entire law—the entire will of God for our lives—in two great commands: to love and live for God rather than ourselves and to love and put the needs of others ahead of our own (Matthew 22:37–40).

All people need to be treated gently and respectfully, especially those who have been wounded. They will be unusually sensitive to rough handling. Nevertheless, all people must be challenged to see that their self-centeredness hasn't been caused by the people who hurt them; it's only been aggravated by the abuse. And they must do something about it, or they're going to be miserable forever.

In Western culture today, you decide to get married because

you feel an attraction to the other person. You think he or she is wonderful. But a year or two later—or, just as often, a month or two—three things usually happen. First, you begin to find out how selfish this wonderful person is. Second, you discover that the wonderful person has been going through a similar experience and he or she begins to tell you how selfish *you* are. And third, though you acknowledge it in part, you conclude that your spouse's selfishness is more problematic than your own. This is especially true if you feel that you've had a hard life and have experienced a lot of hurt. You say silently, "OK, I shouldn't do that—but *you don't understand me.*" The woundedness makes us minimize our own selfishness. And that's the point at which many married couples arrive after a relatively brief period of time.

So what do you do then? There are at least two paths to take. First, you could decide that your woundedness is more fundamental than your self-centeredness and determine that unless your spouse sees the problems you have and takes care of you, it's not going to work out. Of course, your spouse will probably not do this—especially if he or she is thinking almost the exact same thing about you! And so what follows is the development of emotional distance and, perhaps, a slowly negotiated kind of détente or cease-fire. There is an unspoken agreement not to talk about some things. There are some things your spouse does that you hate, but you stop talking about them as long as he or she stops bothering you about certain other things. No one changes for the other; there is only tit-for-tat bargaining. Couples who settle for this kind of relationship may look happily married after forty years, but when it's time for the anniversary photo op, the kiss will be forced.

The alternative to this truce-marriage is to determine to see your own selfishness as a fundamental problem and to treat it more seriously than you do your spouse's. Why? Only you have complete access to your own selfishness, and only you have complete responsibility for it. So each spouse should take the Bible seriously, should make a commitment to "give yourself up." You should stop making excuses for selfishness, you should begin to root it out as it's revealed to you, and you should do so regardless of what your spouse is doing. If two spouses *each* say, "I'm going to treat my self-centeredness as the main problem in the marriage," you have the prospect of a truly great marriage.

It Only Takes One to Begin Healing

Neither of you may take this course of action, or both of you may do it together. But there is a third possibility: It may be that one of you decides to operate on the basis of verse 21 and one of you does not. In this case, let's say, you are the only one who decides, "My selfishness is the thing I am going to work on." What will happen? Usually there is not much immediate response from the other side. But often, over time, your attitude and behavior will begin to soften your partner. He or she can see the pains you are taking. And it will be easier for your spouse to admit his or her faults because you are no longer always talking about them yourself. So if both of you decide to work on your selfishness and minister to the other, the prospects for your marriage are great. But even if only one of you does it, your prospects are still good.

This reminds me of the place in Genesis 4 where God looks at Cain, who is full of self-pity, and says to him, "Cain, sin is crouching at the door. Its desire is for you, but you must master it." What's important to understand is that the principle of self in your life is crouching at your door! It wants to have you, it wants to pounce on you, it wants to devour you. And it's up to you to do something about it. God asks that you deny yourself, that you lose yourself to find yourself. If you try to do this without the work of the Spirit, and without belief in all Christ has done for you, then simply giving up your rights and desires will be galling and hardening. But in Christ and with the Spirit, it will be liberating.

The principle we have been describing serves as a corrective to a couple of the popular models for "having a satisfying marriage."

There is a conservative approach to marriage that puts a great deal of stress on traditional gender roles. It says that the basic problem in marriage is that both husband and wife need to submit to their God-given functions, which are that husbands need to be the head of the family, and wives need to submit to their husbands. There is a lot of emphasis on the differences between men and women. The problem is that an overemphasis could encourage selfishness, especially on the part of the husband.

There is a more secular approach to marriage that says that the real problem in marriage is that you have to get your spouse to recognize your potential and help you to develop it. You must not let your spouse trample all over you. Self-realization is the goal. You've got to develop yourself in your marriage, and if your spouse won't help you do it, you've got to negotiate. And if your spouse won't negotiate, you've got to get out to save yourself. That, of course, also can just pour gas on the fire of selfishness instead of putting it out.[8]

The Christian principle that needs to be at work is Spirit-generated selflessness—not thinking less of yourself or more of yourself but thinking of yourself less. It means taking your mind off yourself and realizing that in Christ your needs are going to be met and are, in fact, being met so that you don't look at your spouse as your savior. People with a deep grasp of the gospel can turn around and admit that their selfishness is the problem and that they're going to work on it. And when they do that, they will often discover an immediate sense of liberation, of waking up from a troubling dream. They see how small-minded they were being, how small the issue is in light of the grand scheme of things. Those who stop concentrating on how unhappy they are find that their happiness is growing. You must lose yourself to find yourself.

The Fear of Christ

There's one more phrase in this crucial introductory verse 21 that we haven't looked at. Paul says that we should submit to one another "out of reverence for Christ." That's what many modern translations say, but literally Paul says we should do it out of the *fear of Christ*. The word "reverence" is too weak to convey what Paul is talking about here, but the word "fear" is also misleading, because to English readers it conveys the idea of fright and dread. What does it mean?

When we go to the Old Testament, where the term "the fear of the Lord" is very common, we come upon some very puzzling usages. Often the fear of the Lord is linked with great joy. Proverbs 28:14 tells us that "Happy is the one who feareth always." How can someone who is constantly in fear be filled with happiness? Perhaps most surprising is Psalm 130:4, where the Psalmist says, "Forgiveness comes from you—therefore you are feared." Forgiveness and grace increase the fear of the Lord. Other passages tell us that we can be instructed and grow in the fear of the Lord (2 Chronicles 26:5; Psalm 34:11), that it is characterized by praise, wonder, and delight (Psalm 40:3; Isaiah 11:3). How can that be? One commentator on Psalm 130 puts it like this: "Servile fear [being scared] would have been diminished, not increased, by forgiveness. . . . The true sense of the 'fear of the Lord' in the Old Testament [then] . . . implies relationship."[9]

Obviously, to be in the fear of the Lord is not to be scared of the Lord, even though the Hebrew word has overtones of respect and awe. "Fear" in the Bible means to be overwhelmed, to be controlled by something. To fear the Lord is to be overwhelmed with wonder before the greatness of God and his love. It means that, because of his bright holiness and magnificent love, you find him "fearfully beautiful." That is why the more we experience God's grace and forgiveness, the more we experience a trembling awe and wonder before the greatness of all that he is and has done for us. Fearing him means bowing before him out of amazement at his glory and beauty. Paul speaks of the love of Christ "constraining" us (2 Corinthians 5:14). What is it that most motivates and moves you? Is it the desire for success? The pursuit of some achievement? The need to prove yourself to your parents? The need for respect from your peers? Are you largely driven by anger against someone or some people who have wronged you? Paul says that if any of these things is a greater controlling influence on you than the reality of God's love for you, you will not be in a position to serve others unselfishly. Only out of the fear of the Lord Jesus will we be liberated to serve one another.

This all seems very theological, but verse 21 shows that it is crucial for how we conduct our relationships.

I once knew a woman in her late thirties who had never married. Her family and her part of the country believed that there was something radically wrong with any woman of that age who was still single. She wrestled greatly with shame and a feeling that she had somehow failed as a woman. Because of this, she also had tremendous unresolved anger against a man she had dated for many years but who had not been willing to marry her.

Finally, she went to a counselor. The therapist told her that she had taken to heart her family's approach to personal value— namely, that a woman had to have a husband and children if she was to have any worth. She was bitter against this man because he had come between her and the thing she felt she *had* to have for her life to have any significance. The counselor then proposed that she throw off such an unenlightened view and devote herself to a career. "If you come to see yourself as a good, accomplished person, then you will see you don't need a man or anyone else to give you a sense of worth." And so she began to shed her family and culture's view of women and to pursue a career. She began to feel better, but she discovered that it didn't enable her to get over her resentment toward her longtime ex-boyfriend.

At about this time, she was going to a church where she was hearing the gospel clearly for the first time. She heard that the gospel was *not* what she had thought—that we amass a good record, give it to God, and then he saves us. Instead, the gospel is that Jesus Christ has amassed a perfect record and when we believe in him, he gives it to us. He lived the life we should have lived and died the death we should have died in our place, so that when we believe, our sins are pardoned and we are "counted righteous in his sight." Then we are completely accepted and loved by the only One in the universe whose opinions really count.

She began to realize that the well-meaning counselor was only half right. Indeed, it was wrong of her to seek self-worth through male affection. That had been a trap. It made her self-regard contingent on what men thought of her. But now she was being asked to look to her career and accomplishments as a way to feel good about herself. That meant that her self-image would be dependent on her success at achieving economic independence. So she said, "Why should I leave the ranks of the many women who make 'family' their whole life to join the ranks of the many men who make 'career' the same thing? Would I not be as devastated then by career setbacks as I have been by romantic ones?

No. I will rest in the righteousness of Christ and learn to rejoice in it. Then I can look at males *or* career and say, 'What makes me beautiful to God is Jesus, not these things.'"

And so she did. Not only did she quickly find that she was much less anxious about her job, but she began to sense more and more the magnitude of God's love through Christ. She began to experience what can be called "emotional wealth"—a sense of being loved so deeply that when someone wrongs us we can afford to be generous, able to forgive. Her anger against her former boyfriend and against men in general subsided. A few years later, to her surprise, she met a man, fell in love, and married. Looking back, there was no doubt in her mind that, if she had married her old boyfriend, it would have been a disaster. She would have looked to him to give her what only Christ can, and therefore she wouldn't have been in a position to serve and care for him.

One of the more dramatic examples of this principle can be found in Laura Hillenbrand's bestselling biography of World War II hero Louis Zamperini. On a mission over the Pacific in 1943, Zamperini's plane crashed into the ocean, killing most on board. After forty-seven days afloat in shark-infested waters, Louie and one other survivor were captured and endured two and a half years of imprisonment, which consisted of almost constant beatings, humiliation, and torture.

Returning after the war, he suffered from severe post-traumatic stress disorder and became an alcoholic. His wife, Cynthia, lost hope for their marriage. Louie spent most of his time dreaming and planning about returning to Japan to murder "the Bird," a Japanese sergeant who had repeatedly assaulted and tormented him in the camps. One night he dreamt that the Bird was looming over him. He reached out to defend himself. A scream woke him up and there he was, straddling Cynthia's chest, his hands locked around the throat of his pregnant wife. Not long afterward, Cynthia announced to him that she was filing for divorce. He was distressed, but even the threat of losing his wife and child could not stop his drinking or his self-destructive behavior. He was too tormented by his past and his bitterness to change, even to save his family.

Then one day in the fall of 1949, Cynthia Zamperini was told by an acquaintance that there was a young evangelist, Billy Graham, preaching downtown at a special series of tent meetings. She attended and "came home alight." She went immediately to Louie and told him she didn't want a divorce, that she had experienced a spiritual awakening, and that she wanted him to accompany her to hear the preaching. After days of resisting, he finally gave in. That night, the young preacher's sermon homed in on the concept of human sin. Louie was indignant. *I am a good man,* he said to himself. But almost as soon as he had the thought, "he felt the lie in it." Several nights later he returned and "walked the aisle," repented, and received Christ as Savior.

Zamperini was immediately delivered of his alcoholism. But more crucially, he felt God's love flood his life and realized that he was able to forgive all those who had imprisoned and tortured him. The shame and sense of powerlessness that had stoked his hate and misery had vanished. His relationship with Cynthia "was renewed and deepened. They were blissful together." In October 1950, Louie was able to return to Japan and speak through an interpreter at the prison where many of his former camp guards were now imprisoned. He spoke about the power of Christ's grace to bring forgiveness, and to the prisoners' shock, he embraced each of them with a loving smile.[10]

I offer this example with hesitation, because dramatic testimonies of instantaneous change can be misleading. Louis Zamperini's emotional wounds were unusually deep and so the work of the Spirit—making God's love in Jesus Christ real to the heart—was also very powerful and dramatic. God's Spirit doesn't always work in such a sudden and obvious way, but he always does this same work. He gave Cynthia hope and Louie release from bitterness, thereby renewing their marriage. He will always have the same influence, whether suddenly or gradually.

> *Therefore, since we have been justified through faith, we have peace with God through our Lord Jesus Christ. . . . And our hope does not put us to shame, because God's love has been poured out into our hearts through the Holy Spirit, who has been given to us.*
>
> (Romans 5:1–2, 5)

Louie Zamperini had been literally tortured, and his inner shame, anger, and fear had eaten up his ability to love and serve others. But each of us comes to marriage with a disordered inner being. Many of us have sought to overcome self-doubts by giving ourselves to our careers. That will mean we will choose our work over our spouse and family to the detriment of our marriage. Others of us hope that unending affection and affirmation from a beautiful, brilliant romantic partner will finally make us feel good about ourselves. That turns the relationship into a form of salvation, and no relationship can live up to that.

Do you see why Paul introduces the subject of marriage with a summons to love one another "out of the fear of Christ"? We come into our marriages driven by all kinds of fears, desires, and needs. If I look to my marriage to fill the God-sized spiritual vacuum in my heart, I will not be in position to serve my spouse. Only God can fill a God-sized hole. Until God has the proper place in my life, I will always be complaining that my spouse is not loving me well enough, not respecting me enough, not supporting me enough.

Growing in the Fear of the Lord

In the end, being filled with the Spirit and the fear of the Lord are basically the same thing. They both refer to an inner spiritual experience and reality, but each phrase brings out different aspects of it.[11] They both take people "out of themselves." Paul says this Spirit-created unselfishness is crucial if we are going to have the marriages we should have. Amazed joy at the sacrifice and love of Christ is the motivation for all New Testament calls to defer, love, and serve. Paul says in Romans 15 that we should not please ourselves because, on the cross, Christ did not please himself. In Philippians 2, the apostle says we should count others better than ourselves, because, in his coming into the world, Christ didn't hold on to his superiority. He came down and emptied himself of his glory and served us, even to the point of dying for us. Let the Holy Spirit bring this home to your heart until you love and sing and wonder. Then, out of this "fear," this fullness of the Spirit, we can turn to our spouses and begin to do what we should do for them.

The question is, then, how can we actually be filled with the Spirit? How can we grow in the fear of the Lord, so we are not controlled by other fears? We could, of course, write many books and only begin to answer the question. But one illustration here will get us thinking in the right direction.

Some years ago, a man who regularly listened to my preaching made a shrewd observation. He said, "When you are well prepared for your sermon, you cite a great variety of sources, but when you aren't well prepared, you just quote C. S. Lewis." He was right. The reason for that is that I have over the years read virtually everything of Lewis that is in print. When I first became a Christian believer, his writings spoke to my questions and concerns more than any other. So I have continually, repeatedly, read his writings until I can recite dozens of passages by heart. I have also read several biographies and lots of his personal letters.

When you dive that deeply into the life and works of a single figure, something interesting happens. You don't just get to know his writings; you get to know how his mind works. You come to know what he *would* have said in answer to a particular question or how he would have responded to a particular incident. The reason that, when I have to speak off the cuff, C. S. Lewis just comes pouring out is because, as it were, he is in there, he is part of my thought life.

What, then, would the effect be if we were to dive even more deeply into *Jesus's* teaching and life and work? What if we were to be so immersed in his promises and summonses, his counsels and encouragements, that they dominated our inner life, capturing our imagination, and simply bubbled out spontaneously when we faced some challenge? How would we live if we instinctively, almost unconsciously, knew Jesus's mind and heart regarding things that confronted us? When you received criticism, you would never be crushed, because Jesus's love and acceptance of you is so deeply "in there." When you gave criticism, you would be gentle and patient, because your whole inner world would be saturated by a sense of Jesus's loving patience and gentleness with you.

This does not mean that every time you are criticized you are consciously, deliberately thinking, "What does Jesus have to say about this?" You won't have to think it out like that, because if Jesus and his Word are so deeply in there, they will just fortify you, lifting you up. They will be part of you. You look at yourself through his eyes; you look at the world through his eyes. It becomes the cast of your whole mind.

This does not happen overnight, of course. It takes years of reflection. It requires disciplined prayer, Bible study and reading, innumerable conversations with friends, and dynamic congregational worship. But unlike learning other thinkers or authors, Jesus's Spirit can come and live within you and spiritually illuminate your heart, so that his gospel becomes glorious in your sight. Then the gospel "dwells in your hearts richly" (Colossians 3:16), and we find the power to serve, to give and take criticism well, to not expect our spouse or our marriage to meet all our needs and heal all our hurts.

Two Ways to "Love"

One of William Blake's "Songs of Experience" shows in the most striking way that there are two ways to conduct a romantic relationship.

> Love seeketh not itself to please,
> Nor for itself hath any care,
> But for another gives its ease,
> And builds a heaven in hell's despair.
>
> Love seeketh only self to please,
> To bind another to its delight,
> Joys in another's loss of ease,
> And builds a hell in heaven's despite.
>
> (from "The Clod and the Pebble")

It is possible to feel you are "madly in love" with someone, when it is really just an attraction to someone who can meet your needs and address the insecurities and doubts you have about yourself. In that kind of relationship, you will demand and control rather than serve and give. The only way to avoid sacrificing your partner's joy and freedom on the altar of your need is to turn to the ultimate lover of your soul. He voluntarily sacrificed himself on the cross, taking what you deserved for your sins against God and others. On the cross he was forsaken and experienced the lostness of hell, but he did it all for us. Because of the loving sacrifice of the Son, you can know the heaven of the Father's love through the work of the Spirit. Jesus truly "built a heaven in hell's despair." And fortified with the love of God in your soul, you likewise can now give yourself in loving service to your spouse.

"We love—because he first loved us" (1 John 4:19).

THREE

THE ESSENCE OF MARRIAGE

For this reason a man shall leave his father and his mother and be united to his wife, and the two shall become one flesh.

Ephesians 5:31 (and Genesis 2:24)

Love and the "Piece of Paper"

I remember some years ago watching a television drama in which a man and a woman who were living together were having an argument over whether to get married. He wanted to go ahead and do it, but she did not. At one point she blew up and said, "Why do we need a piece of paper in order to love one another? I don't need a piece of paper to love you! It only complicates things."

That statement stuck with me, because as a pastor in New York City, I have heard essentially the same thing from younger adults for years. When the woman said, "I don't need a piece of paper to love you," she was using a very specific definition of "love." She was assuming that love is, in its essence, a particular kind of feeling. She was saying, "I feel romantic passion for you, and the piece of paper doesn't enhance that at all, and it may hurt it." She was measuring love mainly by how emotionally desirous she was for his affection. And she was right that the marital legal "piece of paper" would do little or nothing directly to add to the feeling.

But when the Bible speaks of love, it measures it primarily not by how much you want to receive but by how much you are willing to give of yourself to someone. How much are you willing to lose for the sake of this person? How much of your freedom are you willing to forsake? How much of your precious time, emotion, and resources are you willing to invest in this person? And for that, the marriage vow is not just helpful but it is even a test. In so many cases, when one person says to another, "I love you, but let's not ruin it by getting married," that person really means, "I don't love you *enough* to close off all my options. I don't love you enough to give myself to you that thoroughly." To say, "I don't need a piece of paper to love you" is basically to say, "My love for you has not reached the marriage level."

One of the most widely held beliefs in our culture today is that romantic love is all important in order to have a full life but that it almost never lasts. A second, related belief is that marriage should be based on romantic love. Taken together, these convictions lead to the conclusion that marriage and romance are essentially incompatible, that it is cruel to commit people to lifelong connection after the inevitable fading of romantic joy.

The Biblical understanding of love does not preclude deep emotion. As we will see, a marriage devoid of passion and emotional desire for one another doesn't fulfill the Biblical vision. But neither does the Bible pit romantic love against the essence of love, which is sacrificial commitment to the good of the other. If we think of love primarily as emotional desire and not as active, committed service, we end up pitting duty and desire against each other in a way that is unrealistic and destructive. How these two fit together is the subject of this chapter.

The Overly Subjective View of Love

Modern people think of love in such subjective terms that if there is *any* duty involved it is considered unhealthy. Over the years, I have often counseled with people who were quite locked into this conviction. This is particularly true when it comes to sex. Many people believe that if you have sex with your spouse just to please him or her though you are not interested in sex yourself, it would be inauthentic or even oppressive. This is the thoroughly subjective understanding of love-as-passionate-feeling. And often this quickly leads into a vicious cycle. If you won't make love unless you are in a romantic mood at the very same time as your spouse, then sex will not happen that often. This can dampen and quench your partner's interest in sex, which means there will be even fewer opportunities. Therefore, if you never have sex unless there is great mutual passion, there will be fewer and fewer times *of* mutual passion.

One of the reasons we believe in our culture that sex should always and only be the result of great passion is that so many people today have learned how to have sex outside of marriage, and this is a very different experience than having sex inside it. Outside of marriage, sex is accompanied by a desire to impress or entice someone. It is something like the thrill of the hunt. When you are seeking to draw in someone you don't know, it injects risk, uncertainty, and pressure to the lovemaking that quickens the heartbeat and stirs the emotions. If "great sex" is defined in this way, then marriage—the "piece of paper"—will indeed stifle that particular kind of thrill. But this defines sexual sizzle in terms that would be impossible to maintain in any case. The fact is that "the thrill of the hunt" is not the only kind of thrill or passion available, nor is it the best.

Kathy and I were virgins when we married. Even in our day,

that may have been the minority experience, but that meant that on our wedding night we were not in any position to try to impress or entice one another. All we were trying to do was to tenderly express with our bodies the oneness we had first begun feeling as friends and which had then had grown stronger and deeper as we fell in love. Frankly, that night I was clumsy and awkward and fell asleep anxious and discouraged. Sex was frustrating at first. It was the frustration of an artist who has in his head a picture or a story but lacks the skills to express it.

However, we had fortunately not learned to use sex to impress, nor to mix the thrill of the dangerous and the forbidden with sexual stimulation and mistake it for love. With sex, we were trying to be vulnerable to each other, to give each other the gift of barefaced rejoicing in one another, and to know the pleasure of giving one another pleasure. And as the weeks went by, and then the years, we did it better and better. Yes, it means making love sometimes when one or even both of you are not "in the mood." But sex in a marriage, done to give joy rather than to impress, can change your mood on the spot. The best sex makes you want to weep tears of joy, not bask in the glow of a good performance.

Consumer or Covenant?

In sharp contrast with our culture, the Bible teaches that the essence of marriage is a sacrificial commitment to the good of the other. That means that love is more fundamentally action than emotion. But in talking this way, there is a danger of falling into the opposite error that characterized many ancient and traditional societies. It is possible to see marriage as merely a social transaction, a way of doing your duty to family, tribe, and society. Traditional societies made the family the ultimate value in life, and so marriage was a mere transaction that helped your family's interests. By contrast, contemporary Western societies make the individual's happiness the ultimate value, and so marriage becomes primarily an experience of romantic fulfillment. But the Bible sees *God* as the supreme good—not the individual or the family—and that gives us a view of marriage that intimately unites feeling *and* duty, passion *and* promise. That is because at the heart of the Biblical idea of marriage is the covenant.

Throughout history there have always been consumer relationships. Such a relationship lasts only as long as the vendor meets your needs at a cost acceptable to you. If another vendor delivers better services or the same services at a better cost, you have no obligation to stay in a relationship to the original vendor. In consumer relationships, it could be said that the individual's needs are more important than the relationship.

There have also always been covenantal relationships. These are relationships that are binding on us. In a covenant, the good of the relationship takes precedence over the immediate needs of the individual. For example, a parent may get little emotionally out of caring for an infant. But there has always been an enormous social stigma attached to any parent who gives up their children because rearing them is too hard and unrewarding. For most people, the very idea of that is unthinkable. Why? Society still considers the parent-child relationship to be a covenantal one, not a consumer relationship.

Sociologists argue that in contemporary Western society the marketplace has become so dominant that the consumer model increasingly characterizes most relationships that historically were covenantal, including marriage. Today we stay connected to people only as long as they are meeting our particular needs at an acceptable cost to us. When we cease to make a profit—that is, when the relationship appears to require more love and affirmation from us than we are getting back—then we "cut our losses" and drop the relationship. This has also been called "commodifi-cation," a process by which social relationships are reduced to economic exchange relationships, and so the very idea of "cove-nant" is disappearing in our culture. Covenant is therefore a con-cept that is increasingly foreign to us, and yet the Bible says it is the essence of marriage, so we must take some time to under-stand it.

The Vertical and the Horizontal

The serious reader of the Bible will see covenants literally every-where throughout the entire book. "Horizontal" covenants were made between human beings. We see them established between close friends (1 Samuel 18:3; 20:16) as well as between nations. But the most prominent covenants in the Bible are "vertical," covenants made by God with individuals (Genesis 17:2) as well as with families and peoples (Exodus 19:5).

But in several ways, the marriage relationship is unique and is the most deeply covenantal relationship possible between two human beings. In Ephesians 5:31, Paul evokes the idea of the covenant when he fully quotes Genesis 2:24, perhaps the most well-known text in the Old Testament regarding marriage.

> *For this reason a man will leave his father and mother*
> *and cleave to his wife, and the two shall become one flesh.*

There in Genesis 2:22–25 we see the first marriage ceremony. The Genesis text calls what happens "cleaving." This archaic English term (which you can find in the King James Version) conveys the strength of the Hebrew verb, which modern transla-tions render "united to." It is a Hebrew word that literally means to be glued to something. Elsewhere in the Bible, the word "cleave" means to unite to someone through a covenant, a binding promise, or oath.[1]

Why do we say that marriage is the most deeply covenantal relationship? It is because marriage has both strong horizontal *and* vertical aspects to it. In Malachi 2:14, a man is told that his spouse "is your partner, the wife of your marriage covenant" (cf. Ezekiel 16:8). Proverbs 2:17 describes a wayward wife who has "left the partner of her youth, and ignored the covenant she made before God." The covenant made between a husband and a wife is done "before God" and therefore with God as well as the spouse. To break faith with your spouse is to break faith with God at the same time.

This is the reason that so many traditional Christian wedding services have both a set of questions as well as a set of vows. In the questions, each spouse is asked something like this:

> Will you have this woman to be your wife? And will you make your promise to her in all love and honor, in all duty and service, in all faith and tenderness—to live with her, and cherish her, according to the ordinance of God, in the holy bond of marriage?

Each spouse answers "I will" or "I do"—but notice they are not speaking to each other. They are looking forward and technically answering the minister, who asks them the questions. What they are really doing is making a vow to God before they turn and make vows to one another. They are "speaking vertically" before they speak horizontally. They get to hear the other person stand up before God, their families, and all the authority structures of church and state and swear loyalty and faithfulness to the other. Now, building on this foundation, they take one another by the hand and say something like this:

> I take you to be my lawful and wedded husband, and I
> do promise and covenant, before God and these wit-
> nesses, to be your loving and faithful wife. In plenty
> and in want, in joy and in sorrow, in sickness and in
> health, as long as we both shall live.

Imagine a house with an A-frame structure. The two sides of the home meet at the top and hold one another up. But underneath, the foundation holds up both of the sides. So the covenant with and before God strengthens the partners to make a covenant with each other. Marriage is therefore the deepest of human covenants.

Love and Law

What, then, is a covenant? It creates a particular kind of bond that is disappearing in our society. It is a relationship far more intimate and personal than a merely legal, business relationship. Yet at the same time, it is far more durable, binding, and unconditional than one based on mere feeling and affection. A covenant relationship is a stunning blend of law and love.

As we have seen, modern thought does not see duty and passion to be compatible or capable of mutually stimulating interdependence. British philosopher Bertrand Russell made early-twentieth-century arguments for the expression of sexual love outside of marriage. While conceding that we should not dissociate "sex from serious emotion and from feelings of affection," he nevertheless argued that sexual activity should be marked by intense passion and romantic delight, and that can flourish only as long as it is free and spontaneous. "It tends to be killed by the thought it is a duty."[2] This thought is now considered common sense—

namely, that love must be the response to spontaneous desire, never a response to a legal oath or promise.

But the Biblical perspective is radically different. Love needs a framework of binding obligation to make it fully what it should be. A covenant relationship is not just intimate despite being legal. It is a relationship that is *more* intimate *because* it is legal. Why would that be so?

We can begin by observing that making a binding, public marriage vow to another person is an enormous act of love in and of itself. Someone who says, "I love you, but we don't need to be married" may be saying, "I don't love you enough to curtail my freedom for you." The willingness to enter a binding covenant, far from stifling love, is a way of enhancing, even supercharging it. A wedding promise is proof that your love is actually at marriage level as well as a radical act of self-giving all by itself.

There is another way in which the legality of marriage augments its personal nature. When dating or living together, you have to prove your value daily by impressing and enticing. You have to show that the chemistry is there and the relationship is fun and fulfilling or it will be over. We are still basically in a consumer relationship, and that means constant promotion and marketing. The legal bond of marriage, however, creates a space of security where we can open up and reveal our true selves. We can be vulnerable, no longer having to keep up facades. We don't have to keep selling ourselves. We can lay the last layer of our defenses down and be completely naked, both physically and in every other way.

This blending of law and love fits our deepest instincts. G. K. Chesterton pointed out that when we fall in love we have a natural inclination not just to express affection but to make promises to each other. Lovers find themselves almost driven to make vow-like claims. "I will *always* love you," we say when we are at the height of passion, and we know that the other person, if he or she is in love with us, will want to hear those words. Real love, the Bible says, instinctively desires permanence. The great Biblical love poem Song of Solomon ends with these kinds of declarations:

> *"Place me like a seal over your heart, like a seal on your arm, for love is as strong as death, its ardor as unyielding as the grave.*
> *It burns like a blazing fire, like a mighty flame.*
> *Many waters cannot quench love; rivers cannot wash it away."*

(8:6–7)

When two people genuinely love each other, and are not simply using one another for sex, status, or self-actualization, they don't want the situation to ever change. Each wants assurances of enduring commitment, and each delights to give those assurances. So the "law" of vows and promises fits our deepest passions at the present. But it is also something the love of our heart needs in order to have security about the future.

The Promise of Future Love

Years ago I attended a wedding in which the couple wrote their own vows. They said something like this: "I love you, and I want to be with you."[3] The moment I heard it I realized what all historic Christian marriage vows had in common, regardless of their theological and denominational differences. The people I was listening to were expressing their current love for each other, and that was fine and moving. But that is not what marriage vows are. That is not how a covenant works. Wedding vows are not a declaration of present love but a mutually binding promise of future love. A wedding should not be primarily a celebration of how loving you feel now—that can safely be assumed. Rather, in a wedding you stand up before God, your family, and all the main institutions of society, and you promise to *be* loving, faithful, and true to the other person in the future, regardless of undulating internal feelings or external circumstances.

When Ulysses was traveling to the island of the Sirens, he knew that he would go mad when he heard the voices of the women on the rocks. He also learned that the insanity would be temporary, lasting until he could get out of earshot. He didn't want to do something while temporarily insane that would have permanent bad consequences. So he put wax in the ears of his sailors, tied himself to the mast, and told his men to keep him on course no matter what he yelled.

As we observed before, longitudinal studies reveal that two-thirds of unhappy marriages will become happy within five years if people stay married and do not get divorced.[4] Two-thirds! What can keep marriages together during the rough patches? The vows. A public oath, made to the world, keeps you "tied to the mast" until your mind clears and you begin to understand things better. It keeps you in the relationship when your feelings flag, and flag they will. By contrast, consumer relationships cannot possibly endure these inevitable tests of life, because neither party is "tied to the mast."

Does this mean that there are no grounds for leaving a marriage, for divorce? The Bible says that there are. In Matthew 19:3, we are told some Pharisees once asked Jesus, "Is it lawful for a man to divorce his wife for any and every reason?" Some rabbinical schools at the time insisted that a man could divorce his wife simply if she displeased him. He could just walk out for any reason. That, however, would not be a covenant relationship at all; it would essentially be what we have been calling a consumer relationship. Jesus rejected this view, but he did not go to the opposite extreme either.

> *"Haven't you read," he replied, "that at the beginning the Creator 'made them male and female,' and said, 'For this reason a man will leave his father and mother and be united to his wife, and the two will become one flesh'? So they are no longer two, but one. Therefore what God has joined together, let man not separate." "Why then," they asked, "did Moses command that a man give his wife a certificate of divorce and send her away?" Jesus replied, "Moses permitted you to divorce your wives because your hearts were hard. But it was not this way from the beginning. I tell you that anyone who divorces his wife, except for marital unfaithfulness, and marries another woman commits adultery."*
>
> (Matthew 19:4–9)

Jesus denies that you can divorce for any reason. By quoting Genesis 2:24, he confirms that marriage is a covenant. It is not a casual relationship that can be discarded easily. It creates a strong new unity that may only be broken under very serious conditions. But he goes on to say that these serious conditions do exist, because of "the hardness of your hearts." That means that sometimes human hearts become so hard because of sin that it leads a spouse into a severe violation of the covenant, without prospects of repentance and healing, and in such cases divorce is permitted.

The only such violation that Jesus names in this passage is adultery. In 1 Corinthians 7, Paul adds another ground—namely, willful desertion. These actions essentially break the covenant vow so thoroughly, that, as Paul says in 1 Corinthians 7:15, the wronged spouse "is not bound."

There is much more to say about the Bible and divorce,[5] but this one text is sufficient to show us the wisdom of Jesus on the subject. To allow divorce for most any reason is to hollow out the very concept of covenant and vow. Divorce should not be easy; it should not be our first, second, third, or fourth resort. And yet, Jesus knows the depths of human sin and holds out hope for those who find themselves married to someone with an intractably hard heart who has broken his or her vow in these ways. Divorce is terribly difficult, and it should be, but the wronged party should not live in shame. Surprisingly, even God claims to have gone through a divorce (Jeremiah 3:8).[6] He knows what it is like.

The Power of Promising

Divorce is an enormously difficult experience, even today, and that is why marriage vows can still fortify us. Vows keep you from simply running out too quickly. They give love a chance and create stability so the feelings of love, always very fitful and fragile in the early months and years, can grow strong and deep over time. They enable your passion to grow in breadth and depth, because they give us the security necessary to open our hearts and speak vulnerably and truthfully without being afraid that our partner will simply walk away.

W. H. Auden expressed it perfectly in one of his last books, *A Certain World: A Commonplace Book*, where he wrote, "Like everything which is not the involuntary result of fleeting emotion but the creation of time and will, any marriage, happy or unhappy, is infinitely more interesting than any romance, however passionate."[7]

What is this great difference between a romance and a marriage of which Auden speaks? It is the signing of that "piece of paper," or walking through animal parts, or stomping on the glass, or jumping the broomstick, or whatever way your culture provides to make a solemn, public vow to which you are held accountable. Love and law go hand in hand. That's because, according to the Bible, marriage is essentially a covenant.

Why is a binding promise of future love so crucial for creating deep, lasting passion? Christian ethicist Lewis Smedes wrote an article that I read as a young pastor and a still new husband. It helped me enormously as both a counselor and spouse. It is called "Controlling the Unpredictable—The Power of Promising."[8] First, he locates the very basis of our identity in the power of promising:

> Some people ask who they are and expect their feelings to tell them. But feelings are flickering flames that fade after every fitful stimulus. Some people ask who they are and expect their achievements to tell them. But the things we accomplish always leave a core of character unrevealed. Some people ask who they are and expect visions of their ideal self to tell them. But our visions can only tell us what we want to be, not what we are.

Who are we? Smedes answers that we are largely who we become through making wise promises and keeping them. For vivid confirmation, Smedes looks to the great playwright Robert Bolt, who wrote *A Man for All Seasons*, the story of Sir Thomas

More, whose daughter Meg pleaded with him to break the oath he had once made and thereby save his life.

> MORE: You want me to swear to the Act of Succession?
>
> MARGARET: "God more regards the thoughts of the heart than the words of the mouth." Or so you've always told me.
>
> MORE: Yes.
>
> MARGARET: Then say the words of the oath and in your heart think otherwise.
>
> MORE: What is an oath then but words we say to God?
>
> MARGARET: That's very neat.
>
> MORE: Do you mean it isn't true?
>
> MARGARET: No, it's true.
>
> MORE: Then it's a poor argument to call it "neat," Meg. When a man takes an oath, Meg, he's holding his own self in his own hands. Like water. And if he opens his fingers then—he needn't hope to find himself again.

Since promising is the key to identity, it is the very essence of marital love. Why? Because it is our promises that give us a stable identity, and without a stable identity, it is impossible to have stable relationships. Hannah Arendt wrote, "Without being bound to the fulfillment of our promises, we would never be able to keep our identities; we would be condemned to wander helplessly and without direction in the darkness of each person's lonely heart, caught in its contradictions and equivocalities."[7] Smedes uses himself as a case study:

When I married my wife, I had hardly a smidgen of
sense for what I was getting into with her. How could I
know how much she would change over 25 years? How
could I know how much I would change? My wife has
lived with at least five different men since we were
wed—and each of the five has been me.

The connecting link with my old self has always been
the memory of the name I took on back there: "I am he
who will be there with you." When we slough off *that*
name, lose *that* identity, we can hardly find ourselves
again.

The Freedom of Promising

What Auden, Smedes, and Arendt are claiming is illustrated by a
painful account written by Wendy Plump of how her marriage
disintegrated after she had an affair.[10] During an affair, she says,
"The great sex . . . is a given. When you have an affair you already
know you will have passionate sex—the urgency, newness, and
illicit nature of the affair practically guarantee that." Here we
have a perfect example of the attitude toward sex as we discussed
before. The thrill of the forbidden and the ego rush of being
desired was mistaken for love because superficially it made the
sexual encounter crackle with electricity.

But then the affair came to light, and, she relates, her husband
had an affair as well. Finally the marriage fell apart. During the
telling of the story, Plump looked at her parents. "They have this
marriage of fifty years behind them, and it is a monument to success. A few weeks or months of illicit passion could not hold a
candle to it." Finally she asks, "If you were seventy-five, which
would you rather have: years of steady if occasionally strained

devotion, or something that looks a little bit like the Iraqi city of Fallujah, cratered with spent artillery?" Her parents' marriage, the "creation of time and will," was indeed more interesting than her fleeting romance, however passionate.

Some of the comments on this article, posted on the *Times* Web site, were rather scornful. The authors of the comments believed that Plump had capitulated to the oppressive traditional view of marriage as exclusive covenant. "An affair only possesses the destructiveness of a 'bomb,'" one wrote, "if you allow yourself to believe that . . . marriage is the union of two persons for life. . . . In my opinion, we need to . . . begin the long process of re-conditioning ourselves to let go of the culturally imposed obsession with monogamy." Other commenters insisted that striving for permanence through traditional marriage stifles freedom and kills desire.

But Smedes argues eloquently that promising is the *means* to freedom. In promising, you limit options now, in order to have wonderful, fuller options later. You curb your freedom now, so that you can be free to be there in the future for people who trust you. When you make a promise to someone, both of you know that you are going to be there with and for them. "You have created a small sanctuary of trust within the jungle of unpredictability," Smedes says, going on thusly:

> When I make a promise, I bear witness that my future with you is not locked into a bionic beam by which I was stuck with the fateful combinations of X's and Y's in the hand I was dealt out of my parents' genetic deck. When I make a promise, I testify that I was not routed along some unalterable itinerary by the psychic conditioning visited on me by my slightly wacky parents.

When I make a promise, I declare that my future with people who depend on me is not predetermined by the mixed-up culture of my tender years.

I am not fated, I am not determined, I am not a lump of human dough whipped into shape by the contingent reinforcement and aversive conditioning of my past. I know as well as the next person that I cannot create my life *de novo*; I am well aware that much of what I am and what I do is a gift or a curse from my past. But when I make a promise to anyone, I rise above all the conditioning that limits me. No German shepherd ever promised to be there with me. No home computer ever promised to be a loyal help. . . . Only a person can make a promise. And when he does, he is most free.

Promise and Passion

How exactly is the long-term love—the "creation of time and will" produced by the promise—so superior? Wendy Plump saw that her parents had something after fifty years that was not the same as the turbocharged sexual desire of an illicit affair but was ultimately richer and deeper. What was it?

When you first fall in love, you think you love the person, but you don't really. You can't know who the person is right away. That takes years. You actually love your *idea* of the person—and that is always, at first, one-dimensional and somewhat mistaken. In *The Lord of the Rings*, Eowyn falls in love with Aragorn, but he cannot return the love. He says to her brother, Eomer, "She loves you more truly than me; for you she loves and knows; but in me she loves only a shadow and a thought: a hope of glory and great deeds, and lands far. . . ."[11] Aragorn understood that romantic flings are so intoxicating largely because the person is actually in love with a fantasy rather than a real human being.

But not only do you not know the other person, but the other person does not really know you. You have put on your best face (often quite literally.) There are things about yourself that you are ashamed of or afraid of, but you don't let the other person see your flaws. And, of course, you cannot show your partner those parts of your character that you cannot see yourself and which will only be revealed to you in the course of the marriage. There is an emotional "high" that comes to us when someone thinks we are so wonderful and beautiful, and that is part of what fuels the early passion and electricity of falling in love. But the problem is—and you may be semiconsciously aware of this—the person doesn't really know you and therefore doesn't really love you, not yet at least. What you think of as being head over heels in love is in large part a gust of ego gratification, but it's nothing like the profound satisfaction of being known *and* loved.

When over the years someone has seen you at your worst, and knows you with all your strengths and flaws, yet commits him- or herself to you wholly, it is a consummate experience. To be loved but not known is comforting but superficial. To be known and not loved is our greatest fear. But to be fully known and truly loved is, well, a lot like being loved by God. It is what we need more than anything. It liberates us from pretense, humbles us out of our self-righteousness, and fortifies us for any difficulty life can throw at us.

The kind of love life I am talking about is not devoid of passion, but it's not the same kind of passion that is there during the days of naiveté. When Kathy first held my hand, it was an almost electrical thrill. Thirty-seven years later, you don't get the same buzz out of holding your wife's hand that you did the first time.

But as I look back on that initial sensation, I realize that it came not so much from the magnitude of my love for her but from the flattery of her choice of me. In the beginning it goes to your head, and there is some love in that, but there are a lot of other things, too. There is no comparison between that and what it means to hold Kathy's hand now, after all we've been through. We know each other thoroughly now; we have shared innumerable burdens, we have repented, forgiven, and been reconciled to each other over and over. There is certainly passion. But the passion we share now differs from the thrill we had then like a noisy but shallow brook differs from a quieter but much deeper river. Passion may lead you to make a wedding promise, but then that promise over the years makes the passion richer and deeper.

Helping Romantic Love Fulfill Itself

We are now in a position to answer the question of how romantic love can be reconciled with marriage as unconditional commitment. Isn't romantic love something that must be completely free and uncoerced? And isn't it inevitable that intense desire for someone else simply can't be sustained, and therefore it is inevitable that we will need to seek another person who can reawaken the joy of love in us? Isn't it true that fully monogamous, lifelong marriage is the enemy of romantic affection?

No, that is not true. In fact, unconditional covenantal commitment helps romantic love fulfill itself. No one has made a stronger case for this idea than Danish philosopher Soren Kierkegaard.[12]

Kierkegaard writes of three possible outlooks on life—what he calls the *aesthetic*, the *ethical*, and the *religious*. He says that all of us are born aesthetes, and we only can become ethical or religious through our choices. So what is the aesthete? The aesthete doesn't really ask whether something is good or bad but only whether it is *interesting*.[13] Everything is judged as to whether it is fascinating, thrilling, exciting, and entertaining.

An aesthetic aspect is important to any life lived well and happily, but when the aesthetic dominates a life, it creates huge problems. An aesthete often claims to be a free individual. Life should be thrilling, full of "beauty and sparkle," he says. And that means often casting off the shackles of society's expectations and community ties. But Kierkegaard says that this is a very mistaken idea of what freedom is. The person living the aesthetic life is not master of himself at all; in fact, he is leading an accidental life. His temperament, tastes, feelings, and impulses completely drive him.

Looked at another way, the person dominated by the aesthetic sensibility is controlled by circumstances. If a wife loses her beautiful skin and countenance or a husband puts on the pounds, the aesthete begins to look around for someone more beautiful. If a spouse develops a debilitating illness, the aesthete begins to feel that life is pointless. But, says Kierkegaard, such a person is being completely controlled by external circumstances.

The only way for you be truly free is to link your feeling to an obligation. Only if you commit yourself to loving in action, day in and day out, even when feelings and circumstances are in flux, can you truly be a free individual and not a pawn of outside forces. Also, only if you maintain your love for someone when it is not thrilling can you be said to be actually loving a *person*. The aesthete does not really love the person; he or she loves the feelings, thrills, ego rush, and experiences that the other person brings. The proof of that is that when those things are gone, the aesthete has no abiding care or concern for the other.

So far, Kierkegaard has shown us the limitations of romantic passion, but he is not ready to dismiss it as unimportant, not at all. Nor does he pit feeling and obligation against one another, though sometimes they feel opposed to each other. He "argues that marriage actually enhances romantic love, instead of curtailing it. He argues that the ethical commitment to another person in marriage is precisely what enables the spontaneity of romantic love to achieve the stability and longevity that it [longs for but] is unable to provide by itself."[14] Indeed, it is the covenantal commitment that enables married people to *become* people who love each other. Only with time do we really learn who the other person is and come to love the person for him- or herself and not just for the feelings and experiences they give us. Only with time do we learn the particular needs of our spouse and how to meet them. Eventually all this leads to wells of memory and depths of feeling and enjoyment of the other person that frames and enhances the still crucial episodes of romantic, sexual passion in your married life.

Emotion and Action

How does this work itself out in day-to-day married life? Nearly everyone thinks that the Bible's directive to "love your neighbor" is wise, right, and good. But notice that it is a command, and emotions cannot be commanded. The Bible does not call us to *like* our neighbor, to have affection and warm feelings toward him or her. No, the call is to *love* your neighbor, and that must primarily mean displaying a set of behaviors.

The feeling of affection, of course, is a natural part of love, and it can enable us to better perform the actions of love. We are never more satisfied and fulfilled than when affection and action are joined in us, when we are serving someone we delight in. Nevertheless, if we don't distinguish between feelings and actions, it can put huge barriers in the way of loving people.

One reason we need to make this distinction is because of the sheer inconsistency of our feelings. They are tied to complex physical, psychological, and social factors. They wax and then wane, often in infuriating ways. Our emotions are not under our control, but our actions are. Most of our likes and dislikes are neither sins nor virtues—no more than our tastes in food or music. What matters is what we do with them. If, as our culture encourages us, we go so far as to define love *as* "liking"—if we only feel that actions of love are "authentic" if there are strong feelings of love present—we will inevitably be bad friends and even more terrible family members and spouses.

It is a mistake to think that you must feel love to give it. If, for example, I have a child, and I give up my day off to take him to a ballgame to his great joy, at a time when I don't particularly like him, I am in some ways being more loving to him than if my heart were filled with affection. When you feel great delight in someone, meeting their needs and getting their gratitude and affection in return is extremely rewarding to your ego. At those times you may be acting more out of the desire to get that love and satisfaction yourself, rather than out of a desire to seek the good of the other person. As Kierkegaard observed, you may not be loving that person so much as loving yourself. And when we only do the actions of love when we are having strong feelings of love, we often love unwisely. Parents, out of "love," can spoil their children. Spouses, out of "love," can enable destructive behavior in each other. The reason this happens is that we are above all afraid of the displeasure of the beloved. We are afraid that he or she will be angry and say harsh things, and we cannot bear that. This only affirms that we don't really love the person and his or her best interest. We love the affection and esteem we are getting from that person. All this means that you can indeed love, and love truly and wisely, when you lack the feelings of love.

So if your definition of "love" stresses affectionate feelings more than unselfish actions, you will cripple your ability to maintain and grow strong love relationships. On the other hand, if you stress the action of love over the feeling, you enhance and establish the feeling. That is one of the secrets of living life, as well as of marriage.

Actions of Love Lead to Feelings of Love

In one of his BBC radio talks during World War II, C. S. Lewis expounded on the basic Christian virtues, including those of forgiveness and charity (or love). For the British, the world was then unavoidably divided into allies and enemies. In that situation, Lewis said, many of his countrymen and -women found the Christian doctrine of forgiving and loving *all* human beings to be not just impossible but repugnant. "This sort of talk makes me sick," many said to him. But Lewis went on to argue that, despite feelings of indifference and even contempt, you can change your heart over the long haul through your actions:

> [T]hough natural likings should normally be encouraged, it would be quite wrong to think that the way to become charitable is to sit trying to manufacture affectionate feelings. . . . The rule for all of us is perfectly simple. Do not waste time bothering whether you "love" your neighbor; act as if you did. As soon as we do this we find one of the great secrets. When you are behaving as if you loved someone, you will presently come to love him. If you injure someone you dislike, you will find yourself disliking him more. If you do him a good turn, you will find yourself disliking him less. . . . [W]henever we do good to another self, just

because it is a self, made (like us) by God, and desiring its own happiness as we desire ours, we shall have learned to love it a little more or, at least, to dislike it less. . . . The worldly man treats certain people kindly because he "likes" them: The Christian, trying to treat everyone kindly, finds himself liking more and more people as he goes on—including people he could not even have imagined himself liking at the beginning.[15]

Lewis then used an illustration that had great potency, particularly at that time:

This same spiritual law works terribly in the opposite direction. The Germans, perhaps, at first ill-treated the Jews because they hated them: afterwards they hated them much more because they had ill-treated them. The more cruel you are, the more you will hate; and the more you hate, the more cruel you will become—and so on in a vicious circle forever.[16]

Early in my ministry I discovered this practical insight in an unexpected way. A pastor is required to befriend a lot of people that he would never otherwise choose as friends. Doctors and counselors talk sympathetically and personally with people, but that happens within the strict confines of the office and the work week. Pastors live with the people they shepherd. They visit with them and eat and play with them, in restaurants and parks and in their homes, all the while talking to them about their life issues and problems.

As a young minister, I was immediately struck by how different a life this called me to live. Like everyone else, up till that time I had let my likings and affections strictly determine who I spent time with. When I moved to Hopewell, Virginia, and took the church, however, I met plenty of people in the congregation that, if I had moved there with some other job, I would not have pursued as friends. It wasn't that I didn't like them; I just shared no affinities with them. There was no "spark" of the kind you feel when you want to spend more time with someone.

Nevertheless, as their pastor, if anyone needed to talk to me at 3 a.m., I was there. If they went to the hospital, I was there. If a family's son ran away from home, I got in my car and went to find him. I sat in their homes, went to their children's graduations, went to their family picnics. I shared my heart with them as they shared theirs with me. That's what it is to be a pastor, especially in a smaller church in a small town. I was called upon to do all the actions of love with a lot of people to whom I was not emotionally drawn.

And it changed me. This came home to Kathy and me one day after we'd been at the church only a couple of years. We had a mid-week day off, and were deciding how to spend it. I thought of a particular couple in the church and proposed that we visit them or have them over. She looked at me astonished and said, "Why on earth?" This particular couple had few or no friends. They had many personal problems that made them unattractive to others and indeed to each other. Kathy certainly understood the need to see them and spend time with them, but this was our day off, and surely time with this couple was ministry "work."

For a moment I was surprised by her surprise, and then I laughed when I saw what had happened. For months I had been investing much time, thought, and emotion into helping this couple move forward in life. In short, I had been doing various actions of love—listening, serving, sympathizing, confronting, forgiving, affirming, sharing. And after all that, I realized, I'd actually come to like them.

Why did that happen? Was it because I was so holy and spiritual? No, not in the slightest. It was because I'd stumbled on to the practical principle that Lewis named. I had been loving them even when I didn't like them, and the result was that, slowly but surely, my emotions were catching up with my behavior. If you do not give up, but proceed to love the unlovely in a sustained way, they will eventually become lovely to you.

Our culture says that feelings of love are the basis for actions of love. And of course that can be true. But it is truer to say that actions of love can lead consistently to feelings of love. Love between two people must not, in the end, be identified simply with emotion *or* merely with dutiful action. Married love is a symbiotic, complex mixture of both. Having said this, it is important to observe that of the two—emotion and action—it is the latter that we have the most control over. It is the action of love that we can promise to maintain every day.

Deciding to Love

How important is this principle to marriage itself? It is crucial. In Ephesians 5:28, Paul says, "Husbands ought to love their wives." He had already urged them to love their wives in verse 25, but here, just to be clear, Paul uses a verb that stresses obligation. There is no doubt about what Paul is saying. He commands husbands—they *ought* to love their wives. Emotions can't be commanded, only actions, and so it is actions that Paul is demanding. He doesn't care how they feel on a given day or at a given moment—they must love their wives.

Does that mean it doesn't matter who you marry, that you don't have to be in love with the person you wed, or that emotion is unimportant in marriage? No, I am not proposing that you deliberately marry a person you don't like.[17] But I can guarantee that, whoever you marry, you *will* fall "out of like" with them. Powerful feelings of affection and delight will not and cannot be sustained. It is quite typical to lose the head-over-heels feelings for your mate even before you get married, because our emotions are tied to so many things within our physiology, psychology, and environment. Your feelings will ebb and flow, and if you follow our culture's definition of "love," you may conclude that this can't be a person you should marry. Our culture glorifies romantic passion, and so we say, "If this was the person for me to marry, my feelings wouldn't be so up and down." In a chapter called Christian Marriage in *Mere Christianity*, C. S. Lewis writes:

> People get from books the idea that if you have married the right person you may expect to go on "being in love" for ever. As a result, when they find they are not, they think this proves they have made a mistake and are entitled to a change—not realizing that, when they have changed, the glamour will presently go out of the new love just as it went out of the old one. . . .[18]

In any relationship, there will be frightening spells in which your feelings of love seem to dry up. And when that happens you must remember that the essence of a marriage is that it is a covenant, a commitment, a promise of future love. So what do you do? You do the acts of love, despite your lack of feeling. You may not feel tender, sympathetic, and eager to please, but in your actions you must *be* tender, understanding, forgiving, and helpful. And, if you do that, as time goes on you will not only get through the dry spells, but they will become less frequent and deep, and you will become more constant in your feelings. This is what can happen if you decide to love.

This is, I think, one little part of what Christ meant by saying that a thing will not really live unless it first dies. It is simply no good trying to keep any thrill: that is the very worst thing you can do. Let the thrill go— let it die away—go on through that period of death into the quieter interest and happiness that follow— and you will find you are living in a world of new thrills all the time. . . .[19]

How is this transformation possible? I think it may happen something like this: When we first are attracted to someone, we think, "I want it to stay like this! I don't want to lose this passion." But as we have said, that ego rush cannot be sustained and cannot take you very far down the road of learning to love the person you really married. To use Lewis's metaphor, you must let this more immature incarnation of your love "die" if it is to rise again and live. You must stick to your commitment to act and serve in love even when—no, *especially* when—you don't feel much delight and attraction to your spouse. And the more you do that, slowly but surely, you will find your more ego-heavy attraction being transformed into a love that is more characterized by a humble, amazed reception and appreciation of the other person. The love you will grow into will be wiser, richer, deeper, less variable.

Sadly, many people never let this happen, because they have accepted the culture's definition of marriage, and when the thrill wears off, they feel it is time for a change. This view of things leaves married people very vulnerable to affairs, since it is quite natural that you will meet others who are attractive and who will hold out the promise of getting the thrill back that was there in the beginning of your relationship with your spouse.

Another notion we get from novels and plays is that "falling in love" is something quite irresistible; something that just happens to one, like measles. And because they believe this, some married people throw up the sponge and give in when they find themselves attracted by a new acquaintance. . . . But is it not very largely in our own choice whether this love shall, or shall not, turn into what we call "being in love"? No doubt, if our minds are full of novels and plays and sentimental songs, and our bodies full of alcohol, we shall turn any love we feel into that kind of love: just as if you have a rut in your path, all the rainwater will run into that rut, and if you wear blue spectacles, everything you see will turn blue. But that will be our own fault.[20]

So when someone says, "I don't need a piece of paper to show love," you might say, "Yes, you do. If you love the way the Bible describes the love of two people who want to share their lives together, you should have no problem making a legal, permanent, exclusive commitment."

The Bargain

In ancient times there was the bride price. A prospective husband came to the father of a woman and offered him a certain sum, depending on factors such as the woman's beauty and the size of her inheritance. We see that old practice and say, "Oh, how awful that people did that." Today, however, we have moved beyond that, and because we are more democratic—men and women do it now to one another! We look at men and women sizing each other up and say, "She's in the market" and "He got a bad deal there" and "How did she ever fall for that sales pitch?" These offhand comments are telling. We tend to size up potential partners as to their assets and deficits. And in the end we feel that we want to marry this person because he or she brings a lot to the table for us. It is almost impossible not to think in terms of how much I am putting into the marriage and how much my spouse is putting in. And if we are getting out of the relationship as much (or a bit more, we secretly hope) than we put in, then we are happy.

But as time goes on, we come to see our spouse's flaws. And if those flaws persist, and we find that we are now not getting out of the marriage as much as we had hoped for when we made our initial investment, then we begin to do what anyone in a business does. If revenues are down, cut expenditures. And so if my wife is not being the wife she ought to be, I simply will not put in the effort to be the husband I used to be. It seems perfectly fair. "She's not doing this like she used to. So why, then, should I do that? If I'm not getting the same value, I don't need to put as much into this." You tell yourself at some semiconscious level that this behavior is only fair and equitable. But it's really a form of revenge.

This is how you justify your withdrawal in your mind, but, of course, your spouse doesn't see it quite that way. If my wife sees me being emotionally more remote, not being as active in serving her needs or the needs of the family, she will feel warranted to dial back her own involvement and commitment to me. The less you feel love, and the less you act loving, the less you feel loving, and so you both spiral down and down.

Think, for a moment, how different a parent's relationship is with a child. If you have a child, you will find that the Biblical pattern of love is forced on you. Your new child is the neediest human being you have ever met. She needs your care every second of the day, twenty-four hours a day, seven days a week. You make enormous sacrifices in your life, and yet the child, for a very long time, gives you nothing in return. And, while later the child can give you love and respect, never does she give you anything like what you have given her. Often older children go through long stretches during which they rebel and fall apart and need enormous investment from you and again give you nothing in return. But at every turn, whether or not they are giving to you, you give to them.

After eighteen years of this, even if your child is an unattractive person to everyone else, you can't help but love her dearly. Why? Because you've been forced to operate on the Biblical pattern. You have had to do the actions of love regardless of your feelings and therefore now you have deep feelings of love for your child, however loveable she is or not.

It is not surprising, then, that after children leave home, many marriages fall apart. Why? Because while the parents treated their relationship with their children as a covenant relationship— performing the actions of love until their feelings strengthened— they treated their marriages as a consumer relationship and withdrew their actions of love when they weren't having the feelings. As a result, after two decades, their marriages were empty while their love for their children remained strong.

He Stayed

Many people hear this and say, "I'm sorry, I can't give love if I don't feel it! I can't fake it. That's too mechanical for me." I can understand that reaction, but Paul doesn't simply call us to a naked action; he also commands us to think as we act. "Husbands, love your wives just as Christ loved the church and gave himself up for her."

This means we must say to ourselves something like this: "Well, when Jesus looked down from the cross, he didn't think, 'I am giving myself to you because you are so attractive to me.' No, he was in agony, and he looked down at us—denying him, abandoning him, and betraying him—and in the greatest act of love in history, he *stayed*. He said, 'Father, forgive them, they don't know what they are doing.' He loved us, not because we were lovely to him, but to make us lovely. That is why I am going to love my spouse." Speak to your heart like that, and then fulfill the promises you made on your wedding day.

FOUR

THE MISSION OF MARRIAGE

*Husbands, love your wives, just as Christ loved the church
and gave himself up for her to make her holy, cleansing
her by the washing with water through the word, and to
present her to himself as a radiant church, without stain
or wrinkle or any other blemish, but holy and blameless.*

Ephesians 5:25–27

We have spent time discussing what marriage is, but now let's ask, "What is it *for*?" What is the purpose of marriage? The Bible's answer to this question starts with the principle that marriage is a friendship.

Loneliness in Paradise

In Genesis 1–2, as God was creating the world, he looked at what he had done and repeatedly said that "it was good." This assessment is given seven times in the first chapter alone, emphasizing in the strongest possible manner how great and glorious the created material world is.[1] It is striking, then, that after God created the first man, he said, "It is *not* good that the man should be alone" (Genesis 2:18). It is striking not just by contrast with all we have read so far, but it raises a question: How could Adam be in a "not good" condition when he was in a perfect world and had, evidently, a perfect relationship with God?

The answer may lie in the statement of God in Genesis 1:26: "Let us make man in our own image." Readers instantly ask the question, "Who is *us*? Who is God talking to?" One answer is that God is talking to the angels around him, but there is no indication anywhere in the Bible that the angels participated with God in the creation of human beings. Christian theologians over the centuries have seen here an allusion to a truth only revealed after the coming of Jesus into the world—namely, that God is triune, that the one God has existed from all eternity as three persons—Father, Son, and Spirit—who know and love one another. And therefore, among other things, being created in God's image means that we were designed for relationships.[2]

So here is Adam, created by God and put into the garden of paradise, and yet his aloneness is "not good." The Genesis narrative is implying that our intense relational capacity, created and given to us by God, was not fulfilled completely by our "vertical" relationship with him. God designed us to need "horizontal" relationships with other human beings. That is why even in paradise, loneliness was a terrible thing. We should therefore not be surprised to find that all the money, comforts, and pleasures in the world—our efforts to re-create a paradise for ourselves—are unable to fulfill us like love can. This is confirmation of our intuition that family and relationships are a greater blessing and provide greater satisfaction than anything money can buy.

In response to being alone, God created what the text calls an *'ezer*, a word that means a "helper-companion," a friend.[3] When the man sees the woman, he responds in poetry. "At last!" he says. "This is bone of my bone and flesh of my flesh!" Some have proposed that he is saying, "Meeting you fills a void in me." And so we see that, in the beginning, God gave the man a companion to be his spouse. The female speaker in Song of Solomon echoes Adam when she says, "This is my lover, this is my friend" (5:16).

The Character of Friendship

What is friendship? The Bible, and particularly the book of Proverbs, spends much time describing and defining it. One of the prime qualities of a friend is constancy. Friends "love at *all* times" and especially during "adversity" (Proverbs 17:17). The counterfeit is a "fair-weather friend" who comes over when you are successful but goes away if prosperity, status, or influence wanes (Proverbs 14:20; 19:4,6,7). True friends stick closer than a brother (Proverbs 18:24). They are always there for you. Another of the essential characteristics of friendship is transparency and candor. Real friends encourage and affectionately affirm one another (Proverbs 27:9; cf. 1 Samuel 23:16–18), yet real friends also offer bracing critiques: "Faithful are the wounds of a friend" (Proverbs 27:5–6). Like a surgeon, friends cut you in order to heal you. Friends become wiser together through a healthy clash of viewpoints. "As iron sharpens iron, so friend sharpens friend" (Proverbs 27:17).

There are two features of real friendship—constancy and transparency. Real friends always let you in, and they never let you down. A writer once described a relationship that united these two things. She spoke of:

> the inexpressible comfort of feeling safe with a person—
> having neither to weigh thoughts nor measure words,
> but pouring them all right out, just as they are, chaff
> and grain together; certain that a faithful hand will
> take and sift them, keep what is worth keeping, and
> then with the breath of kindness blow the rest away.[4]

However, there is a third quality to friendship, and it is not as easy to put into a single word. The right word, literally, is "sympathy"—*sym-pathos*, common passion. This means that friendships are discovered more than they are created at will. They arise between people who discover that they have common interests in and longings for the same things.

Ralph Waldo Emerson[5] and C. S. Lewis each wrote well-known essays about how a common vision can unite people of very different temperaments. Lewis insisted that the essence of friendship is the exclamation "You, too?" While erotic love can be depicted as two people looking at one another, friendship can be depicted as two people standing side by side looking at the same object and being stirred and entranced by it together. Lewis speaks of a "secret thread" that runs through the movies, books, art, music, pastimes, ideas, and scenery that most deeply move us. When we meet another person who shares this thread with us, there is the potential for a real friendship, if nurtured with transparency and constancy. The paradox is that friendship cannot be merely about itself. It must be about something else, something that both friends are committed to and passionate about besides one another.

> Friendship arises . . . when two or more . . . discover that they have in common some insight or interest. . . . [A]s Emerson said, *Do you love me?* means *Do you see the same truth?*—or at least, *Do you care about the same truth?* The man who agrees with us that some question, little regarded by others, is of great importance can be our Friend. . . . That is why those pathetic people who simply "want friends" can never make any. The very condition of having friends is that we should

want something else besides friends. Where the truthful answer to the question *"Do you see the same truth?"* would be *"I don't care about the truth—I only want [you to be my] friend,"* no friendship can arise. Friendship must be *about* something, even if it were only an enthusiasm for dominoes or white mice. Those who have nothing can share nothing; those who are going nowhere can have no fellow-travelers.[6]

Christian Friendship

When we come to the New Testament, there is a new layer added to our understanding of friendship. Friendship is only possible when there is a common vision and passion—think of what that means for all Christians. For believers in Christ, despite enormous differences in class, temperament, culture, race, sensibility, and personal history, there is an underlying commonality that is more powerful than them all. This is not so much a "thread" as an indestructible steel cable. Christians have all experienced the grace of God in the gospel of Jesus. We have all had our identity changed at the root, so now God's calling and love are more foundational to who we are than any other thing. And we also long for the same future, journey to the same horizon, what the Bible calls the "new creation." Paul speaks of "the good work" God is doing in believers that will be complete at the end of time (Philippians 1:6). We will become our true selves, the persons we were created to be, freed from all flaws, imperfections, and weaknesses. He speaks of "the glory that will be revealed in us," a liberation from our "bondage to decay . . . the glorious freedom of the children of God" (Romans 8:18, 20). We "hope" and "wait eagerly" for this final and full redemption (Romans 8:23).

What does this mean? It means that any two Christians, with

nothing else but a common faith in Christ, can have a robust friendship, helping each other on their journey toward the new creation, as well as doing ministry together in the world. How can they do that?

They do it through spiritual transparency. Christian friends are not only to honestly confess their own sins to each other (James 5:16), but they are to lovingly point out their friend's sins if he or she is blind to them (Romans 15:14). You should give your Christian friends "hunting licenses" to confront you if you are failing to live in line with your commitments (Galatians 6:1). Christian friends are to stir one another up, even provoking one another to get them off dead center (Hebrews 10:24). This isn't to happen infrequently but should happen at a very concrete level every day (Hebrews 3:13). Christian friends admit wrongs, offer or ask forgiveness (Ephesians 4:32), and take steps to reconcile when one disappoints another (Matthew 5:23ff; 18:15ff).

The other way is spiritual *constancy*. Christian friends bear each other's burdens (Galatians 6:2). They should be there for each other through thick and thin (1 Thessalonians 5:11,14–15), sharing their goods and their very lives with each other if there is need (Hebrews 13:16; Philippians 4:14; 2 Corinthians 9:13). Friends must encourage each other through honor and affirmation (Romans 12:3–6,10; Proverbs 27:2). They are to identify and call out one another's gifts, strengths, and abilities. They are to build up each other's faith through study and common worship (Colossians 3:16; Ephesians 5:19).

The picture that the Bible draws of spiritual friendship is remarkable. Christian friendship is not simply about going to concerts together or enjoying the same sporting event. It is the deep oneness that develops as two people journey together toward the same destination, helping one another through the dangers and challenges along the way. There have been numerous "buddy movies" made over the years, of all types and all levels of artistic merit, from the Leatherstocking tales of James Fenimore Cooper to the 1960s film *The Dirty Dozen* to the classic *The Lord of the Rings*. In each story, a disparate group of people are brought together. They may come from different races and classes and may hate one another, but because some common goal and mission is thrust on them, they become a team, a unit. They rescue each other, push, provoke, and exhort each other and win through because their common mission turns them into friends and their differences become their strengths.

How does this supernatural friendship that can exist between any two Christians relate to the natural human friendship described by Emerson and Lewis, which is based on the common thread of similar loves and passions? The answer is that they can overlap or coincide. A Christian can become great friends with a non-Christian who, for example, shares her enthusiasm for an author. They read the author's books and meet to talk enthusiastically and joyfully about what they loved in the books. If the two friends are also, say, young mothers, then they have another basis for friendship, and the friendship can become warm and close, despite the lack of common Christian faith. As we have shown, two Christians can have the spiritual friendship described in the "one anothering" directives of the New Testament, even if temperamentally and in every other way the two are extremely different and, humanly speaking, incompatible. Perhaps the richest and best relationships, however, are those that combine both the natural and the supernatural elements. Marriage, of course, can add the power of romantic love to the natural and supernatural bonds of friendship, and this is what can make marriage the richest of all human relationships.

Friendship is a deep oneness that develops as two people, speaking the truth in love to each other, journey together to the same horizon. Spiritual friendship is the greatest journey of all, because the horizon is so high and far, yet sure—it is nothing less than "the day of Jesus Christ" and what we will be like when we finally see him face-to-face. The apostle John writes,

> *Dear friends, now we are children of God, and what we will be has not yet been made known. But we know that when Christ appears, we shall be like him, for we shall see him as he is. All who have this hope in him purify themselves, just as he is pure.*
>
> (1 John 3:2–3)

Your Spouse as Your Best Friend

When God brought the first man his spouse, he brought him not just a lover but the friend his heart had been seeking. Proverbs 2:17 speaks of one's spouse as your *'allup*, a unique word that the lexicons define as your "special confidant" or "best friend." In an age where women were often seen as the husband's property, and marriages were mainly business deals and transactions seeking to increase the family's social status and security, it was startling for the Bible to describe a spouse in this way. But in today's society, with its emphasis on romance and sex, it is just as radical to insist that your spouse should be your best friend, though for a different reason. In tribal societies, romance doesn't matter as much as social status, and in individualistic Western societies, romance and great sex matter far more than anything else. The Bible, however, without ignoring responsibility to the community or the importance of romance, puts great emphasis on marriage as companionship.

We see it in our text, Ephesians 5. Here Paul is speaking to people from pagan backgrounds and to their view that marriage is mainly a social transaction. In that time, you had to marry as well as you could for the sake of your family's social status. Your wife's job was to link your family to another good family and then bear children. That was what marriage was supposed to accomplish.

Paul, however, gives his readers a vision for marriage that must have completely astonished them. The primary goal of Christian marriage is not social status and stability, as it was in ancient cultures, nor is it primarily romantic and emotional happiness, as it is in our culture today. Paul points husbands to Jesus's sacrificial love toward us, his "bride." But Paul does not stop there; he goes on to speak of the goal of that sacrificial love for his bride. It is "to sanctify her" (verse 26) to "present her to himself" in radiant beauty and splendor (verse 27a), to bring her to be perfectly "holy and blameless" (verse 27c). He wants the new creation for us! He wants to remove all spiritual stains, flaws, sins, and blemishes, to make us "holy," "glorious," and "blameless."[7]

In another place, Paul tells all the Christians in Philippi that "He who began a good work in you will carry it on to completion in the day of Christ Jesus" (1:6). This speaks of a process, begun the day we believed in Jesus, that has traditionally been named "sanctification." Paul is saying we should not think that process will be complete before the end of time—we should never think we can achieve perfection here and now. But he also warns us against losing hope. He *will* bring the work to completion. Slowly but surely, by the power of the Spirit, we will put on our "new self, created to be like God" (Ephesians 4:24). During this life, as we trust in God and come to know him, we are "being transformed into [Christ's] likeness from one degree of splendor to the next" (2 Corinthians 3:18). Even (or especially) the sufferings we experience can make us wiser, deeper, stronger, better.

Therefore we do not lose heart. Though outwardly we are wasting away, yet inwardly we are being renewed day by day. For our light and momentary troubles are achieving for us an eternal glory that far outweighs them all. Therefore we fix our eyes not on what is seen, but what is unseen.

(2 Corinthians 4:16–18)

How can Paul say to all Christians that the work of new creation that was begun in us *will* be brought to completion? Because Jesus is present with us, overseeing the work. He is the ultimate friend "who sticks closer than a brother." He will never let us down. He is committed to making us into the glorious, unique person that we can be in him. In John 15:9–15 this is accomplished because he is our Divine Friend, but in Ephesians 5, he accomplishes this because he is our Divine Husband. In his redemptive work, Jesus is both Friend and Lover, and this is to be the model for spouses in marriage. Husband and wife are to be both lovers and friends to one another as Jesus is to us. Jesus has a vision of our future glory (Colossians 1:27; 1 John 3:2) and everything he does in our lives moves us toward that goal. Ephesians 5:28 directly links the purpose of every marriage to the purpose of the Ultimate Marriage. "In this same way, husbands ought to love their wives. . . ." And how could it be otherwise? If any two unrelated Christians are to provoke each other toward love and goodness (Hebrews 10:24), are to affirm each other's gifts and hold each other accountable to grow out of their sins (Hebrews 3:13), how much more should a husband and wife do that?[8]

This principle—that your spouse should be capable of becoming your best friend—is a game changer when you address the question of compatibility in a prospective spouse. If you think of marriage largely in terms of erotic love, then compatibility means sexual chemistry and appeal. If you think of marriage largely as a way to move into the kind of social status in life you desire, then compatibility means being part of the desired social class, and perhaps common tastes and aspirations for lifestyle. The problem with these factors is that they are not durable. Physical attractiveness will wane, no matter how hard you work to delay its departure. And socio-economic status unfortunately can change almost overnight. When people think they have found compatibility based on these things, they often make the painful discovery that they have built their relationship on unstable ground. A woman "lets herself go" or a man loses his job, and the compatibility foundation falls apart.

But worst of all, sexual attraction and social class relatability do not give you any common vision. What is your marriage *for*? Where are you going? If you have mainly mutual material and financial goals, that will serve to bring unity, for a while. But such goals do not create deep oneness, for eventually you reach them (or you don't), and then what? If you marry mainly a sexual partner, or mainly a financial partner, you are going nowhere together, really. And those who are going nowhere can have no fellow travelers.

The Great Horizon

What, then, is marriage for? It is for helping each other to become our future glory-selves, the new creations that God will eventually make us. The common horizon husband and wife look toward is the Throne, and the holy, spotless, and blameless nature we will have. I can think of no more powerful common horizon than that, and that is why putting a Christian friendship at the heart of a marriage relationship can lift it to a level that no other vision for marriage approaches.

Have you ever traveled to a mountainous part of the world when it was cloudy and rainy? You look out your windows and you can see almost nothing but the ground. Then the rain stops and the clouds part and you catch your breath because there, towering right over you, is this magnificent peak. But a couple of hours later the clouds roll in and it has vanished, and you don't see it again for a good while. That is what it is like to get to know a Christian. You have an old self and a new self (Ephesians 4:24). The old self is crippled with anxieties, the need to prove yourself, bad habits you can't break, and many besetting sins and entrenched character flaws. The new self is still you, but you liberated from all your sins and flaws. This new self is always a work in progress, and sometimes the clouds of the old self make it almost completely invisible. But sometimes the clouds really part, and you see the wisdom, courage, and love of which you are capable. It is a glimpse of where you are going.

Within this Christian vision for marriage, here's what it means to fall in love. It is to look at another person and get a glimpse of the person God is creating, and to say, "I see who God is making you, and it excites me! I want to be part of that. I want to partner with you and God in the journey you are taking to his throne. And when we get there, I will look at your magnificence and say, 'I always knew you could be like this. I got glimpses of it on earth, but now look at you!'" Each spouse should see the great thing that Jesus is doing in the life of their mate through the Word, the gospel. Each spouse then should give him- or herself to be a vehicle for that work and envision the day that you will stand together before God, seeing each other presented in spotless beauty and glory.

My wife, Kathy, often says that most people, when they are

looking for a spouse, are looking for a finished statue when they should be looking for a wonderful block of marble. Not so you can create the kind of person *you* want, but rather because you see what kind of person Jesus is making. When Michelangelo was asked how he carved his magnificent *David*, his reply is reputed to have been, "I looked inside the marble and just took away the bits that weren't David." When looking for a marriage partner, each must be able to look inside the other and see what God is doing and be excited about being part of the process of liberating the emerging "new you."

> If we let Him . . . He will make the feeblest and filthiest of us into a god or goddess, a dazzling, radiant, immortal creature, pulsating all through with such energy and joy and wisdom and love as we cannot now imagine, a bright stainless mirror which reflects back to God perfectly (though, of course, on a smaller scale) His own boundless power and delight and goodness. The process will be long and in parts very painful; but that is what we are in for. Nothing less.[9]

This is by no means a naïve, romanticized approach—rather it is brutally realistic. In this view of marriage, each person says to the other, "I see all your flaws, imperfections, weaknesses, dependencies. But underneath them all I see growing the person God wants you to be." This is radically different from the search for "compatibility." As we have seen, researchers have discovered that this term means we are looking for a partner who accepts us just as we are. This is the very opposite of that! The search for an ideal mate is a hopeless quest. This is also a radically different approach from the cynical or cold method of finding a spouse who can just deliver social status, financial security, or great sex.

If you don't see your mate's deep flaws and weaknesses and dependencies, you're not even in the game. But if you don't get excited about the person your spouse has already grown into and will become, you aren't tapping into the power of marriage as spiritual friendship. The goal is to see something absolutely ravishing that God is making of the beloved. You see even now flashes of glory. You want to help your spouse become the person God wants him or her to be.

When two Christians who fully understand this stand before the minister all decked out in their wedding finery, they realize they're not just playing dress-up. What they're saying is that someday they are going to be standing not before the minister but before the Lord. And they will turn to see each other without spot and blemish. And they hope to hear God say, "Well done, good and faithful servants. Over the years you have lifted one another up to me. You sacrificed for one another. You held one another up with prayer and with thanksgiving. You confronted each other. You rebuked each other. You hugged and you loved each other and continually pushed each other toward me. And now look at you. You're radiant."

Romance, sex, laughter, and plain fun are the by-products of this process of sanctification, refinement, glorification. Those things are important, but they can't keep the marriage going through years and years of ordinary life. What keeps the marriage going is your commitment to your spouse's holiness. You're committed to his or her beauty. You're committed to his greatness and perfection. You're committed to her honesty and passion for the things of God. That's your job as a spouse. Any lesser goal than that, any smaller purpose, and you're just playing at being married.

Now we can see how marriage-as-friendship agrees so well with love-as-commitment. On the cross, Jesus did not look down on us with a heart full of admiration and affection. He felt no "chemistry." But he gave himself. He put our needs ahead of his own; he sacrificed for us. But the Bible tells spouses not only to imitate the quality and manner of Christ's love but also the *goal* of it. Jesus died not because we were lovely, but to make us lovely. He died, Paul says, to "make us *holy*." Paradoxically, this means Paul is urging spouses to help their mates love Jesus more than them.[10] It's a paradox but not a contradiction. The simple fact is that only if I love Jesus more than my wife will I be able to serve her needs ahead of my own. Only if my emotional tank is filled with love from God will I be able to be patient, faithful, tender, and open with my wife when things are not going well in life or in the relationship. And the more joy I get from my relationship with Christ, the more I can share that joy with my wife and family.

A Message for Our Culture

Paul's teaching about marriage was certainly radical for ancient, traditional cultures. But it may be just as radical a message for today's society.

It often happens that you have a good friend of the opposite sex with whom you share common commitments. You trust this person's wisdom and you find you can open up and share many intimate things without fear. He or she understands you well and listens to you and gives you great advice. But the person doesn't attract you romantically. Maybe he or she doesn't have the body type that you find appealing. You feel no sexual chemistry at all. Then imagine that you meet someone else to whom you feel *very* attracted. This person has the physical and social attributes you have been looking for and is interested in you, too. So you start seeing each other and you have a lot of fun together and things are moving along into more and more romantic intimacy. But if you are honest with yourself, this person you say you are falling in love with does not make nearly as good a friend as the one you already have, nor is that likely to change.[11]

You are in trouble. Your spouse has got to be your best friend, or be on the way to becoming your best friend, or you won't have a strong, rich marriage that endures and that makes you both vastly better persons for having been in it.

I'm not saying that you should marry someone when you feel no attraction. The Bible does indicate that your spouse must be more than your dearest friend, but not less. Most of us know that there is some truth in the stereotype that men overvalue beauty in a prospective spouse and that women overvalue wealth in a potential mate. But if you marry someone more for these things than for friendship, you not only are setting yourself up for future failure—wealth may and sexual appeal *will* decrease—but you are also setting yourself up for loneliness. For what Adam in the garden needed was not just a sexual partner but a companion, bone of his bones, and flesh of his flesh.

If singles accepted this principle, it would drastically change the way people seek a marriage partner in our day. It is typical for a single person to walk into a room and see a number of people of the opposite sex and immediately begin to screen them, not for companionship but for attractiveness. Let's say three out of the ten look appealing. The next step is to approach those three to see what rapport there may be. If one of them will agree to go out on a date, and you get romantically involved, perhaps you'll see if you can turn that person into a friend as well. The problem is many of your best prospects for friendship were likely among those you ruled out because they were too tall or too short, too fat or too skinny.

We think of a prospective spouse as primarily a lover (or a provider), and if he or she can be a friend on top of that, well isn't that nice! We should be going at it the other way around. Screen first for friendship. Look for someone who understands you better than you do yourself, who makes you a better person just by being around them. And then explore whether that friendship could become a romance and a marriage.

So many people go about their dating starting from the wrong end, and they end up in marriages that aren't really about anything and aren't going anywhere.

The Priority of Marriage

There is one very important implication of this principle of marriage-as-friendship. If you see your spouse as mainly a sexual partner or a financial partner, you will find that you will need pursuits outside of marriage to really engage your whole soul. In that case, children, parents, career, political or social activism, hobbies, or a network of close friends—one or more of these things—will capture your imagination, provide joy and meaning, and absorb emotional energy more than your marriage. And that will be deadly. Your marriage will slowly die if your spouse senses that he or she is not the first priority in your life. But only if your spouse is not just your lover and financial partner but your best friend is it possible for your marriage to be your most important and fulfilling relationship.

In Ephesians 5, Paul quotes Genesis 2:24—namely, that when a man marries, he "leaves his father and mother and cleaves to his wife." Western people are not shocked when they read this command, but they should be. Think of the historical and social context of that statement. Ancient cultures put enormous emphasis on the parent-child relationship. Pleasing your parents, being faithful to the wishes of your parents, was all important. In more traditional cultures even today, parents and grandparents are given great authority and children are expected to heed their parents' wishes above all other requests. And there is a certain warrant for this kind of respect. By the time you are a young adult, you should be willing to admit that the single relationship that has most shaped who you are—for good and ill—is your relationship to your parents. You wouldn't be alive without them, and all but a few parents have made enormous sacrifices for the well-being of their children.

And yet right in the midst of these patriarchal cultures, and in the face of these realities, God says, "I didn't put a parent and a child in the Garden, I put a husband and a wife. When you marry your spouse, that must supersede all other relationships, even the parental relationship. Your spouse and your marriage must be the number one priority in your life."

Your marriage must be more important to you than anything else. No other human being should get more of your love, energy, industry, and commitment than your spouse. God asks that a man leave his father and mother, as powerful as that relationship may have been, to forge a new union that must be an even more important and powerful force in his life.

Pseudo-Spouses

When I was a young pastor in a small Southern town, I did a lot of marriage counseling. Some marriages were harmed by things like drink, drugs, pornography, or an extramarital affair. But in most of the troubled marriages I saw, the problem stemmed not from bad things but from very good things that had become too important. When some good thing becomes more engrossing and important than your spouse, it can destroy the marriage.

There were many varieties. Sometimes I heard a wife say, "His parents' opinions are more important to him than mine. Pleasing them is far more important to him than pleasing me." Or I would hear a husband say, "She's totally wrapped up in the kids, in their needs, programs, school, social life. If I need something, she shrugs and says, 'OK,' but it's the kids and their needs that really excite her. Being a mother is much more enjoyable to her than being a wife." I could also hear either husband or wife say about the other, "His (or her) career is what's really important. The career is the real spouse—the career gets all the ingenuity and time and energy." If your spouse does not feel that you are putting him or her first, then by definition, you aren't. And when that happens, your marriage is dying.

Plenty of people have marital problems because they haven't "left" to cleave to their spouses. You have failed to leave your parents if you are more driven by their wishes and expectations than by your spouse's. But you can also fail to leave your parents if you resent or hate them too much. For example, you may say, "I won't bring my kids to church because my parents did that and I hated it!" But this means you are being controlled by your parents. You aren't making the choice based on what your children need but based on repudiating your parents. Or you may say, "I can't marry him—he reminds me of my father." So what if a man resembles your father? You should be judging him on what he is *in toto* and how he relates to you. Don't let your bad relationship with your father control how you relate to your partner. You must leave it behind.

Some spouses have constant arguments over a variety of practical issues, from how decisions are made to how vacations are taken to how children are disciplined. Look carefully to see whether you are insisting that you do things exactly the way your parents did them. Maybe your family's way of operating was wise in a particular regard, but you should only carry it into your new family if it makes sense to your spouse, too. You shouldn't do it simply because "my family did it that way." When you marry, you commit to becoming a new decision-making unit and to developing new patterns and ways of doing things. If you rigidly impose the patterns that you saw in your own family rather than working together with your spouse to create new ones that fit both of you, you haven't "left home" yet.

Over-commitment to parents is one problem that sinks many marriages. Arguably, over-commitment to children is even more of a problem. There are a lot of reasons why this is a major temptation today. First, your children do need you desperately. They are part of your new family, not your former family, so it is right to consider parenting a very high and important calling in life. Also, if a marriage cools, it is natural to get your primary need for love and affection met through the parent-child relationship rather than the husband-wife relationship.

But if you love your children more than your spouse, the entire family will be pulled out of joint and everyone will suffer. And I do mean everyone. I know of a woman who was giving her life for her daughter, but in such a way that it was creating great stress and strain between her and her husband. The husband resented the time and effort the mother was putting into their daughter's musical career. It was clear to nearly everyone that the mother was fulfilling some of her own unrealized dreams through her daughter, but in the process she was killing her marriage. The irony was, this was the worst possible thing for her daughter, who was very anxious about the crumbling marriage. A strong marriage between parents makes children grow up feeling the world is a safe place and love is possible. Also, her daughter was not learning from observation how a good marriage worked or how men and women can relate together well. By putting her daughter before her husband, she was harming her daughter.

A breakthrough came when a counselor said to her, "The best

way for you to be a great mother to your daughter is by being a great wife to your husband. That is the main thing your daughter needs from you." When she began to see this, she began to give her marriage the priority it should have.

Research on child abuse has revealed that many of the people who physically abuse their children don't do so because they hate their children. Often it is because their children are the ones on whom they rely for most of their love. And if their children don't love them back by behaving properly, their anger explodes; they snap. But children are children. They shouldn't be expected to give you the friendship and love that a spouse can.

The Power of Marriage

Marriage is so much like salvation and our relationship with Christ that Paul says you can't understand marriage without looking at the gospel. So let's do that. Salvation is a fresh start. Old things have passed away—behold, the new has come. And when through the gospel we enter into a marriage-like relationship with Jesus as our Divine Spouse, that means giving Christ the supremacy in your life (Colossians 1:15ff). In other words, Jesus asks for nothing that any spouse doesn't ask for. "Put me first," he says, "have no other pseudo-gods before me." It is the same with marriage. Marriage won't work unless you put your marriage and your spouse first, and you don't turn good things, like parents, children, career, and hobbies, into pseudo-spouses.

In Ephesians 5:28, Paul introduces another metaphor. He says that a husband ought to love his wife as he does his own body. Paul is referring to the fact that your health is foundational to everything else you do. What if you decide that making a lot of money will make you happy, so you put your work ahead of your health? You work enormously long hours so that you get no exercise or sleep, you eat very poorly, and you put yourself under a lot of stress. Yes, you are making a lot of money, but the heart attack you bring on will make it impossible to enjoy your wealth. In other words, if you think you can put your "happiness" ahead of your health, you actually won't be happy at all. Good health, then, is more fundamental to happiness than great wealth, as most rich people will tell you when their health has broken down.

Paul likens marriage to the health of your body. As we have said, it must be the most fundamental human relationship of your life. When you marry, you've gotten into something that was invented by God. And if you determine to run your marriage your way, you're in for a lot of trouble, because marriage is God's institution. He built it to be the primary relationship in your life. If you think that marriage is going to be a sidebar to your great career, that it is going to come second or third in your life and that your spouse had better get used to it, watch out. Marriage isn't built that way. Once you're married, your marriage has to take priority.

The reason it must have priority is because of the power of marriage. Marriage has the power to set the course of your life as a whole. If your marriage is strong, even if all the circumstances in your life around you are filled with trouble and weakness, it won't matter. You will be able to move out into the world in strength. However, if your marriage is weak, even if all the circumstances in your life around you are marked by success and strength, it won't matter. You will move out into the world in weakness. Marriage has that kind of power—the power to set the course of your whole life. It has that power because it was instituted by God. And because it has that unequalled power, it must have an unequalled, supreme priority.

And the main message of this chapter is that the key to giving marriage that kind of priority is spiritual friendship. So many

THE MEANING OF MARRIAGE

marriages are begun with the journey to God only as an after-thought. Many Christians congratulate themselves that they have married another believer, but they look at their prospective spouse's faith as simply one more factor that makes him or her compatible, like common interests and hobbies. But that is not what spiritual friendship is. It is eagerly helping one another know, serve, love, and resemble God in deeper and deeper ways.

A parishioner heard me preach on Ephesians 5, where Paul says that the purpose of marriage is to "sanctify" us. She said, "I thought the whole point of marriage was to be happy! You make it sound like a lot of work." She was right—marriage is a lot of work—but she was wrong to pit that against happiness, and here is why. Paul is saying that one of the main purposes of marriage is to make us "holy . . . without stain or wrinkle or any other blemish . . ." (verses 26–27). What does that mean? It means to have Jesus's character reproduced in us, outlined as the "fruit of the Spirit"—love, joy, peace, patience, kindness, goodness, faith-ful integrity, gentle humility, and self-control—in Galatians 5:22–25. When Jesus's love, wisdom, and greatness are formed in us, each with our own unique gifts and callings, we become our "true selves," the persons we were created to be. Every page in the Bible cries that the journey to this horizon cannot be accom-plished alone. We must face it and share it with brothers and sis-ters, friends of our heart. And the very best human friendship possible for that adventure is with the lover-friend who is your spouse.

Is all this a lot of work? Indeed it is—but it is the work we were built to do. Does this mean "marriage is not about being happy; it's about being holy"? Yes and no. As we have seen, that is too stark a contrast. If you understand what holiness is, you come to see that real happiness is on the far side of holiness, not the near side. Holiness gives us new desires and brings old desires into line with one another. So if we want to be happy in marriage, we will accept that marriage is designed to make us holy.

As C. S. Lewis writes:

> He gives the happiness that there is, not the happiness that is not. To be God—to be like God and to share his goodness in creaturely response—to be miserable— these are the only three alternatives. If we will not learn to eat the only food that the universe grows—the only food that any possible universe can ever grow— then we must starve eternally.[12]

Now we are ready to get specific. How exactly can spouses help one another on this journey to God? The answers will come in the next chapter.

FIVE

LOVING THE STRANGER

. . . and gave himself up for her to make her holy, cleans-
ing her by the washing with water through the word.

Ephesians 5:25–26

L et's recall the point made by Stanley Hauerwas:

> We never know whom we marry; we just think we do.
> Or even if we first marry the right person, just give it a
> while and he or she will change. For marriage, being
> [the enormous thing it is] means we are not the same
> person after we have entered it. The primary problem
> is . . . learning how to love and care for the stranger to
> whom you find yourself married.[1]

Hauerwas's realism rings true to people who have been married for a long time. Marriage changes us. Having children changes us. A career switch changes us. Age changes us. On top of everything else, marriage brings out and reveals traits in you that were there all along but were hidden from everyone including you, but now they are all seen by your spouse.

Most people enter marriage through the "in-love" experience, and at its peak it is euphoric. Two people can become almost obsessed with each other. Marriage counselor and author Gary Chapman argues that the in-love phase, which he believes usually lasts several months to two years, includes the illusion that the beloved is perfect in every aspect that matters. Describing one of his counselees, Jen, he writes: "Her best friend could see the flaws [in her fiancé]—it bothers her how he talks to Jen sometimes, but Jen won't listen. Her mother, noting the young man seems unable to hold a steady job, keeps her concerns to herself but asks polite questions about 'Ryan's plans.'"

Chapman goes on to describe the condition:

> Of course we are not totally naïve. We know intellectually that we will eventually have differences. But we are certain that . . . we will [quickly] reach agreement. . . . We are caught up in the beauty and charm of the other's personality. Our love is the most wonderful thing we have ever experienced. We observe that some married couples seem to have lost that feeling but it will never happen to us. "Maybe they didn't have the real thing," we reason.[2]

The in-love experience passes when the flaws in the other person come home to us. Things that seemed small and inconsequential now loom large. We begin to feel that we did not really know the person after all. And this presents us with the challenge of loving a person who, at the moment, seems in large part a stranger, not the person you remember marrying.

When this happens, people respond in a number of different ways. If your purpose in marriage was to acquire a "soul mate"—a person who would not change you and would supportively help you reach your life goals—then this particular reality of marriage will be deeply disorienting. You wake up to the realization that your marriage will take a huge investment of time just to make it work. Just as distressing will be the discovery that your spouse finds *you* a stranger and has begun to confront you with a list of your serious shortcomings. Your first response will be to tell yourself you made a bad choice and failed to find someone truly compatible.

What if, however, you began your marriage understanding its purpose as spiritual friendship for the journey to the new creation? What if you expected marriage to be about helping each other grow out of your sins and flaws into the new self God is creating? Then you will actually be expecting the "stranger" seasons, and when you come to one you will roll up your sleeves and get to work.

What are the "tools" for this work? How can we engage one another in spiritual friendship to help us on our journey toward our future selves? How do we love each other so that our marriage goes on from strength to strength rather than stalling out in repetitive arguments that end in fruitless silence? The basic answer is that you must speak the truth in love with the power of God's grace.

> *Speaking the truth in love, we will in all things grow up*
> *into him who is the Head, that is, Christ.*
>
> (Ephesians 4:15)

That statement sounds platitudinous, until we break it down. As a divine institution, marriage has several inherent powers that we must accept and use—the power of truth, the power of love, and the power of grace. As we use each power in the life of our spouse, we will help him or her grow into a person who not only reflects the character of Christ but who also can love us and help us in the same way. These three powers will do their best work in us during times when we find it hard to love the semi-stranger to whom we are married.

The Power of Truth—Facing the Worst

There's a passage in Soren Kierkegaard's work where he likens all of us to people at a costume ball. "Do you not know that there comes a midnight hour when every one has to throw off his mask?"[3] At the time, the custom was to keep your mask on for the first part of festivities. During that time, you danced, ate, and talked with the other guests, but no one knew who anyone else was. But then at midnight all masks had to be stripped off and everyone's true identity was revealed. In some ways, the Cinderella story is an extension of this theme, that an hour comes in which all the layers of glitter are taken away and the real, unvarnished you stands there, unfiltered for all to see. That sounds like Judgment Day, doesn't it? But it also sounds like marriage. In marriage you can't hide. You are exposed. You finally have your mask and finery stripped away, as it were. How so?

Marriage brings two human beings into closer contact than any other relationship can bring them. The parent-child relationship is of course very close—they live together and see one another's character—but there is a major power differential there. The child and the parents are on such different planes that it is easy for either the parent to dismiss the child's criticism or the child to dismiss the parent's. Besides, it is expected that children grow up and leave.

Marriage is also a more inescapable relationship than cohabitation. When unmarried people live together, they certainly see one another "up close," but each party knows that the other one does not have the same claims on him or her that would be true if they were married. They don't merge their entire lives—socially, economically, legally—and so either one can walk away with relatively few complications if they don't like what they are being told.

Marriage is different from these others. The merged life of marriage brings you into the closest, most inescapable contact with another person possible. And that means not only that you see each other close up, but that you are forced to deal with the flaws and sins of one another.

What are the flaws that your spouse will see? You may be a fearful person, with a tendency toward great anxiety. You may be a proud person, with a tendency to be opinionated and selfish. You may be an inflexible person, with a tendency to be demanding and sulky if you don't get your way. You may be an abrasive or harsh person, who people tend to respect more than they love. You may be an undisciplined person, with a tendency to be unreliable and disorganized. You may be an oblivious person, who tends to be distracted, insensitive, and unaware of how you come across to others. You may be a perfectionist, with a tendency to be judgmental and critical of others and also to get down on yourself. You may be an impatient, irritable person, with a tendency to hold grudges or to lose your temper too often. You may be a highly independent person, who does not like to be responsible for the needs of others, who dislikes having to make joint decisions, and who most definitely hates to ask for any help yourself. You may be a person who wants far too much to be liked, and so you tend to shade the truth, you can't keep secrets, and you work too hard to please everyone. You may be thrifty but at the same time miserly with money, too unwilling to spend it on your own needs appropriately, and ungenerous to others.

Others have seen these flaws in you. Your parents certainly have, and others that have lived with you, such as siblings or college roommates or friends, have seen them, too. But if they spoke to you about them, you could either write them off as being biased or mistaken, or you could escape from the weight of the criticism by vaguely promising to do better in the future. However, your confronters didn't keep up their confrontations, and you haven't really admitted the severity of the problem. The reason was that the flaw did not pose the same kind of problem for them as it will for your spouse.

But while your character flaws may have created mild problems for other people, they will create major problems for your spouse and your marriage. For example, a tendency to hold grudges could be a problem within friendships, but within marriage it can kill the relationship. No one else is as inconvenienced and hurt by your flaws as your spouse is. And therefore your spouse becomes more keenly aware of what is wrong with you than anyone else ever has been.

When conducting marriage services, I like to explain this aspect of marriage using the analogy of a bridge. Think of an old bridge over a stream. Imagine that there are structural defects in the bridge that are hard to see. There may be hairline fractures that a very close inspection would reveal, but to the naked eye there is nothing wrong. But now see a ten-ton Mack truck drive onto the bridge. What will happen? The pressure from the weight of the truck will open those hairline fractures so they can be seen. The structural defects will be exposed for all to see because of the strain the truck puts on the bridge. Suddenly, you can see where all the flaws are. The truck didn't create the weaknesses; it revealed them.

When you get married, your spouse is a big truck driving right through your heart. Marriage brings out the worst in you. It doesn't create your weaknesses (though you may blame your spouse for your blow-ups)—it reveals them. This is not a bad thing, though. How can you change into your "glory-self" if you assume that you're already pretty close to perfect as it is?

When I was diagnosed with thyroid cancer in 2002, it was during a routine checkup. My doctor just happened to feel a tiny lump in my neck. Though the surgery and subsequent treatments were painful and frightening, at no time did the thought ever cross my mind, "Oh, I wish the doctor had never found that lump. It was so small, why couldn't he just have missed it and spared me all this trouble!" That was because the consequences of being "spared all the trouble" would have been, in the end, far more deadly, far more trouble, than finding and treating the cancer while it was small and confined.

The first part of making your marriage into a relationship that enhances growth is to accept this inherent feature of married life. Marriage by its very nature has the "power of truth"—the power to show you the truth about who you are. People are appalled when they get sharp, far-reaching criticisms from their spouses. They immediately begin to think they married the wrong person. But you must realize that it isn't ultimately your spouse who is exposing the sinfulness of your heart—it's marriage itself. Marriage does not so much bring you into confrontation with your spouse as confront you with yourself. Marriage shows you a realistic, unflattering picture of who you are and then takes you by the scruff of the neck and forces you to pay attention to it.

This may sound discouraging, but it is really the road to liberation. Counselors will tell you that the only flaws that can enslave you are the ones that you are blind to. If you are in denial about some feature of your character, that feature will control you. But marriage blows the lid off, turns the lights on. Now there is hope. Finally you can begin dealing with the real you. Don't resist this power that marriage has. Give your spouse the right to talk to you about what is wrong with you. Paul talks about how Jesus "washes" and "cleanses" us of stains and blemishes. Give your spouse the right to do that.

All his life, Rob had few friends. One reason for this was that since childhood, Rob had a real problem putting himself into the shoes of others. He had little or no empathy and often was surprised at people's negative reactions to his words or deeds. When he was in fourth grade, a school counselor told his parents that he thought Rob was a "mild sociopath," someone who often trampled on the feelings of others because he couldn't sympathetically imagine what they were feeling. This character flaw had created problems for Rob for years, but he couldn't see it for what it was. Few of his acquaintances ripened into friendships, and in his first jobs he regularly made missteps that infuriated both superiors and those reporting to him. He lost one job over it.

Then he met Jessica, and by the second date they both were deep into the in-love experience. She thought he was a brilliant conversationalist, and he was, and he loved the fact that she was an assertive kind of woman who didn't easily get her feelings hurt. Several times, his sense of humor strayed into the realm of the hurtful and the insulting. This was a problem that he had had all his life, but unlike so many others, Jessica just told him off and put him in his place. He liked that! Finally a woman who wasn't a shrinking violet.

And so they married, but as the months went by, Rob's insensitive humor and semi-abusive remarks got worse. When we are in love, we are on our best behavior, but at home and with someone becoming more and more familiar, our natural instincts take over. We no longer catch ourselves. Soon the full extent of Rob's problem character was there for Jessica to see in all its ugly detail. Jessica began to see how he spoke to other people, and most of them were not as resilient and thick skinned as she was. She realized the kind of relational problems that he was going to have all his life. She became deeply disillusioned with him, and, just a year after their wedding, she found herself fantasizing about being single again and free from him.

When Rob realized the depth of her unhappiness, he became alarmed, and together they sought counseling from the pastor of their church. That began a long journey. After many weeks of meetings with their pastoral counselor, they had their first breakthrough. One evening, both Rob and Jessica began to see that she had been brought into Rob's life for this very purpose. She *was* a strong woman who was not fragile. She was *exactly* the person who could stand toe-to-toe with Rob and say, "That hurt me. I'm going to tell you exactly how it felt until you learn what your words do to people. I'm not going to clam up on you and just withdraw, and I'm not going to attack you back. I'm going to be like Jesus has been with us—accepting us in love but not allowing us to just destroy ourselves with sin."

Rob had never had anyone love him like this. People had either just given up and withdrawn from him or had simply attacked him. Here was someone who calmly but candidly described the devastating effect of his words. And most transforming of all was the fact that the person who was telling him about his hurtfulness was the person he loved most in the world. The more Jessica loved him so nobly and well, the less he wanted to see her hurt. And so, slowly but surely, Rob began to listen, learn, and change.

Jessica herself came to see that she also had a need for radical change. "I had a fiercely independent spirit that made it hard for me to depend on anyone," she said. "If anyone let me down, I simply dropped them. I was completely impatient with them." When she saw the depths of Rob's problems, she wanted to flee as she always had, but her marriage vow wouldn't allow her to do that. For the first time in her life, she couldn't run from a damaged person.

Three years after their wedding, Rob's parents hardly recognized him. He was more thoughtful and empathetic than they ever thought he could be. Jessica's parents noticed a gentleness and a graciousness toward weakness that they hadn't seen in her before. Marriage's "power of truth" had done its work.

"Someone Better" Is Your Spouse

We see, then, that the "power of truth" that comes with marriage is a gift, but it truly is a hard gift to receive. When you are seeing some new flaws in your spouse, or if you are always being told what is wrong with you, it takes a toll on the feelings. We are like ore right out of the mine. When you got married you saw the gold in your spouse, but as time goes on you see all the impurities. You see attitudes and personality traits and sinful habits that are going to be burned off as "dross" in the light of God's glory over time. These flaws are not permanent. But they can loom large in your mind and create big problems, and that is hard to take.

And yet if two people learn to make the distinction between the dross and the gold, it can be a great help. Instead of saying, "That's just the way he is, and I hate it," remember that the part of him you hate isn't the real, permanent him. In Romans 7:14–25, Paul speaks about this dynamic in himself: "I do the very things I hate" (7:15) and therefore "it's not really me doing it, it's the sin living within me" (7:20). This does not mean that Paul doesn't take full responsibility for his actions, but he knows that the sinful actions are not from his "innermost being" where he "delights in the law of God" (7:22). Christian spouses must make the same distinction.

It will help a great deal to say, "I hate it when he does that, but that is not truly *him*. That is not permanent." It will help even more to work together to agree on what is the dross and what is the gold in each other so you can say, "This is the real you, this is the real me, this is what God wants us to be, and this is what has got to go. And we've got to work together against it."

I won't minimize the disappointment of seeing the dross. When people first begin to see the flaws in their spouses, some flee the marriage. Others just withdraw, downscaling their expectations of happiness almost completely and just learn to get along. Others go into a long period of fighting and blaming their spouses for their unhappiness. All of these approaches share one thing in common, however. One spouse looks at his or her spouse's weaknesses and says, "I need to find someone better than this."

But the great thing about the model of Christian marriage we are presenting here is that when you envision the "someone better," you can think of the future version of the person to whom you are already married. The someone better is the spouse you already have. God has indeed given us a desire for the perfect spouse, but you should seek it in the one to whom you're married. Why discard this partner for someone else only to discover *that* person's deep, hidden flaws? Some people with serial marriages go through the cycle of infatuation, disillusionment, rejection, and flight to someone else—over and over. The only way you're going to actually begin to see another person's glory-self is to stick with him or her.

Many people have asked me, "How can you tell whether you've got a friendship on which you can base a marriage?" The answer that Kathy and I have always given is this. When you see the problems in each other, do you just want to run away, or do you find a desire to work on them together? If the second impulse is yours, then you have the makings of a marriage. Do you obsess over your partner's external shortcomings, or can you see the beauty within, and do you want to see it increasingly released? Then move forward. The power of truth that marriage has should hold no fear for you.[4]

The Godly Tantrum

Before we move on from the power of truth to that of love, let me encourage readers not to shrink from really telling the truth to one another. Kathy talks of what she calls the "godly tantrum." By this she means not an emotional loss of temper but an unrelenting insistence on being heard.

When my family moved to New York City to start Redeemer Presbyterian Church, we knew that it would be very time-consuming, especially given my tendency to overwork. From what I learned from other church planters, my life would be out of balance for about three years. That is, I'd be working longer hours than I could sustain permanently without endangering my health or my family relationships. So I asked Kathy to grant me these long hours for three years. After that, I promised, things would change. I'd cut back. OK? OK, she said.

But the three-year mark came and went, and Kathy asked me, as we agreed, to cut back on my work hours. "Just a couple more months," I said. "I have this and that commitment that I have to see through. Just a couple of more months." I kept saying that. The months flew by with no change.

One day I came home from work. It was a nice day outside and I noticed that the door to our apartment's balcony was open. Just as I was taking off my jacket I heard a smashing noise coming from the balcony. In another couple of seconds I heard another one. I walked out on to the balcony and to my surprise saw Kathy sitting on the floor. She had a hammer, and next to her was a stack of our wedding china. On the ground were the shards of two smashed saucers.

"What are you doing?" I asked.

She looked up and said, "You aren't listening to me. You don't realize that if you keep working these hours you are going to destroy this family. I don't know how to get through to you. You aren't seeing how serious this is. This is what you are doing." And she brought the hammer down on the third saucer. It splintered into pieces.

I sat down trembling. I thought she had snapped. "I'm listening. I'm listening," I said. As we talked it became clear that she was intense and laser focused, but she was not in a rage or out of control emotionally. She spoke calmly but forcefully. Her arguments were the same as they had been for months, but I realized how deluded I had been. There would never be a convenient time to cut back. I was addicted to the level of productivity I had achieved. I had to do something. She saw me listening for the first time and we hugged.

Finally I inquired, "When I first came out here I thought you were having an emotional meltdown. How did you get control of yourself so fast?"

With a grin she answered, "It was no meltdown. Do you see these three saucers I smashed?" I nodded. "I have no cups for them. The cups have broken over the years. I had three saucers to spare. I'm glad you sat down before I had to break any more!"

Give each other the right to hold one another accountable. "Exhort one another daily, lest you become hardened by the deceitfulness of sin" (Hebrews 3:13).[5]

The Power of Love—Renewing the Heart

Marriage has the power of truth, the ability to reveal to you who you really are, with all your flaws. How wonderful that it also has the "power of love"—an unmatched power to affirm you and heal you of the deepest wounds and hurts of your life.

You come into marriage with a self-image, an assessment of your worth. It is the sign of many verdicts passed upon you over the years by a great variety of people. Parents, siblings, boyfriends and girlfriends, teachers, and coaches have all passed judgments on you, called you good and bad, worthy and unworthy, promising and hopeless. We have sifted through them and tried to forget some, but that is hard. Statements of affirmation make a far lighter and less lasting impression upon the human heart than criticisms and condemnations. We may have been wounded by things that have been said to us—they have left an indelible impression. So there are many layers to this self-image, and many of them are contradictory. Your self-view has been stitched together often without a unifying theme. If it were made visible, it might look something like the Frankenstein monster, with many disparate parts.

However, perhaps the most damaging statements that have ever been said about us are those things we have said about ourselves to ourselves. Many people have a never-ending loop of self-talk that berates them for being foolish, stupid, a failure, a loser.

But now into your life comes someone who has the power to overturn all the accumulated verdicts that have ever been passed upon you by others or by you yourself.[6] Marriage puts into your spouse's hand a massive power to reprogram your own self-appreciation. He or she can overturn anything previously said about you, to a great degree redeeming the past. The love and affirmation of your spouse has the power to heal you of many of the deepest wounds. Why? If all the world says you are ugly, but your spouse says you are beautiful, you feel beautiful. To paraphrase a passage of Scripture, your heart may condemn you, but your spouse's opinion is greater than your heart.

In my own life, I must confess that I had never felt "manly" until I got married. I was a nerd before it was fashionable, playing trumpet in the marching band and staying in the Boy Scouts through high school. Good things, no doubt, but not cool or macho. I was often mocked and excluded, especially during high school, for my uncoolness. But Kathy looked at me like her knight in shining armor. She has always told me, and continues to tell me, that though all the world may look at me and see Clark Kent, she knows that underneath I have on blue underwear. She has always been very quick to point out and celebrate anything I have done that is courageous. Over the years, bit by bit, it has sunk in. To my wife, I'm Superman, and it makes me feel like a man in a way nothing else could.

The same aspect of marriage that entails the power of truth also contributes to this power of love. That is, because marriage merges two lives and brings you into the closest possible contact, a positive assessment by your spouse has ultimate credibility. If someone I know a little comes up to me and says, "You are one of the kindest men I know," I will certainly feel complimented and pleased. But how deeply will it sink in? Not too far. Why? Because a part of my heart says, "Well, nice. But he doesn't really know me at all." But if my wife, after years of living with me, says, "You are one of the kindest men I know," that goes in. That affirmation is profoundly comforting. Why? Because she knows me better than anyone. And if, over the years, you have grown to love and admire your spouse more and more, then his or her praise will get more and more strengthening and healing. As Faramir says to Sam Gamgee in *The Lord of the Rings: The Two Towers*, "The praise of the praiseworthy is above all rewards." To be highly esteemed by someone you highly esteem is the greatest thing in the world.

This principle explains why, ultimately, to know that the Lord of the universe loves you is the strongest foundation that any human being can have. A growing awareness of God's love in Christ is the greatest reward. And yet we must not forget Adam in the garden. Though he had a perfect relationship with God, his humanity's relational nature was designed also for human love. Your spouse's love for you and Christ's love work together in your life with powerful interaction.

The power of healing love in marriage is a miniature version of the same power that Jesus has with us. In Christ, God sees us as righteous, holy, and beautiful (2 Corinthians 5:21). The world tells us about our faults, and we know they are there, but God's love for us covers our sins and continues despite them. So Jesus has the ability to overcome everything anyone has ever said about or to you. In a Christian marriage, you're living that out in miniature. Sometimes your spouse points you directly to Jesus's love. Sometimes your spouse's affirmation imitates Jesus's love and stimulates us to more fully believe and accept the love we have in Christ.

So, more than any other human relationship, marriage has a unique power to heal all hurts and convince us of our own distinctive beauty and worth.

Love Me—No, You Love Me

How do you give this life-healing love to your spouse so he or she actually feels loved? That is a very crucial subject and skill. Let me start with an illustration before I begin to lay out the principles.

In Kathy's family, her father regularly helped her mother with the chores. He was very involved in the day-to-day domestic operations, including the care and feeding of the children. In my family, however, my father was never asked to do much in the way of chores inside the home, and in particular he wasn't involved in clothing or feeding the kids. When we got married, we were barely aware of these differences in our family backgrounds, even though there had been one incident that should have tipped us off.

Once when I came to visit Kathy in her home, I ate dinner in the kitchen with her family. (We'd progressed beyond the "dining room and fine china" stage.) And when the meal was over I simply stood up and walked out of the room. My future mother-in-law was appalled. In Kathy's household, *every*one helped with the cleanup. At the very least, everyone was expected to take their plates and silverware and cups and any other item on the table next to their place and bring it to the sink or refrigerator. When she saw that I never even gave this a thought, she muttered something to Kathy about my wanting people to wait on me. But in my family, my mother would have been insulted if even family members—let alone a guest—helped with the dishes. That was her job—to serve and do all those menial tasks so that others did not have to do them.

This family background difference did not show itself in our marriage until the birth of our first child. I remember one day I was sitting holding David when Kathy was working in the kitchen. I noticed a funny smell and said, "Kathy, his diaper needs to be changed."

And Kathy said, "Well you know what we say around our house, don't you?"

"What?"

"Finders keepers!" She laughed. This meant, "Don't look at me; I'm busy. You've got the child. You change his dirty diaper."

But I found myself becoming quite angry. I felt—well, I couldn't immediately put my finger on it. It seemed like a lack of respect. This shouldn't be my job. When I resisted, then it was Kathy's turn to feel annoyed. Hey, it's just a dirty diaper. You aren't busy and I am, she said. We didn't resolve the issue that day, because we didn't really understand what was going on. The care of the children in general, and smelly, poopy diapers in particular, became a bone of contention for a good while until we began to understand the underlying dynamics operating in our hearts.

Kathy's mother had had a stroke when she was only in her forties, and her father had stepped in to do many practical household chores in a way that was atypical for our parents' generation of working fathers and stay-at-home mothers. Her mother was deeply grateful for this and admired her husband's love and humility. Kathy heard her mother say, "This is how my husband loves me: He helps me with the chores and children." In my family, however, my father was never asked to do those kinds of chores. I'm not sure he ever saw the inside of a dirty diaper. He worked extremely long hours and was often very tired. My mother was grateful for his being a good provider and felt that the only way she could make an equal contribution to the family's welfare was if she asked him to do absolutely nothing around the home. And I heard my mother say, "This is how I love your father. He works so hard. He provides for the family, so when he comes home, I don't ask him to do those things. I take care of them."

This difference in our families was not merely a different domestic division of labor. This was a difference in what we could call "love currency." Kathy's father was a man of few words; he was not verbally expressive. But he gave his wife love in the particular way that she needed it and that she knew was costly to him. It was far more valuable to her than if he had bought her flowers and jewelry. She appreciated it deeply, and it made her feel loved. My father, on the other hand, who worked such long hours, could have had a wife who complained about virtually raising the children on her own. She did not, and he appreciated it deeply and felt like a "king in his castle."

We had observed these patterns of love currency in our respective families, and they had become part of our unconscious assumptions. And that is why we had an abiding conflict over "Who changes the diapers in this family?" It was perplexing to us at first. It seemed like a pretty simple issue. Why was there so much emotional heat around it?

Eventually we realized that when Kathy asked me to change our son's diaper, I heard her saying that she didn't love me, that she didn't think I worked that hard. And when I asked her to be the one to change the diapers, she heard me saying that it was women's work, not really important. In short, Kathy was actually saying, at a semiconscious level: "If you love me the way my father loved my mother, you would change the diaper." And I was saying in my heart, "If you love me the way my mother loved my father, you wouldn't even be asking me." Each of us heard the other one saying, "I don't love you," because each of us was failing to get love in the particular way we felt was emotionally valuable to us.

What happened? We realized what was going on, and in that particular instance it was I who made the change, because I didn't want to fall into a pattern of pitting my work against involvement with my children. But the lesson was one that we never forgot. It is not enough to simply say, "I love you." Nor is it enough to give love to your spouse in the way to which *you* feel most accustomed. If you want to give a person $100, there are many ways to do so. You can give it in cash or by check or in gold or in kind. You can give it in different currencies. So you ask, "In which form do you want the hundred dollars?" In the same way you learn to give your spouse love in the way he or she finds most emotionally valuable and powerful. That is the only way to bring the remaking and healing power of love into your spouse's life.[7]

The Currencies of Love

What we call love currencies are often called "love languages." This metaphor is also very helpful. If we say "I love you" to someone who does not understand a word of English, then the love does not get through. We are sending it, but it is not being received. We must learn to send love in forms that the other person can comprehend. I will dare to use one more metaphor. A radio signal may be sent out on one frequency, but the radio receiver does not respond if it is tuned to another frequency. In the same way, a husband may be sending out the message "I love you" by being very sensual and romantic toward his wife, but that might not be where her love receiver is tuned. He doesn't listen sympathetically to her when she wants to talk about the things that discourage her. She desperately wants an understanding listener, but he is impatient, usually barking out some brief advice. So she tells her husband, "I don't feel you love me!" He retorts, "But I do love you!" Why the discrepancy? He is sending his love over a channel to which she is not tuned. This is why, so often, love is being sent in a marriage but is not received.

There are many different ways to express love. You can buy a present, say "I love you" out loud, give a compliment, be romantic and tender physically, abide by your loved one's wishes, and spend time in focused attention. That's just the beginning of the list. For centuries, thinkers have discerned forms of love. The Greeks had words to distinguish affection (*storge*), love between friends (*philos*), erotic love (*eros*), and service (*agape*). There are other ways of breaking down expressions of love into categories. All forms of love are necessary, and none are to be ignored, but all of us find some forms of love to be more emotionally valuable to us. They are a currency that we find particularly precious, a language that delivers the message of love to our hearts with the most power. Some types of love are more thrilling and fulfilling to us when we receive them.

Why? Sometimes a particular form of love is more valuable because some significant person in your life was particularly inept at it. Perhaps a form of love is crucial now because of your life circumstances. At any rate, some forms of love especially delight your heart. Anyone who wants to give you love needs to know what those forms are and to express his or her love in those ways.

We should do this for our spouses because God did this for us. When Moses asked to see God's glory, he was told that he couldn't see it, that it would be lethal. Yet in the gospel of John we read that God has come in human form, so that in Jesus "we beheld his glory, glory of the only begotten of the Father, full of grace and truth" (John 1:14). That is amazing. God expressed his glory to us in a form we could relate to—a human form. In the incarnation, God came to us in a manner that we could grasp. So we, too, must clothe our love in the forms to which our spouse can relate. We must communicate love in the way our spouse needs it. Here are some practical principles for doing that.

First, realize you have a "filter" on. You tend to only "hear" certain kinds of love language. For example, your spouse may be working hard to provide you with material things, but you wish he were more verbal. There is a tendency to say, "He doesn't love me!" because he is not communicating love in your most valuable language. Take off your filter and recognize the love your spouse is giving you.

Theologian R. C. Sproul once told us a story about himself and his wife, Vesta, that illustrates this principle. "What I really wanted for my birthday was something I wouldn't buy for myself. I was hoping for new golf clubs. Vesta, a practical person, knew I needed white shirts. So she bought me six beautiful white shirts. I tried not to show my disappointment." When it came time for Vesta's birthday, however, he didn't do any better. Wanting to give her something lavish and extravagant, he bought her a fur coat, not realizing that what she really wanted was a new washer and dryer. They were both trying hard to express love to each other, but they were speaking their own languages to a person who needed to hear love in a different dialect.

Consider whether some of the running conflicts you have with your spouse are not love language conflicts. That can soften your attitude and change your strategy. You could, like Kathy and I, have an intractable conflict over child-care responsibilities. But it could be that the husband is thinking (as I did), "If you love me like my mother loved my father, you'd not ask me to change diapers," and the wife could be thinking (as Kathy did), "If you love me like my father loved my mother, you'd volunteer." Instead of thinking about the other person, "He (she) is so selfish," each should think, "He (she) is feeling particularly unloved."

Learn the primary languages of your spouse and send love over those channels, not over the channels you prefer for yourself. We tend to give love through the channels in which we like to receive it.

Remember that improper love languages can be "heard in reverse." For example, if you give material gifts to a person who wants some other form, she may say, "You are trying to buy my love!"

Never abuse the primary love language. Never withhold it to hurt the other, for the hurt will go deep. A man who greatly values getting respect from his wife in public will not be able to take it when she mocks him in front of their friends. A woman who needs lots of verbal affirmation will be devastated by the silent treatment.

Transitioning from In Love to Love

We have spoken often about how the early experience of romantic love tends to wear off and bring us back to reality. When that

THE MEANING OF MARRIAGE

happens, how do we make a good transition to loving our spouse deliberately and well over the long term?

Author Gary Chapman provides an account from his marriage counseling experience that answers this question well.[8]

Becky came alone to see the counselor and through tears told him that her husband, Brent, was leaving. Brent later came to see the counselor at his wife's request, but he said, "I just don't love her anymore. I don't want to hurt her, and I wish it were different, but I don't have any feelings for her." At first, Brent and Becky had been euphorically in love with each other. But in the months that followed the wedding, both had come to see one another's flaws and the feelings cooled. In Brent's case, the feelings of love cooled the fastest and then simply vanished. Now he said he wanted out. He admitted that he had been in love with someone else for several months. He said he could not imagine living without this new woman's love, and he was intent on getting a divorce.

The counselor proceeded to ask him to consider a particular way to look at things. He said most marriages start with an in-love "high" during which time both partners feel profoundly loved by the very presence of the other. But eventually that high wears off and then love must become a deliberate choice. He said to Brent:

> [After the euphoria wears off] if our spouse has learned to speak our primary love language, our need for love will continue to be satisfied. If, on the other hand, he or she does not speak our love language, our tank will slowly drain, and we will no longer feel loved. Meeting that need is definitely a choice. If I learn the emotional love language of my spouse and speak it frequently . . . when she comes down from the obsession of the in-love experience, she will hardly even miss it because her

emotional love tank will continue to be filled. However, if I have not learned her primary love language or have chosen not to speak it, when she descends from the emotional high, she will have the natural yearnings of unmet emotional needs. After some years of living with an empty love tank, she will likely "fall in love" with someone else, and the cycle will begin again.[9]

Brent was unmoved. He was not convinced that his new in-love experience was the same as the one he had with Becky. This one was "the real thing," the love that would last. He courteously thanked the counselor for his concern and asked that he do everything he could to help Becky. But he was leaving.

Several weeks later Brent called and asked for a meeting with the counselor. When he came in, he was visibly disturbed—he was not the calm and self-assured man who had come in before. He explained that his new love seemed to have turned on him. She was beginning to criticize many of the same things in his character that Becky had pointed out to him, but she was considerably more harsh and angry about it than Becky had been. It looked like the new relationship was collapsing.

The counselor restated the paradigm—at first love sweeps you up involuntarily, but eventually love is a deliberate choice. It will seem mechanical at first, he reiterated, but if both spouses do it together, eventually the experience of being loved richly and well will sweeten their lives. Brent committed himself to try, and nearly a year later he and Becky had a renewed marriage.

We should not think that this example teaches that all marriage problems can be solved by the discipline of discerning love languages and of providing love in the most fitting forms. The human heart is infinitely complex (Jeremiah 17:9). Marriage difficulties can come from deep-seated patterns of idolatry, from semiconscious anger, and from fear that needs to be rooted out with counseling and God's grace. Nevertheless, the hard and deliberate work of knowing your spouse and loving him or her *fittingly* is foundational to any good marriage. Because our culture thinks of love as mainly an involuntary feeling and not a conscious action, this foundational skill is often missed entirely.

Affection

It is helpful to simply list examples of different kinds of love languages.[10] Just looking at a list can begin the process of discernment. Looking over the items, a spouse may say, "If you did *that* for me every week, things would be different in our marriage!" And then you are on your way.

I'll start with the category of Affection. Love can be given through eye contact, caresses, sitting closely together, and holding hands. This must not be done only when preparing for sex or it loses its integrity as a way of showing affection. Love can also be expressed through creatively finding situations that make focused attention easier. Plan walks, sitting before fireplaces, scenic drives, and picnics. Even making the effort to arrange these are an important sign and expression of love. Also, we can work on our own personal appearance as a gift to our spouse. Playfulness and fun are part of creating affectionate climates as well.

Love should be expressed verbally, not by simply saying, "Of course I love you." We must learn to send messages of love in direct, personal, specific, and ever-fresh ways. Discern the strengths and gifts of your partner and communicate honest praise, appreciation, and thankfulness for him or her. The flip side of this form of love is refraining from harsh, critical words. Send love not just through the spoken word but through notes, cards, letters, and thoughtful reflections on special occasions, such as anniversaries.

Finally, affection can be expressed through considerate, personal, useful, and beautiful gifts.

Friendship

As we have said, friendship is essential to marriage, and this form of love has its own range of specific expressions. Friendship love can be cultivated by spending quality time together. That means doing something that at least one of you loves doing and that enables you to communicate while doing it. Most people immediately think of recreation and entertainment, and that is right, but doing common work tasks—like gardening or chores—bonds you together, too. Above all, show your spouse that time with him or her has priority in your life.

Friendship love can also be expressed through showing supportive loyalty for, as well as interest and pride in, the work world of your spouse. If both have careers outside the home, it means each learning about each other's work and appreciating it. If the wife is at home engaged in raising children and housekeeping, it is crucial for the husband to be emotionally engaged and deeply interested in helping his wife make the house a home and a haven.

Love can additionally be expressed by sharing each others' mental world. Reading books together (even aloud), discussing changes in one's thinking, studying a subject together—all these are included.

Finally, friendship love is expressed and grows through both listening and opening up to the other. Friendship is above all a relationship in which it is safe to share fears, hurts, and weaknesses—an emotional refuge. Listening takes concentration. Some people are good at listening but not at opening up themselves, and vice versa. Trust is also built by following through on commitments, being reliable.

Service

Serving each other begins with the most practical and menial tasks. If the wife is largely or fully engaged in childcare and housekeeping, that may entail the husband's participation in that work as much as possible. For example, it means happily changing diapers or helping with the house cleaning without being asked.

But serving your spouse also means showing him or her great respect. It means giving your spouse the confidence that you will always speak up and stand up for him, that you will show loyalty and appreciation for her before other family and friends.

Serving your spouse also means showing that you are committed to his or her well-being and flourishing. This kind of love is given when you seek to help your spouse develop gifts and pursue aspirations for growth.

One of the greatest expressions of love is the willingness to change, to make a commitment to change attitudes and behaviors in yourself that trouble or hurt your spouse. There must be an ability to take correction and to be accountable for real concrete changes. This kind of change is always hard, and nearly impossible without the grace of God, but it is also one of the most powerful signs of love in a marriage.

Finally, there is no greater way for Christian spouses to serve one another than to help each other grow spiritually, as we discussed in chapter 4. This means encouraging each other to participate together actively in church, in Christian community. It means reading and digesting Christian books together as well as studying the Bible together. And it means praying together. For centuries, Christian spouses have observed various forms of daily family prayer.

Praying daily with and for each other is a love language that in many ways brings the other love languages together. It means being tenderly affectionate and transparent with each other. And you hear your spouse lifting you up to God for blessing. If you do that every day, or most days, it seasons your entire relationship with the love of God and of one another.

This is by no means a definitive list of love languages or currencies. Another example might be allowing your spouse privacy, either for brief or longer periods, depending on emotional needs. There can be no excuses for shutting one's spouse out of one's life, but different people have different capacities and needs for time alone or outside interests. Lists like these help partners identify and articulate what is often semiconscious and hard to put into words. The task before you is difficult but simple. Learn your spouse's love languages. Figure out together what they are, then brainstorm a handful of concrete ways to regularly give love in those forms. Then execute. Concretely give love to each other in deliberate ways every week.

The Great Problem

We have seen how marriage by its very nature has the power of truth and the power of love. The power of truth is marriage's ability to show you who you really are. The power of love is marriage's capacity for reprogramming your self-image, redeeming the past, and healing your deepest hurts. And now a warning is in order.

We said that if everyone else says you're ugly, and your spouse says you're beautiful, you feel beautiful, because your spouse's words have that kind of power. But that means that the reverse is also true. If everyone else says you are beautiful and your spouse says you're ugly, you will feel ugly. Your spouse's opinion of you can be a terrible weapon. Early in your marriage you will realize what power you have to hurt your spouse. You will know his or her sensitivities like no one else. And cutting remarks from you will go deeper than any knife.

In this fallen world, marriage's power of truth and power of love can be at loggerheads. The reason marriage has the power to show me what's wrong with me is because my spouse sees me to the bottom in a way that even I can't see myself. That is why her affirmation, verdict, and blessing have so much credibility and power. But here's the problem. My wife does not learn about my sins like my physician learns about my diseases or like my counselor learns about my anger and fear. She knows my sins because they so often are committed against *her*. She knows I'm insensitive because I'm insensitive to her. She knows I'm selfish because I'm selfish to her.

And there's the Great Problem of marriage. The one person in the whole world who holds your heart in her hand, whose approval and affirmation you most long for and need, is the one who is hurt more deeply by your sins than anyone else on the planet. When we are first sinned against by our spouses in a serious way, we use the power of truth. We tell our spouses what fools, what messes, what selfish pigs they are. The first few times we do it, however, we may learn to our surprise how shattering our criticism can be. Sometimes we let fly some real harsh, insulting remarks, and the next thing we know there's nothing left of our spouses but a pair of sneakers with smoke coming out of them. What happened? Because of our spousal power of love and affirmation, when that love is withheld, the statement of the truth doesn't help—it destroys.

When we see how devastating truth-telling in marriage can be, it can push us into the opposite error. We may then decide that our job is to just affirm. We avoid telling our spouses how disappointed we are. We shut up. We stuff and hide what we really think and feel. We exercise the power of love, but not the power of truth.

But then marriage's enormous potential for spiritual growth is lost. If I come to realize that my spouse is not really being truthful with me, then her loving affirmations become less powerful in my life. Only when I know that my spouse regularly tells me the truth will her loving affirmations really change me.

The point is this—truth and love need to be kept together, but it is very hard. When we are hurt, we use the power of truth without love. The fury and pain of such encounters can lead to the mistake of trying to just love without telling the truth, though in the end this does not lead to anyone feeling loved at all.

What we need is the two together, intertwined. We need to feel so loved by our partners that when they criticize us, we have the security to admit our faults. Then we can come to know and face who we are and grow. That's what should happen, but it usually doesn't. Why not? Because when we see our spouse's flaws we get too angry. It is extremely difficult to use the truth in a loving way, to keep truth and love together. What is the answer?

The Power of Grace—Reconciling

Truth without love ruins the oneness, and love without truth gives the illusion of unity but actually stops the journey and the growth. The solution is grace. The experience of Jesus's grace makes it possible to practice the two most important skills in marriage: forgiveness and repentance. Only if we are very good at forgiving and very good at repenting can truth and love be kept together.

Arvin Engelson, a fellow student with Kathy and me at seminary years ago, likened marriage to a gem tumbler. You put gems into the tumbler and they are brought into constructive, creative contact with each other. They knock the rough edges off of each other until each gem is smooth and beautiful. But if you don't put a special compound into the tumbler with the gems, the stones will either bounce off of one another without any effects or may crack and shatter each other. The grinding compound in the gem tumbler is like God's grace in a marriage. Without the power of grace, truth and love can't be combined. Spouses either stay away from the truth—they "bounce off each other"—or else they attack one another and they shatter.

In Mark 11:25, Jesus says that if you are praying, and you realize that you have something against someone, you must forgive him or her right there. Does that mean you should not confront the person? No, you should, since Jesus in Matthew 18—as well as Paul in Galatians 6 and elsewhere—tells Christians that if someone wrongs them, they should go to the person and discuss their sin. Wait, we say. The Bible says we are supposed to forgive people and *then* go and confront them? Yes! The reason we are surprised by this is almost always because *we confront people who have wronged us as a way of paying them back*. By telling them off, we are actually getting revenge. They made us feel bad and now we are going to make them feel bad, too. But this is absolutely deadly. The person you are confronting knows you are doing payback, and he or she will either be devastated or infuriated—or both. You are not really telling the truth for their sake; you are telling it for your sake, and the fruit of that will be grief, bitterness, and despair.

Jesus gives us the solution. He says that Christians, knowing that they live only by the forgiving grace of God, must do the work of forgiving wrongdoers in their hearts and then go to confront them. If you do that, the confrontation will be so different. In other words, without the "compound"—the power of forgiving grace in your life—you will use the truth to hurt. The other person will either attack you back or withdraw. Your marriage will go either into a truth-without-love mode, with constant fighting, or a shallow love-without-truth mode, in which both partners simply avoid the underlying problems.

One of the most basic skills in marriage is the ability to tell the straight, unvarnished truth about what your spouse has done—and then, completely, unself-righteously, and joyously express forgiveness without a shred of superiority, without making the other person feel small. This does not mean you cannot express anger. In fact, if you never express anger, your truth-telling probably won't sink in. But forgiving grace must always be present, and if it is, it will, like salt in meat, keep the anger from going bad. Then truth and love can live together because, beneath them both, you have forgiven your spouse as Christ forgave you.

What does it take to know the power of grace? First it takes humility. If you have trouble forgiving someone, it is at least partly because deep in your heart you are thinking, "*I* would never do anything like *that*!" As long as you feel superior to someone, feel like you are a much better kind of person, you will find it very hard if not impossible to forgive. If you stay superior and disdainful of the person, truth will eat up love. You will only criticize, and not in a way that the person can hear. You will be too scornful and harsh.

But speaking the truth in love requires not just emotional humility but also "emotional wealth," a fundamental inner joy and confidence. If you are very down on yourself, if you struggle with self-loathing, then it may be far too important for you to have your spouse always pleased with you. You will not be able to bear to have your spouse upset with you at all, and that will mean you will not be able to criticize your spouse or explain how much he or she hurt you. You won't be able to confront and forgive.

You will stay resentful but will hide it, unable to be open about it. You will just affirm; you won't confront. In this case, we have love eating up truth.

See, then, that to wield both the power of truth and the power of love in the life-changing, integrative, balanced way that they should be used, it takes deep humility and yet profound joy and confidence. Where in the world can you get that? The answer is that it must come from outside of this world. Unaided, our human nature is incapable of producing them in combination. Without an experience of God's grace, people who feel they have succeeded in life feel confident but are not humble before others who are wrongdoers. People who feel they have largely failed in life are humble but not confident and joyful.

But the gospel transforms us so our self-understanding is no longer based on our performance in life. We are so evil and sinful and flawed that Jesus had to die for us. We were so lost that nothing less than the death of the divine Son of God could save us. But we are so loved and valued that he was willing to die for us. The Lord of the universe loved us enough to do that! So the gospel humbles us into the dust and at the very same time exalts us to the heavens. We are sinners but completely loved and accepted in Christ at the same time.

How do you get the power of grace? You can't create this power; you can only reflect it to others if you have received it. If you see Jesus dying on the cross for others, forgiving the people who killed him, that can be just a crushing example of forgiving love that you will never be able to live up to. But if instead you see Jesus dying on the cross for *you*, forgiving you, putting away your sin, that changes everything. He saw your heart to the bottom but loved you to the skies. And the joy and freedom that comes from knowing that the Son of God did that for you enables you to do the same for your spouse. It gives you both the emotional humility and wealth to exercise the power of grace.

The Ultimate Power

Marriage has unique power to show us the truth of who we really are. Marriage has unique power to redeem our past and heal our self-image through love. And marriage has unique power to show us the grace of what God did for us in Jesus Christ. In Ephesians 5, Paul tells us that Jesus laid down his life for us, forgiving at great cost us to make us something beautiful. And because he has done it for us, we can do the same for others.

Our sins hurt Jesus infinitely more than your spouse's sins hurt you. You may feel your spouse is crucifying you, but our sins really did put Jesus on the cross, yet he forgave us.

It is said that one of the old czars of Russia had a trusted general who was dying of his wounds. When the soldier was on his deathbed, the czar promised to raise the soldier's young son and provide for him. After his death, the czar made good on his word. He gave the young boy the best of places to live and the best education. He was given a commission and entered the army. However, the young man had an addiction to gambling. Because he couldn't cover his gambling debts, he began to embezzle from his regiment's funds. One night he was sitting in the tent looking at the books and he realized that his embezzlement was about to be discovered. He could hide it no longer from the accountants. He sat drinking heavily as he prepared to kill himself. He had the revolver by his side and he took a few more drinks to strengthen his resolve for the suicide. But the drink was too potent and he passed out on the table.

That night the czar was doing what he often did. Disguised as a simple soldier, he was walking through the camp and the ranks, trying to assess the morale of his army, hearing what he could hear. He walked into his foster son's tent and saw him slumped over the book. He read the book and realized what he had done and what he was about to do.

When the young man awoke hours later, to his surprise the revolver was gone. Then he saw a letter by his hand. To his shock, it was a promissory note, saying, "I, the czar, will pay the full amount from my own personal funds to make up the difference found in this book." And it was sealed with the czar's personal seal. The czar had seen the young man's sin clearly, the full dimensions of what he had done. But he had covered and paid for the sin personally.

Here is why you can say to your spouse who has wronged you, "I see your sin, but I can cover it with forgiveness, because Jesus saw my sin and covered it." It is because the Lord of the universe came into the world in disguise, in the person of Jesus Christ, and he looked into our hearts and saw the worst. And it wasn't an abstract exercise for Jesus—our sins put him to death. When Jesus was up there, nailed to the cross, he looked down and saw us, some denying him, some betraying him, and all forsaking him. He saw our sin and covered it.

I do not know of any more powerful resource for granting forgiveness than that, and I don't know of anything more necessary in marriage than the ability to forgive fully, freely, unpunishingly, from the heart. A deep experience of the grace of God—a knowledge that you are a sinner saved by grace—will enable the power of truth and love to work together in your marriage.

And by wielding this power in the knowledge of his grace, you are helping your spouse become something glorious.

Kathy and I have a picture of us on our wedding day on our bedroom wall. It is now thirty-seven years old. Physically, we looked a lot better then. I had hair, and, shall we say, we were a lot sleeker. When I've done weddings and I look at the bride and groom standing there looking fabulous in their finery, I've often been tempted to quip, "You look terrific, but it's all downhill from here. You'll never look this good again."

But that's not ultimately true, not if you and your spouse wield the power of truth and love with grace in each other's lives. Not if you are committed to the adventure of spiritual companionship, to partner with God in the journey to the new creation. Then, to the eye of God, as the years go by, you are making each other more and more beautiful, like a diamond being cut and polished and set.

> *Therefore we do not lose heart. Though outwardly we are wasting away, yet inwardly we are being renewed day by day. For our slight momentary troubles are achieving for us an eternal weight of glory beyond all comparison. So we fix our eyes not on what is seen, but on what is unseen. For what is seen is temporary, but what is unseen is eternal.*
>
> (2 Corinthians 4:16–18)

Spiritually discerning spouses can see a bit of what God sees in their partners, and it excites them. The rest of the world sees us wrinkling up, but using marriage's powers in the grace of Jesus, we see each other become more and more spiritually gorgeous. We are clothing, washing, adorning each other. And someday the whole universe will see what God sees in us.

What we should say to each other on our wedding day is, "As great as you look today, someday you will stand with me before God in such beauty that it will make these clothes look like rags."

SIX

EMBRACING THE OTHER

Wives, submit to your husbands as to the Lord. For the
husband is the head of the wife as Christ is the head of the
church, his body, of which he is the Savior. Husbands, love
your wives, just as Christ loved the church and gave him-
self up for her.

Ephesians 5:22–23, 25

Although Tim and I (Kathy) have collaborated throughout this book, we thought it made more sense for me to write this chapter in my own, singular voice, as I have had more direct experience in talking about and struggling with the difference in gender roles between men and women. No surprise there—under the influence of the curse in Genesis, every human culture has found a way to interpret male headship in a way that has marginalized and oppressed women, and it's usually the women who notice, and object, to this treatment first.

Whether you identify yourself as an egalitarian, a feminist, a traditionalist, a complementarian, or any other variety on the interpretive spectrum, the differences between men and women will become an unavoidable issue in every marriage. Failure to come to terms with it is like tiptoeing around the proverbial elephant in the living room. Everyone comes into marriage with an idea of roles—of how a husband should behave to his wife, a wife to her husband, and children to their parents. This may be the sum of impressions gathered from one's family of origin, current cultural norms, observations of friends' marriages, and even the flotsam and jetsam of one's fictional reading or television and movie habits.

There's no denying that the subject of gender roles in marriage is a contentious and controversial one. I have personally lived at the heart of the controversy myself for more than forty years. I have seen Bible verses used as weapons of both oppression and rebellion. I have also seen the healing and flourishing that can happen in a marriage when hot-button words like "headship" and "submission" are understood correctly, with Jesus as the model for both.

Tim and I did not come into our marriage with any well-articulated thoughts about how the roles of men and women played out in a real-life relationship. In fact, despite many major conversations on the theoretical level in our seminary classes, I was unprepared for the first morning in our new church when Tim packed up his briefcase, kissed me good-bye, and "went off to work." I remember standing in the kitchen saying, "Now what am I supposed to do all day?" Up until then, we had pretty much lived in a unisex world, as students taking the same classes, competing for grades on a level playing field, rarely forced into any consideration of what God's intention may have been in making us male and female. Suddenly I had to think both practically and Biblically about my role as a woman and a wife.

Though Tim and I have been both clumsy and clueless at times, we have found that in submitting to our own divinely assigned gender roles that we discovered one of God's great gifts for getting in touch with our deepest selves, as well as entering into the Great Dance of the universe. And no, this did not involve me developing a taste for frilly clothing, nor Tim taking up car maintenance. No wise person rejects a gift from someone who loves them without at least giving it a look. So we hope that even if you are not comfortable with the idea of distinct, divinely ordained gender roles within marriage, that you will suspend judgment just for the space of this chapter and consider how God may have intended them for our good.[1]

In the Beginning

A discussion of how gender roles work in marriage must begin with a look at the good that God originally intended, how men and women have corrupted that good, and what Jesus has done to redeem gender roles; only then can we move on to the hazardous concepts of authority, submission, and headship and the idea of the helpmate.

The first mention of gender in the Bible occurs with the very first mention of humanity itself.[2] "In the image of God he created him; male and female he created them" (Genesis 1:27). This means that our maleness or our femaleness is not incidental to our humanness but constitutes its very essence. God does not make us into a generic humanity that is later differentiated; rather from the start we are male or female. Every cell in our body is stamped as XX or XY. This means I cannot understand myself if I try to ignore the way God has designed me or if I despise the gifts he may have given to help me fulfill my calling. If the postmodern view that gender is wholly a "social construct" were true, then we could follow whatever path seemed good to us. If our gender is at the heart of our nature, however, we risk losing a key part of ourselves if we abandon our distinctive male and female roles.

At the same time, Genesis shows us that men and women were

created with absolute equality. Both are equally made in the image of God, equally blessed, and equally given "dominion" over the earth. This means that men and women together, in full participation, must carry out God's mandate to build civilization and culture. Both men and women are called to do science and art, to build families and human communities.[3]

Immediately after making us male and female, God tells us to be "fruitful" and "fill the earth." Here God gives the human race the mandate to procreate, which is a reflection of his own boundless life-giving creativity. But, obviously, this wonderful gift of creating new human life is something we can only carry out together. Neither sex has all the characteristics necessary—only in complementary union can we do it. These verses suggest strongly that the sexes, while equal in dignity and worth, are complementary.

When God sees Adam alone, a male without a female, God says it is "not good."[4] It is the first thing in the universe that God finds imperfect. Adam is the physical source of Eve, and he is given the responsibility of naming her. Both of these elements in the narrative lay the basis for later New Testament statements about a husband's "headship."[5] However, despite giving authority to the man, the woman is not described in the expected way—as an inferior. She is called "a helper suitable for him" (Genesis 2:18, NIV).

The English word "helper" is not the best translation for the Hebrew word *'ezer*. "Helper" connotes merely assisting someone who could do the task almost as well without help. But *'ezer* is almost always used in the Bible to describe God himself. Other times it is used to describe military help, such as reinforcements, without which a battle would be lost. To "help" someone, then, is to make up what is lacking in him with your strength.[6] Woman was made to be a "strong helper."

The word "suitable" is just as unhelpful a translation. This translates a compound phrase that is literally "like opposite him."[7] The entire narrative of Genesis 2, in which a piece of the man is removed to create the woman, strongly implies that each is incomplete without the other.[8]

Male and female are "like opposite" to one another. They are like two pieces of a puzzle that fit together because they are not exactly alike nor randomly different, but they are differentiated such that together they can create a complete whole. Each sex is gifted for different steps in the same Great Dance.

Genesis 3 recounts the Fall, in which both man and woman sin against God and are expelled from the garden of Eden. We immediately see the catastrophic change in the unity between man and woman. The air is filled with blameshifting, finger pointing, and accusation.[9] Rather than their Otherness becoming a source of completion, it becomes an occasion for oppression and exploitation. The woman remains dependent and desirous of her husband, but it turns into an idolatrous desire, and his protection and love become a selfish lust and exploitation.

The Dance of the Trinity

In Jesus Christ's person and work we begin to see a restoration of the original unity and love between the sexes. Jesus both elevates and underlines the equality of women as co-bearers of the image of God and the creation mandate,[10] and he also redeems the roles given to man and woman at the beginning by inhabiting them, both as servant-head and 'ezer-subordinate.

In Philippians 2:5–11,[11] we have one of the earliest hymns to Jesus sung by the church, which celebrates that although Jesus was equal with God, he emptied himself of his glory and took on the role of a servant. Jesus shed his divine privileges without becoming any less divine, and he took on the most submissive role—that of a servant who dies in his master's service. In this passage we see taught both the essential equality of the First and Second Persons of the Godhead, and yet the voluntary submission of the Son to the Father to secure our salvation. Let me emphasize that Jesus's willing acceptance of this role was wholly voluntary, a gift to his Father. I discovered here that my submission in marriage was a gift I offered, not a duty coerced from me.

As I personally struggled with understanding gender *equality* within gender roles, it was this passage that entirely took the sting out of the subordinate role assigned to the female sex. If a child of the fifties can be said to have been raised "gender neutral," my siblings and I were. My mother was one of the only college-educated women among her acquaintances. I had grown up not even considering whether I was the equal of any boy—it just never occurred to me to divide the world into boys and girls, except when it came to restrooms. So, in some ways, the whole feminist movement was a terrible shock to me. You mean, I thought, there are women who have been mistreated, abused, exploited, marginalized, made to feel inferior? The proposed cure revealed to me that I had been oblivious to the disease.

Nevertheless, when I first heard Christians talk about male and female as "different but equal," it sounded a little too much like the "separate, but equal" motto of segregation. So my first encounter with the ideas of headship and submission was both intellectually and morally traumatic. But fortunately I had some gifted teachers who steered me to the Philippians 2 passage. And then I saw it. If it was not an assault on the dignity and divinity (but rather led to the greater glory) of the Second Person of the Godhead to submit himself, and assume the role of a servant, then how could it possibly injure me to be asked to play out the "Jesus role" in my marriage?

This passage is one of the primary places that the "dance of the

Trinity" becomes visible. The Son defers to his Father, taking the subordinate role. The Father accepts the gift, but then exalts the Son to the highest place. Each wishes to please the other; each wishes to exalt the other. Love and honor are given, accepted, and given again. In 1 Corinthians 11:3, Paul says directly what is implied in Philippians 2—namely, that the relationship of the Father and the Son is a pattern for the relationship of husband to wife.[12] The Son submits to the Father's headship with free, voluntary, and joyful eagerness, not out of coercion or inferiority. The Father's headship is acknowledged in reciprocal delight, respect, and love. There is no inequality of ability or dignity. We are differently gendered to reflect this life within the Trinity. Male and female are invited to mirror and reflect the "dance" of the Trinity, loving, self-sacrificing authority and loving, courageous submission. The Son takes a subordinate role, and in that movement he shows not his weakness but his greatness. This is one of the reasons why Paul can say that the marriage "mystery" gives us insight into the very heart of God in the work of our salvation (Ephesians 5:32). C. S. Lewis writes, "In the imagery describing Christ and the church, we're dealing with male and female, not merely as facts of nature, but as the live and awe-full shadows of realities utterly beyond our control and largely beyond our knowledge."[13]

But What about Headship?

Understanding that submission to my role was neither demeaning nor dangerous was a big step for me. I was a woman living in the heady days of early feminism, albeit one who had never personally felt the need for its advocacy and protection. To choose willingly to "submit," or to "be submissive," didn't sound like me in the slightest, nor was it a choice that was either understood or encouraged by anyone around me.[14]

But an even bigger leap was required to understand that it took an equal degree of submission for *men* to submit to their gender roles. They are called to be "servant-leaders."

In our world, we are accustomed to seeing the perks and the privileges accrue to those who have higher status—Platinum mileage flyers receive free upgrades to first class and, along with that, free food and drink and free baggage checking. Those with bigger bank accounts than the rest of us are ushered into the (shorter and faster) premium banking line at the bank.

But in the dance of the Trinity, the greatest is the one who is most self-effacing, most sacrificial, most devoted to the good of the Other. Jesus redefined—or, more truly, defined properly— headship and authority, thus taking the toxicity of it away, at least for those who live by his definition rather than by the world's understanding.

In John 13:1–17, Jesus, on the night before his death, famously washed his disciples' feet, both showing and teaching them how he was redefining authority and headship. He said:

> *Do you understand what I have done for you? . . . You call me "Teacher" and "Lord" and rightly so, for that is what I am. Now that I, your Lord and Teacher, have washed your feet, you also should wash one another's feet. I have set you an example that you should do as I have done for you. I tell you the truth, no servant is greater than his master.*
>
> (12–16)

The master has just made himself into a servant who has washed his disciples' feet, thus demonstrating in the most dramatic way that authority and leadership mean that you become the servant, you die to self in order to love and serve the Other. Jesus redefined all authority as servant-authority. Any exercise of power can only be done in service to the Other, not to please oneself. Jesus is the one who did not come to be served, as the world's authority figures expect to be, but to serve, to the point of giving his life.

His disciples, writing in the gospels, candidly reveal how thoroughly they did not get this, arguing practically on the eve of his crucifixion about who would get the honor of sitting at his right and left hand, positions of power in his soon-to-be inaugurated rule. Jesus clearly states his position on the meaning of authority and headship: In the world, rulers and high officials exercise their authority by "lording it" over others. *Not so with you.* Those tasked with leadership must be the slaves of all, following their master, who "did not come to be served but to serve. . . ."[15]

Following the resurrection and the coming of the Holy Spirit, Jesus's words seemed to have finally sunk in. By the time Paul wrote to the Ephesians, the relationship of Jesus to the church had been made the model for that of a husband and wife. We, the church, submit to Christ in everything, and the parallel of a wife submitting "everything" to her husband is no longer daunting, since we know what kind of behavior the husband has been called on to imitate. To what role must he submit? To that of savior, a servant-leader, who uses his authority and power to express a love that doesn't even stop at dying for the beloved.

In Jesus we see all the authoritarianism of authority laid to rest, and all the humility of submission glorified. Rather than demeaning Christ, his submission leads to his ultimate glorification, where God "exalted him to the highest place and gave him the name that is above every name." By analogy, does that mean that a husband is grooming his wife, in her submission to him, to be lifted in glory above himself? I don't know, but I do know that if a wife's role in relation to her husband is analogous to the church's submission to Christ, then we have nothing to fear.

Both women *and* men get to "play the Jesus role" in marriage—Jesus in his sacrificial authority, Jesus in his sacrificial submission. By accepting our gender roles, and operating within them, we are able to demonstrate to the world concepts that are so counterintuitive as to be completely unintelligible unless they are lived out by men and women in Christian marriages.

Embracing the Other

Since God called woman specifically to be a "helper" suited for her husband, it would be strange if he did not endow both men and women with distinguishable abilities to better fulfill their distinguishable calls. The most obvious are physical characteristics that enable women to bear and nurture children, but more subtle emotional and psychological endowments would be natural accompaniments to those physical differences, albeit on a spectrum.

This is where, surprisingly, some feminist theory echoes Biblical teaching about gender difference. Men and women are not interchangeable, unisex beings, but they have different strengths that result in men and women solving problems, building consensus, and performing leadership functions in distinct ways. In one interesting case study in the op-ed pages of the *New York Times*, "When Women Make Music," a female conductor and music director outlined how gender differences in each of these three areas meant that she directed her orchestra differently than a man would.[16] She said at one point that women's style of management is "perhaps better" than men's, and at another she insisted that musicians who are treated the way a woman conductor treats them "perform better over the long run." Not surprisingly, some believed the author was guilty of a kind of reverse sexism. However, the main point—that men and woman approach the same task in significantly distinct ways—has been verified by a great wave of empirical studies in the last twenty years that support the depth of gender differences in the way we think, feel, behave, work, and conduct relationships.

One of the first feminist studies that argued for such irreducible gender differences was Carol Gilligan's *In a Different Voice* in 1982. Harvard University Press, the book's publisher, describes it as "the little book that started a revolution." Before then, social scientific theorizing emphasized the superficiality of gender differences, but Gilligan insisted that female psychological development, motivations, and even moral reasoning were different from those of males.[17] Gilligan argued that while men seek maturity by detaching themselves, women see themselves maturing as they attach.[18]

Using all the qualifiers in the world, in general, as a whole and across the spectrum, men have a gift of independence, a "sending" gift. They look outward. They initiate. Under sin, these traits can become either an alpha male individualism, if this capacity is turned into an idol, or dependence, if the calling is utterly rejected and the opposite embraced in rebellion. The first sin is hypermasculinity, while the second sin is a rejection of masculinity.

Using all the qualifiers in the world, on the whole and across the spectrum, women have a gift of interdependence, a "receiving" gift. They are inwardly perceptive. They nurture. Under sin, these traits can become either a clinging dependence, if attachment is turned into an idol, or individualism, if the calling is utterly rejected and the opposite embraced in rebellion. The first sin is hyperfemininity, while the second sin is a rejection of femininity.

The dance of the Trinity would lead us to expect differences such as these, as well as others, if we are made in the image of the triune, dancing God.[19]

Sadly, those who most deny innate differences between men and women (fewer now than before medical and scientific research joined sociological and psychological studies) may end up devaluing women at the very point where they are trying to protect them. Dominant, swaggering (and sinful) male behavior is assumed to be the default mode if one wishes to get ahead or be taken seriously in the world. Women are asked to shed their feminine qualities and become faux men in order to be "one of the boys." The strengths of gender-distinct leadership, creativity, and insight that women bring to the world, to name only a few, are lost to the business world, romantic relationships, and even ministry within the church.

Over the last thirty years, many philosophers and social theorists have reflected on the "problem of Otherness."[20] It is natural to define one's identity against others who are different. Many have argued that this process automatically leads people to strengthen their sense of worth and uniqueness by excluding and subordinating those who are Other, who are not like us. Christians can acknowledge that our sinful drive for self-justification often leads us to despise those who think, feel, and behave differently than we do. Personal, racial, and class pride naturally grow out of the human heart's alienation from God and therefore our need to prove ourselves and win an identity based on our specialness, superiority, and performance.

One of the main places where "exclusion of the Other" happens is between the sexes. Loving someone of the other sex is *hard*. Misunderstandings, angry explosions, and tears abound. Men tend to look down on women as they gather around the water cooler and snicker about female foibles. Women return the favor, skewering male pretensions and weaknesses. Does anyone not know how to say "Men!" or "Women!" with that particular sneering tone? And indeed, the gap between the sexes often looks like a chasm. We cannot understand each other. And since the default mode of the human heart is self-justification, where we cannot understand the other sex we assume inferiority. Yet as men and women lose or deny their "peculiar honors,"[21] knowledge of how to relate to and relish the Other is also lost.

However, this is where the Christian understanding of marriage comes in. Marriage, in the Biblical view, addresses the chasm between the sexes. Marriage is a full embrace of the other sex. We accept and yet struggle with the gendered "otherness" of our spouse, and in the process, we grow and flourish in ways otherwise impossible. Because, as Genesis says, male and female are "like-opposite" each other—both radically different and yet incomplete without each other. I have had homosexual friends, both men and women, tell me that one of the factors that made homosexual love attractive to them was how much easier it was than dealing with someone of a different sex. I have no doubt this is true. A person of one's own sex is not as likely to have as much Otherness to embrace. But God's plan for married couples involves embracing the otherness to make us unified, and that can only happen between a man and a woman.[22] Even at the atomic level, all the universe is held together by the attraction of positive and negative forces. The embrace of the Other, as it turns out, really *is* what makes the world go around.

The Cross and the Other

Inside a real marriage there will be conflicts rooted in gender differences that are seismic. It is not simply that the other gender is different; it's that his or her differences *make no sense*. And once we come up against this wall of incomprehensibility, the sin in our heart tends to respond by assigning moral significance to what is simply a deep temperamental difference. Men see women's need for "interdependence" as sheer *dependence*, and women see men's need for independence as pure ego. Husbands and wives grow distant from one another because they allow themselves to engage in a constant, daily drumbeat of thoughts of inner disdain for the gendered difference of their spouse.

But Jesus gives both a pattern and a power to change all of this.

Miroslav Volf, writing in *Exclusion and Embrace*, shows that the God of the Bible embraces the Other, and it is us. Quoting another theologian, Volf writes:

> On the cross of Christ, [the love of God] is there *for the others*, for sinners—the recalcitrant—enemies. The reciprocal self-surrender to one another within the Trinity is manifested in Christ's self-surrender in a world which is in contradiction to God; and this self-giving draws all those who believe in him into the eternal life of divine love.[23]

Christ embraced the ultimate "Other"—sinful humanity. He didn't exclude us by simply consigning us to judgment. He embraced us by dying on the cross for our sins. To love the Other, especially an Other that is hostile, entails sacrifice. It means sometimes experiencing betrayal, rejection, and attacks.[24] The easiest thing is to leave. But Jesus did not do that. He embraced and loved us, the Other, and brought us into a new unity with himself.

Knowing this kind of gracious, sin-covering love gives believers in the gospel of Christ the basis for an identity that does not need superiority and exclusion to form itself. In Christ we have a profound security. We know who we are in him, and that frees us from the natural human impulse to despise anyone who is significantly different from us. This enables us to embrace rather than exclude those who differ from us, and that especially goes for our spouse, with all his or her mysterious and often infuriating differences.

This is one part of the glory of marriage, in the Biblical conception. Two people of different sexes make the commitment and sacrifice that is involved in embracing the Other. It is often painful and always complicated, but it helps us grow and mature in ways no other experience can produce, and it brings about deep unity because of the profound complementarity between the sexes. This has nothing to do with who brings home the biggest salary or makes the most sacrifices to care for the children. The family model in which the man went out to work and the woman stayed home with the children is really a rather recent development. For centuries, husband and wife (and often children) worked together on the farm or in the shop. The external details of a family's division of labor may be worked out differently across marriages and societies. But the tender, serving authority of a husband's headship and the strong, gracious gift of a wife's submission restore us to who we were meant to be at creation.

Embracing the Other at Home

This all may sound inspiring on paper, but how does this idea work itself out in the actual life of a marriage?

First, you have to find a very safe place to practice headship and submission. I say this because I am not unaware of God's warning that sin will lead men to try to dominate women (Genesis 3:16).[25] Therefore it is crucial that women who want to accept gender-differentiated roles within marriage find a husband who will truly be a *servant*-leader to match her as a strong helper.

We are all familiar with watching stunts or action sequences on television or in movies that come with the "Do not try this at home" disclaimer attached.[26] Gender roles are the exact opposite: "Only try this at home or within the community of believers, the church."[27] It is only safe for us sinners to attempt to resume our royal heritage and our creation gifts of gender roles where resources such as repentance and forgiveness can be (and very often will need to be) accessed.

I will never be one to dismiss or make light of the horrible record of abuse suffered by women at the hands of men who wielded twisted and unbiblical definitions of "headship" and "submission" as their primary weapon. The church should not overlook or minimize one iota of that suffering, but I would beg that we not throw the baby out along with the dirty bathwater. Bail bathwater, by all means available, but save the baby, which in this case is the rightful acceptance of gender roles as Jesus has both defined and embodied them.

The home, then, can become a window into a restored and redeemed human society in which our different gender roles lead to a deeper understanding of ourselves and a deeper melding with the Other.[28] Within that context of marriage-as-ministry, wives are told to "submit" to husbands and husbands are told to "head" their wives.

Second, you and your spouse should grasp one of the most startling aspects of the Biblical teaching on gender roles in marriage. While the principle is clear—that the husband is to be the servant-leader and have ultimate responsibility and authority in the family—the Bible gives almost no details about how that is expressed in concrete behavior. Should wives never work outside the home? Should wives never create culture or be scientists?

Should husbands never wash clothes or clean the home? Should women take primary responsibility for daily child care while men oversee the finances? Traditionally minded people are tempted to nod yes to these questions until it is pointed out that nowhere does the Bible say such things. The Scripture does not give us a list of things men and women must and must not do. It gives *no* such specific directions at all.

Why would this be? Well, consider that the Bible was written for all centuries and all cultures. If it had written rules for the roles of wife and husband in ancient agrarian cultures, they would be hard to apply today. But the Scripture doesn't do that.

What does that mean for us? It means that rigid cultural gender roles have no Biblical warrant. Christians cannot make a scriptural case for masculine and feminine stereotypes. Though social scientists have made good cases about abiding gender differences with regard to the expression of emotion, the conduct of relationships, the making of decisions, different individual personalities and different cultures will express those distinctions in somewhat different ways. A man considered an authoritative father in America may look rather passive in a non-Western country. We must find ways to honor and express our gender roles, but the Bible allows for freedom in the particulars, while still upholding the obligatory nature of the principle.[29]

When we moved to Philadelphia for Tim to teach at Westminster Theological Seminary, we bought a home for the first (and only) time. We shortly discovered that Tim's salary was not big enough to cover our living expenses plus a mortgage payment, so I took part-time employment with Great Commission Publications as an editor. I had to go out to work in the mornings, year round, while Tim's more flexible daily and summer schedule meant that he could be the "Mr. Mom" who got the kids off to school and watched them during the summer break. An outsider looking at our marriage might have thought a role reversal was going on, or at least a negation of our gender roles. Quite the contrary, in fact. Although the superficial details of who did what had changed, I was still bringing my gifts as a strong helper to Tim, making it possible for him to teach.

I can imagine two objections to what I've been saying. The first comes from a person who wants more definition: "I need more direction than this! What exactly does a husband do that the wife does not? What does a wife do that the husband does not? I need details!" The answer is that the Bible deliberately does not give answers to you, and that helps couples with more traditional mind-sets to avoid falling into the pattern of simply saying, "Well in *my* family, this is how it was done." But you and your spouse are different people and live in a different time and probably a different place. The basic roles—of leader and helper—are binding, but every couple must work out how that will be expressed within their marriage. The very process of making these decisions is a key part of what it is to think out and honor your gender differences.

But some women might chafe under the idea of male headship: "I agree that men and women are profoundly different according to their sex, but why does the *man* get to lead? If men and women are equal in dignity but different, why is the husband the head?" I think the truest answer is that we simply don't know. Why was Jesus, the Son, the one who submitted and served (Philippians 2:4ff)? Why wasn't it the Father? We don't know, but we do know that it was a sign of his greatness, not his weakness.

I think there is also a more practical answer to the second objection and even to the first. It is our very effort to submit to the roles of servant-leader and strong helper that will help us get in touch with and honor our gender differences.

In the home, the Bible directs male and female to reflect our different gifts in our family functions—our job descriptions in the team. Wives are *more directly and more often* exhorted to be gentle supporters, to be encouragers (1 Peter 3:1–2, 4), and *more directly and more often* to be nurturing children and the home life (Titus 2:4–5). Husbands are exhorted *more directly and more often* to lead, provide for and protect the family, but are not let off the hook for the education and nurture of the children (1 Timothy 3:4; 5:8).

These gifts can be stronger or weaker along the spectrum, but if we accept our gender roles as a gift from God, we will try to nourish our weaker abilities rather than deny them. Tim and I, for instance, both come from homes that had domineering wives and passive husbands, so our default mode, when we married, was to duplicate what we had grown up with. It took a great deal of swimming against the tide of our own predilections for me to give Tim the headship (and for Tim to assume those responsibilities) and for him to likewise help me not to usurp his headship while ignoring my own call to nurture and support.

So Tim had to work on the *leader* side of being a servant-leader. Seeing this role as a gift of God matured and strengthened him. But some men may need to work on the *servant* side of being a servant-leader. Then submitting to the role will become a good gift for them. (For more thoughts on how gender roles bear on practical decision-making in marriage, see the appendix at the end of this volume.)

Embracing the Other Increases Wisdom

Submission to God's pattern in marriage gets you more in touch with some deep things in yourself, your primary maleness or femaleness, yet marriage balances you and broadens you, too. The qualities of the other sex "rub off" on you, making you each strong and tender, serving each other in distinct ways. Tim likes to say that after years and years of marriage he often finds himself in situations where he is about to respond, but he knows instinctively what I would say or do if I were there. "In that split second, I have the opportunity to ask myself, 'Would Kathy's typical reaction be more wise and appropriate than mine?' And I realize my repertoire of possible words and actions has been greatly expanded. My wife has taught me how to look at life as she does, and now I have a greater range of responses and a greater likelihood of doing the right thing."

Therefore, marriage is for both the overly gender-typed and the under gender-typed. It broadens us and deepens us.

In some ways Tim is under–gender typed (such as in his desire not to offend others). But in other ways he's quite frustratingly masculine. Sometimes I'll say to him, "You're mad, aren't you?" And he'll reply, "Not at all. I'm fine." But three days later he'll come back to me and say, "You were right. I was furious and resentful." And I will think, "How can an *adult* be that out of touch with his feelings?" He tends to look outward; he doesn't look inside his own feelings very well. Over the years, I have needed to respectfully teach him. But other times I have found myself saying, "You are going to have to lead on this one, because you are much better at detaching your feelings."

Somebody might object: "These are sexual stereotypes"—the insensitive male and the emotional female. But they are not stereotypes; they are us—Tim and me. And what do you think stereotypes are? They are unbalanced and unredeemed masculinity and femininity. But husband and wife are there to complete each other. It's a "great mystery," as St. Paul says, but at some deep level, this person who is so Other is healing me, and I him.

Remember, this person is utterly unlike you. He acts differently, thinks differently, and operates differently, and in some cases, dealing with him is not only frustrating and scary, but it's downright incomprehensible. But at a deeper level, you're finding out who you really are. You're seeing him as your other half. You see how God is completing you in your husband. The result of completion is personal ease. Adam and Eve were naked and unashamed with each other before the Fall. There was no anxiety, no hiding. There was a sense of a primordial, ancient unity and accord that Adam and Eve had then that we've not experienced since, because sin entered and disrupted the unity that they had. When you see marriage as completion, submission finds its place.

What about a Marriage in which One Party Doesn't Get It?

Agreeing on gender roles as a foundational part of your marriage takes two people, but what if your spouse persists in a wrong interpretation of his or her role? Wouldn't it just be better to assume the egalitarian, unisex roles that we use in the world as a protection against misuse and outright abuse?

Although it is true that sin has changed and twisted everything, the problem in jettisoning gender roles is this: Since every mention of gender roles in the Bible is tied to the creation story, it is not that easy to just lightly dispense with them. Further, if our assigned roles are rooted in the nature of the relationships within the Trinity, tampering with the revelation of that mystery that God intends within marriage is surely not our prerogative.

Instructions in the New Testament regarding the situation of believers who find themselves married to unbelievers are one place to start. But suppose a husband in a putatively Christian marriage has a wife who wants no part of a gender role that requires her to be "submissive" to her husband, the "head"? Or a wife whose churchgoing husband uses a misreading of the Bible to dismiss and marginalize her opinion, her contribution, even her person?

Though I have never been in those situations, I have friends whose marriages are all that and even worse. Furthermore, I am a sinner, married to another sinner, so we don't always inhabit our gender roles perfectly, either.

One of the pillars of wise counseling is the statement, "The only person over whom you have control is yourself." You can change no one's behavior but your own. If a man or a woman wishes to bring him- or herself more fully into the biblically defined gender roles, it does not actually require assent from the other person. Since both the headship role of a husband and the submission role as a wife are *servant* roles, one can always begin to serve without waiting for permission.

Often this will be an invisible change of attitude before it is ever visible in action. For a husband to begin to channel his energies into helping his wife to flourish spiritually (no matter where she is at the moment), may mean that he begins a prayer life where before he had none. Or a wife accustomed to resenting every Archie Bunker–like behavior of her husband may begin offering her submission with graciousness rather than resenting the lack of honor she receives from her husband.

Just as working out the particulars of how to inhabit gender roles when both spouses are eager to do so will differ from couple to couple, so will the particulars of glorifying God in the more difficult situation of an unbalanced marriage. But you can be sure that if you aren't getting any satisfaction from obeying God, you surely will get none from avoiding his pattern.

Why not give it a try, and inhabit the "Jesus role" that your part of the marriage calls you to?

SEVEN

SINGLENESS AND MARRIAGE

When Kathy and I (Tim) first came to Manhattan to plant a new church, we soon found ourselves in a congregation that was over 80 percent single. That surprised us until we realized that Redeemer was simply reflecting the demographics of center-city Manhattan. For the first several months of preaching, I assumed that a congregation of singles would not require the ordinary number of annual sermons on marriage and family. I soon realized I was wrong, and in the late summer and fall of 1991 I preached nine sermons on the topic of marriage, the core content of which is appearing in this book.

So what motivated me to preach about marriage to the unmarried? The answer is that single people cannot live their lives well as singles without a balanced, informed view of marriage. If they do not have that, they will either over-desire or under-desire marriage, and either of those ways of thinking will distort their lives.

In 1 Corinthians 7, St. Paul writes, "Are you unmarried? Do not look for a wife. But if you do marry, you have not sinned, and if a virgin marries, she has not sinned. But those who marry will face many troubles in this life, and I want to spare you this. What I mean is that the time is short" (7:27–28). This passage is very confusing on its surface. This view of marriage seems at profound variance with the exalted picture of marriage in Ephesians 5:21ff. Was Paul just having a bad day when he wrote this chapter? Others have pointed out that his view of marriage seems to have been conditioned by a conviction that Jesus was coming back any day ("The time is short."). Doesn't history show that he was wrong?

But immediately following, Paul writes:

> *From now on, those who have wives should live as if they had none. Those who mourn as if they did not. Those who are happy as if they were not. Those who buy as if it was not theirs. Those who use the things of the world as if not engrossed in them. For this world in its present form is passing away.*

(1 Corinthians 7:29–31)[1]

Here we see that behind "the time is short" phrase is a sophisticated view of history. Paul taught the "overlap" of the ages.[2] The prophets of the Old Testament preached that the Messiah would end the old order—the world of "swift death and little bliss"—and then begin the new age of God's kingdom, in which all things would be put right and death and decay banished. When Jesus came, he announced that he was the Messiah, but to everyone's surprise, he did not ascend a throne. Instead he went to a cross. He did not come to bring judgment but to bear it. What did this mean? It meant that Jesus *did* bring the kingdom of God. Through repentance and faith, we enter it now (John 3:3, 5). His reigning power is among us now, healing people by putting them right with God and each other (Luke 11:20; 12:32). And yet, this present world is not over. We still live in a world of decay, disease, and death. This is what is meant by the "overlap of the ages." The kingdom of God—God's power to renew the whole of creation—has broken into the old world through Christ's first coming, but it is not fully here. The old order is still here, though it is doomed and living on borrowed time. It is "passing away," as Paul says.

What are the implications of this? On the one hand, it means that all the social and material concerns of this world still exist. The world goes on and we live in it. We must take thought for tomorrow. Yet our assurance about God's future world transforms our attitudes toward all our earthly activities. We should be glad of success, but not overly glad, and saddened by failure, but not too downcast, because our true joy in the future is guaranteed by God. So we are to enjoy but not be "engrossed" (I Corinthians 7:31) in things of this world.[3]

What does this mean for our attitude toward marriage and family? Paul says it means that both being married and not being married are good conditions to be in. We should be neither overly elated by getting married nor overly disappointed by not being so—because Christ is the only spouse that can truly fulfill us and God's family the only family that will truly embrace and satisfy us.

The Goodness of Singleness

With this background, we can better understand how radical Paul's statements are regarding singleness and marriage. Stanley Hauerwas argues that Christianity was the very first religion that held up single adulthood as a viable way of life. He writes, "One . . . clear difference between Christianity and Judaism [and all other traditional religions] is the former's entertainment of the idea of singleness as the paradigm way of life for its followers."[4] Nearly all ancient religions and cultures made an absolute value of the family and of the bearing of children. There was no honor without family honor, and there was no real lasting significance or legacy without leaving heirs. Without children, you essentially vanished—you had no future. The main hope for the future, then, was to have children. In ancient cultures, long-term single adults were considered to be living a human life that was less than fully realized.

But Christianity's founder, Jesus Christ, and leading theologian, St. Paul, were both single their entire lives. Single adults cannot be seen as somehow less fully formed or realized human beings than married persons because Jesus Christ, a single man, was the perfect man (Hebrews 4:15; 1 Peter 2:22). Paul's assessment in 1 Corinthians 7 is that singleness is a good condition blessed by God, and in many circumstances, it is actually better than marriage. As a result of this revolutionary attitude, the early church did not pressure people to marry (as we see in Paul's letter) and institutionally supported poor widows so they did not have to remarry. A social historian described the practice:

> Should they be widowed, Christian women enjoyed substantial advantages. Pagan widows faced great social pressure to remarry; Augustus even had widows fined if they failed to marry within two years. In contrast, among Christians, widowhood was highly respected and remarriage was, if anything, mildly discouraged. The church stood ready to sustain poor widows, allowing them a choice as to whether or not to remarry. [Single widows were active in care-giving and good deeds in the neighborhood.][5]

Why did the early church have this attitude? The Christian gospel and hope of the future kingdom de-idolized marriage. There was no more radical act in that day and time than to live a life that did not produce heirs. Having children was the main way to achieve significance for an adult, since children would remember you. They also gave you security, since they would care for you in old age. Christians who remained single, then, were making the statement that our future is not guaranteed by the family but by God.

Single adult Christians were bearing testimony that God, not family, was their hope. God would guarantee their future, first by giving them their truest family—the church—so they never lacked for brothers and sisters, fathers and mothers, in Christ. But ultimately, Christians' inheritance is nothing less than the fullness of the kingdom of God in the new heavens and new earth. Hauerwas goes on to point out that Christian hope not only made it possible for singles to live fulfilled lives without spouse and children, but it also was an impetus for people to marry and *have* children and not be afraid to bring them into this dark world. "For Christians do not place their hope in their children, but rather their children are a sign of their hope . . . that God has not abandoned this world. . . ."[6]

The Christian church in the West, unfortunately, does not seem to have maintained its grasp on the goodness of singleness. Instead it has labeled it "Plan B for the Christian life." Paige Benton Brown, in her classic article "Singled Out by God for Good," lists a number of common ways that Christian churches try to "explain" singleness:

- "As soon as you're satisfied with God alone, he'll bring someone special into your life"—as though God's blessings are ever earned by our contentment.
- "You're too picky"—as though God is frustrated by our fickle whims and needs broader parameters in which to work.
- "As a single you can commit yourself wholeheartedly to the Lord's work"—as though God requires emotional martyrs to do his work, of which marriage must be no part.

- "Before you can marry someone wonderful, the Lord has to make you someone wonderful"—as though God grants marriage as a second blessing to the satisfactorily sanctified.

Beneath these statements is the premise that single life is a state of deprivation for people who are not yet fully formed enough for marriage. Brown responds along the lines of Paul's 1 Corinthians passage: "I am not single because I am too spiritually unstable to possibly deserve a husband, nor because I am too spiritually mature to possibly need one. I am single because God is so abundantly good to me, because this is his best for me."[7] That fits perfectly with the reasoning and attitude of St Paul. Christianity affirmed the goodness of single life as no other faith or worldview ever has.

The Penultimate Character of Marriage

What about today? In non-Western, traditional cultures, there continues to be strong social pressure to build one's hope on family and heirs. This is not generally the case in Western societies, but that does not mean there is no pressure to marry. As we discussed earlier, Western culture tempts us to put our hopes in "apocalyptic romance," in finding complete spiritual and emotional fulfillment in the perfect mate. Innumerable Disney-style popular culture narratives begin telling life stories only when two parties are about to find True Love and then, once they do, the story fades out. The message is that what matters in life is finding romance and marriage. Everything else is prologue and afterword. So both traditional and Western cultures can make singleness seem like a grim and subhuman condition.

However, the New Testament is different. In fact, when we turn from 1 Corinthians 7 to Ephesians 5, with its seemingly more exalted view of marriage, we actually get even more support for the idea of the goodness of singleness. How? As we have seen, Ephesians 5 tells us that marriage is not ultimately about sex or social stability or personal fulfillment. Marriage was created to be a reflection on the human level of our ultimate love relationship and union with the Lord. It is a sign and foretaste of the future kingdom of God.

But this high view of marriage tells us that marriage, therefore, is penultimate. It points us to the Real Marriage that our souls need and the Real Family our hearts were made for. Married couples will do a bad job of conducting their marriage if they don't see this penultimate status. Even the best marriage cannot by itself fill the void in our souls left by God. Without a deeply fulfilling love relationship with Christ now, and hope in a perfect love relationship with him in the future, married Christians will put too much pressure on their marriage to fulfill them, and that will always create pathology in their lives.

But singles, too, must see the penultimate status of marriage. If single Christians don't develop a deeply fulfilling love relationship with Jesus, they will put too much pressure on their *dream* of marriage, and that will create pathology in their lives as well.

However, if singles learn to rest in and rejoice in their marriage to Christ, that means they will be able to handle single life without a devastating sense of being unfulfilled and unformed. And they might as well tackle this spiritual project right away. Why? Because the same idolatry of marriage that is distorting their single lives will eventually distort their married lives if they find a partner. So there's no reason to wait. Demote marriage and family in your heart, put God first, and begin to enjoy the goodness of single life.

Gender "Completeness" and Singleness

How can we claim that long-term singleness is a good condition in light of the previous chapter's argument that males and females are in some ways incomplete without the other? The answer is the same. It has to do, again, with our hope in Christ and our experience of Christian community. Just as Christian singles find their "heirs" and family within the church, so do brothers find their sisters and sisters find their brothers.

Christian hope turns the church into something far more profound than a club or interest organization. Gospel beliefs and experience create a bond between Christians that is stronger than any other connection, whether it be blood relationship or racial and national identity (Ephesians 2; 1 Peter 2:9–10). The experience of deep repentance and salvation by grace through the cross of Christ means that my most foundational beliefs about the world and myself now align with those of other Christians. I love my biological siblings, my neighbors, and the other members of my ethnic or racial group, yet we no longer share in common our deepest instincts and beliefs about reality. This means, in short, that I am a Christian first and I'm black or white second. I'm a Christian first and I'm European or Latin American or Asian second. I'm a Christian first and I'm a Keller, or Smith, or Jones second.

This doesn't mean that if I am Asian I cease to be Asian and become something else. If I am Asian when I believe in Jesus, I become an Asian Christian, not a Latino Christian. My primary beliefs are those that I share with all Christians, but I share with others of my home culture many important and vital habits of heart and mind. The Bible speaks strongly of love and care for my family, regardless of their beliefs. Nevertheless, in the end, the gospel creates a bond with other believers that makes the church into a Christian's ultimate family (1 Peter 4:17) and nation (1 Peter 2:9–10).

This means that single people within a strong Christian community can experience much of the unique enrichment of cross-gender relationships within a family, particularly the sibling relationships between brothers and sisters.[8] It is my experience that it is nearly impossible to come up with a single, detailed, and very specific set of "manly" or "womanly" characteristics that fits every temperament and culture. Rather than defining "masculinity" and "femininity" (a traditional approach) or denying and suppressing them (a secular approach), I propose that within each Christian community you watch for and appreciate the inevitable differences that will appear between male and female in your particular generation, culture, people, and place.

Wait for them to appear, and know them. Talk about them among yourselves. Notice the distinct idols women have and men have in your generation, culture, and place. Notice the strengths women have and men have in your generation, culture, and place. Notice communication modes, decision-making skills, leadership styles, life priorities, and the balance of work and family. Once you see them, respect and appreciate them. Without the gospel, people often turn temperamental, cultural, and gender differences into moral virtues. This is one of the ways we bolster our self-esteem—a form of "works-righteousness," a way to earn our superior status. And so men and women scorn and mock the other gender's distinctive traits. But the gospel should remove that kind of attitude.

Kathy pointed out in the last chapter that marriage forces you over the years to learn how a person of the other sex habitually looks at and reacts to people and situations. Eventually you can instinctively identify the way your spouse would react to a situation, assess its wisdom in this situation, and adopt it sometimes in a way that you never would have been able to pre-marriage. Let's call this "cross-gender enrichment." In this way, male and female "complete" each other and reflect the image of God together (Genesis 1:26–28). But this is not something that only married people can do. It happens quite naturally in strong Christian community, where the sharing of our hearts and lives goes beyond the superficial down to what God is teaching us and how he is forming and growing us. In settings where brothers and sisters are doing this kind of mutual "one-another"[9] ministry, a kind of cross-gender enrichment happens naturally. Of course it is less intense than in marriage. And yet the more corporate experience is not a poor second to marriage, since in marriage you are put together with just one member of the opposite sex. Marriage does and should somewhat limit the extent of friendships you have with others of the opposite sex. In Christian community, however, singles can have a greater range of friendships among both sexes.

The Goodness of Seeking Marriage

The Christian perspective on singleness is almost unique. Unlike traditional societies, Christianity sees singleness as good because the kingdom of God provides the most lasting possible legacy and heirs. Unlike sex-and-romance-saturated Western society, Christians see singleness as good because our union with Christ can fulfill our deepest longings.

And yet, unlike our commitment-averse, postmodern society, Christianity does not fear or avoid marriage either. Adults in Western society are deeply shaped by individualism, a fear and even hatred of limiting options for the sake of others. Many people are living single lives today not in the conscious, lonely misery of wanting marriage too much but rather in the largely unconscious, lonely misery of wanting marriage too little, out of fear of it.

While traditional societies tend to make an idol out of marriage (because they make an idol out of the family and tribe), contemporary societies tend to make an idol of independence (because they make an idol out of individual choice and happiness). While the traditional motive for marriage has been social duty, stability, and status, the contemporary motive for marriage is personal fulfillment. Both of these motives are partially right, of course, but they tend to become ultimates if the gospel has not changed your mind and heart.

As a pastor in New York City, I have noticed an interesting sociological phenomenon. Some Christian singles in my church were raised in parts of the United States that are very traditional culturally, and there they got the "You aren't a whole person until you are married" mentality. Then they moved to NYC, where they were bombarded with the "You shouldn't marry until you have professionally made it big and you find the perfect partner who won't try to change you in any way" message. Their first culture made them over-desirous of marriage. Their second culture made them over-afraid of marriage. Both the longing and the fear live in their hearts, sometimes in about equal strengths, at war with each other.

The fear of marriage brings with it pathologies. One major fruit of the contemporary culture's fear of marriage is that singles become perfectionistic and virtually impossible to satisfy as they look at prospective spouses. Unfortunately, this perfectionism often supports gender stereotypes, because both anecdotal evidence and empirical studies show that males will look for near perfection in physical looks while women will look for partners who are financially well off. In other words, when contemporary people say they want the perfect mate, sexual and financial factors dominate the thinking. As a result, modern dating can become a remarkably crass form of self-merchandising. You must look good and make money if you are to attract dates, a partner, or a spouse. And the reason you want a good-looking or affluent partner is for your own self-esteem.

I think it is only fair to say that while there have been many happy exceptions, Christian singles tend to operate in pretty much the same way. In the Christian single's mind, most candidates are immediately eliminated from consideration on the basis of looks, polish, and financial or social status. This is simply another way in which Christian singles are being shaped by the culture's idolatry of sexual beauty and money. They are looking for someone already "beautiful" in the most superficial way.[10]

How different seeking marriage would be if, as we argued earlier in this book, we were to view marriage as a vehicle for spouses helping each other become their glorious future-selves through sacrificial service and spiritual friendship. What happens if we see the mission of marriage to teach us about our sins in unique and profound ways and to grow us out of them through providing someone who speaks the truth in love to us? How different it would be if we were to fall in love especially with the glorious thing God is doing in our spouse's life? Ironically, this view of marriage eventually does provide unbelievable personal fulfillment, but not in the sacrifice-free and superficial way that contemporary people want it to come. Instead, it gives the unique, breathtaking fulfillment of visible character growth (Ephesians 5:25–27) into love, peace, joy, and hope (Colossians 1; Galatians 5, 1 Corinthians 13).

Many singles are looking for a highly compatible, brilliant, and beautiful partner. For others, singleness has become at best a purgatory, where you live waiting for your real life to begin, or at worst a misery. The first kind of single looks right past all sorts of good prospective spouses because of fear and perfectionism. The second kind of single can scare people away because of his or her neediness and sometimes can make terrible choices in marital partners out of desperation. Sometimes the first kind of single dates the second kind of single, and that combination can be deeply painful.

Paige Brown strikes the unique Christian balance with the last line of her article on singleness:

> Let's face it: singleness is not an inherently inferior state of affairs. . . . But I want to be married. I pray to that end every day. I may meet someone and walk down the aisle in the next couple of years because God is so good to me. I may never have another date . . . because God is so good to me.[11]

There's the balance.

The History of Dating

So what practical guidance can we give single adults who are interested in seeking a spouse?

To begin, it is helpful to do a quick survey of how this question has been answered in different times and generations.[12] In ancient times, and into eighteenth- and nineteenth-century America, marriages were ordinarily arranged. Certainly (as the novels of Jane Austen show us) romantic love was one of the reasons for marriage, but only one. Even more prominent were social and financial motives. You had to marry into a family with which your family wanted a connection. You had to marry someone with whom you could afford a home and children.

But by the late nineteenth century, the motive of marrying for love became more culturally dominant, and a system of "calling" (sometimes called "courtship") came into being. A man was invited to call on a young woman, and they spent their time together on her family's front porch or in the parlor. In short, the man was invited *in* to the woman's home. There he saw her in the context of her family and her family saw him. Interestingly, it was the young woman's privilege to initiate and invite young men to call.[13]

Somewhere after the turn of the century, modern "dating" developed. The word first appeared in print in this context in 1914.[14] Now the young man did not so much come in but instead took the woman *out* to places of entertainment to get to know her. As dating spread throughout society, it not only individualized the whole process, removing the couple from family context, but it also changed the focus of romance from friendship and character assessment to spending money, being seen, and having fun.

The last social change is more recent. Not long after the turn of the twenty-first century, the "hook-up" culture emerged. In one of the first reports on the shift, a *New York Times Magazine* article reported how teenagers found members of the opposite sex to be annoying and difficult, and dating involved you in the hard work of give-and-take, communication, and learning to deal with someone who was different. In other words, they rightly perceived that dating involved you, in a preliminary way, in the difficult but rewarding work of building a marriage relationship. To avoid all this, a new form of meeting partners was developed, one that went straight to sex. A hook-up is a simple sexual encounter, without the condition of conducting a relationship. After a hook-up, you may want to start a dating relationship, or maybe not, but that is no condition for a hook-up.[15]

The advent of hook-up culture has meant to some that we have one of the first societies with no clear culturally supported pathways for single adults to meet and marry. In response, many traditional religious communities are springing up in which there are efforts to return to more family and community involvement in seeking marriage. Orthodox Jewish communities, for example, have a traditional process called *shidduch* dating in which friends and relatives propose suitable mates for a single woman or man, and then they meet to assess one another.[16] There are some evangelical Christian communities that have sought to reestablish the kinds of pathways that were prevalent in former times. Some have proposed a very father-directed form of courtship in which a young woman's father chooses mates and directs the process.

I believe that by and large these "return to courtship" movements are beset with many problems. They don't take into consideration the idols that were inherent in traditional societies and they each institutionalize one particular moment in human social history. Why courtship? Why not go all the way back to completely arranged marriages? They also assume very stable communities where everyone has known everyone else for a long time. As Lauren Winner says, "If you are a twenty-six-year-old who has just moved across the country for grad school, the role your community can play in your romantic life will be different from the place of community in the life of a twenty-six-year-old who grew up in a small town, went to the local college, and now works at the local bookstore."[17] Winner points to a story about a couple who conduct an "acquaintanceship." She coins the term because it describes an orthodox Jewish couple who discover and are attracted to each other but who then after the fact find friends to help them arrange a series of *shidduch* dates and courtship.[18]

I mention this example because I think it is an interesting way to think about how Christians can move forward in this confusing time. We do live in a far more mobile world, and so traditional neighborhoods and social and family networks are fading in their influence. But can we apply some older approaches to contemporary realities? Can we move the focus away from money and sex back to character? From personal fulfillment to building community? Can we involve the community around us more in seeking marriage? In the following section I will lay out some practical guidelines for doing so.

Some Practical Counsel for Marriage Seekers

Recognize that there are seasons for not seeking marriage. There are many times or "seasons" in which active dating and seeking marriage do not have to occur. Anyone who always needs to "have somebody" is probably into marriage idolatry. When you are going through a significant transition—starting a new job, starting a new school, dealing with the death of a parent, or some other absorbing time or event—it might not be a good time to begin a relationship. After some emotionally charged times in your life, you might want to deliberately avoid seeking marriage. In such situations, your judgment may be cloudy. During times of healing or regrouping, you probably need deep Christian friendship more than dates and ideas of marriage.

Understand the "gift of singleness." Paul calls singleness a *gift* in 1 Corinthians 7:7. Many have thought that Paul is talking about a complete lack of interest in or desire for marriage. In this view, to have the gift of singleness is to experience no emotional struggle, no restlessness or wish to be married. No wonder so many joke and say, "I don't think I have that gift!" It is important to discern Paul's meaning here, or we may be too quick to think that any lack of romantic desire is a gift from God. There are many bad reasons for a person to lack interest in marriage, including a selfish spirit, an inability to maintain friendships, and a disdain for the opposite sex.

In his writings, Paul always uses the word "gift" to mean an ability God gives to build others up. Paul is not speaking, then, of some kind of elusive, stress-free state. The "gift-ness" of being single for Paul lay in the freedom it gave him to concentrate on ministry in ways that a married man could not. Paul may very well, then, have experienced what we today would call an "emotional struggle" with singleness. He might have wanted to be married. He not only found an ability to live a life of service to God and others in that situation, he discovered (and capitalized on) the unique features of single life (such as time flexibility) to minister with very great effectiveness.[19]

Consider, then, that the "single calling" Paul speaks of is neither a condition without any struggle nor on the other hand an experience of misery. It is fruitfulness in life and ministry *through* the single state. When you have this gift, there may indeed be struggles, but the main thing is that God is helping you to grow spiritually and be fruitful in the lives of others despite them. That means a single gift is not just for a select few, and it is not necessarily lifelong, though it may be. It may be a grace given for a finite period of time.

Get more serious about seeking marriage as you get older. There is a spectrum of dating experiences. At one end of the spectrum is dating that means going out to various entertaining events, but it is mainly an excuse for getting together with a particular person to spend time with him or her. At the other extreme, dating entails going to some desired event—a prom, a movie, or a concert—and simply needing an escort, someone to go along with you. Especially when we are younger, the latter kind of dating is more appropriate, and it will have almost nothing to do with assessing the other person for a future marriage. As we get older, however, there is a tendency for most people more and more to think, "If you are going out with me, you are thinking about a serious relationship with me or marriage." If you then maintain the latter kind of dating as you get older, it can become very tricky. One of the most painful situations you can be in is when one of you thinks the dating is to consider a serious relationship and the other person thinks it is just for social fun and entertainment.

So here is some advice. First, act your age. Teenagers generally shouldn't try to "awaken emotional and physical desires that can't be fulfilled for years to come"—that is, can't responsibly find their fulfillment in marriage.[20] However, if you are single and in your thirties, you should recognize that if you insist on trying to continue the entertainment category of dating with others of your age, you will be often playing with people's emotions. The older you are, and the more often you go out, the quicker both people must be to acknowledge that you are seeking marriage.

Do not allow yourself deep emotional involvement with a non-believing person. This is a controversial point to make, though no reader of this book up to this point should be surprised. The Bible everywhere assumes that Christians should marry other Christians. For example, in 1 Corinthians 7:39, Paul writes, "A woman is bound to her husband as long as he lives. But if her husband dies, she is free to marry anyone she wishes, but he must belong to the Lord." Other passages in the Bible, such as 2 Corinthians 6:14, are invoked for this principle, and rightly so. The many prohibitions in the Old Testament against Jews marrying non-Jews at first sight seem to be telling people to marry within one's race, but passages such as Numbers 12—where Moses marries a member of another race—indicate that God's concern is not about marrying outside of one's race but outside one's *faith.*

Many think it is very narrow-minded indeed to discourage Christians from marrying outside of their faith, but there are strong reasons for this Biblical rule. If your partner doesn't share your Christian faith, then he or she doesn't truly understand it as you do, from the inside. And if Jesus is central to you, then that means that your partner doesn't truly understand *you*. He or she doesn't understand the mainspring of your life, the ground motive of all you do. As we observed in previous chapters, no one can perfectly know your spouse before you marry. But when two people marry who have a common faith in Christ, each one knows something significant about the other's fundamental motivations and views of life. If, however, you marry someone who doesn't share your most deeply held and core beliefs, then you will repeatedly make decisions that your partner won't be able to fathom at all. That part of your life—and it is the most important part—will forever be opaque and mysterious to your spouse.

The essence of intimacy in marriage is that finally you have someone who will eventually come to understand you and accept you as you are. Your spouse should be someone you don't have to hide from or always be "spinning"; it should be someone who "gets" you. But if the person is not a believer, he or she can't understand your very essence and heart.

If you do marry someone who does not share your faith, then there are only two ways to proceed. One is that you will more and more have to lose your transparency. In the normal, healthy Christian life, you relate Christ and the gospel to everything. You will think of Christ when watching a movie. You will base decisions on Christian principles. You will think about what you read in the Bible that day. But if you are natural and transparent about all of these thoughts, your partner will find it at least tedious or annoying and even offensive. He or she will say, "I had no idea you were this overboard about your faith." You will just have to hide it all.

The other, worse possibility is that you move Christ out of a central place in your consciousness. You will have to let your heart's ardor for Christ cool. You will have to deliberately *not* think out how your Christian commitment relates to every area of your life. You will demote Christ in your mind and heart, because if you keep him central, you will feel isolated from your spouse.

Both of these possible outcomes are, of course, terrible. That is why you should not deliberately marry someone who does not share your Christian faith.

Feel "attraction" in the most comprehensive sense. One of the more misunderstood passages in Paul's writings about marriage is 1 Corinthians 7:9, where he says that you should get married rather than "burn with passion." Many have seen this as a negative view. Paul seems to be saying, "Oh, if you really *have* to get married because you are too undisciplined to control your urges, go ahead and get married!" But Paul was not really being negative at all. He was saying that if you find yourself having passionate attraction to someone, by all means you should marry that person.

He is also saying that it is quite okay to "marry for love." Bible scholars Roy Ciampa and Brian Rosner argue that here Paul is rejecting the late Stoic view that marriage should be something you do not for romantic passion but strictly for business and producing children and heirs. And also he does not, as did most pagan authors of the time, teach that you can get release for sexual passion merely through nonmarital sexual liaisons. No, let your passion find its fulfillment in marriage and only there. So Paul teaches that attraction is an important factor in choosing to be married.[21]

But let us go a step further toward what we have been saying throughout this book about the mission of marriage. Yes, physical attraction is something that must definitely grow between marriage partners, and it will grow (rather than diminish) as time goes on if you start with a deeper attraction than merely the physical. Let me call it "comprehensive attraction." What is that?

Partly it is being attracted to the person's "character" or spiritual fruit (Galatians 5:22ff). Early American philosopher Jonathan Edwards said that "true virtue" in any person—contentment, peace, and joy from the gospel—is beautiful. We have been exploring marriage as a means to help one another become the glorious, unique persons God is making us. Marriage partners can say, "I see what you are becoming and what you *will* be (even though, frankly, you aren't there yet). The flashes of your future attract me."

Ultimately, your marriage partner should be part of what could be called your "mythos." C. S. Lewis spoke of a "secret thread" that unites every person's favorite books, music, places, or pastimes. Certain things trigger an "inconsolable longing" that gets you in touch with the Joy that is God. Leonard Bernstein said that listening to Beethoven's Fifth always made him sure (despite his intellectual agnosticism) that there was a God. Beethoven's Fifth doesn't do that for me. But everyone has something that moves them so that they long for heaven or the future kingdom of God (though many nonbelievers know it only as bittersweet longing for "something more").

Sometimes you will meet a person who so shares the same mythos thread with you that he or she becomes part of the thread itself. This is very hard to describe, obviously.

This is the kind of comprehensive attraction you should be looking for in a future partner. So many people choose their marriage partner on the basis of looks and money—rather than on character, mission, future self, and mythos—that they often find themselves married to a person they don't really respect that much. Comprehensive attraction is something that you can begin to sense with people if you deliberately disable the default "money, looks, and polish" screening mode. If you do that, you may find (perhaps to your initial horror) that you have that attraction to persons who didn't make the grade under your old evaluation policy.

Don't let things get too passionate too quickly. One of the great advantages of the old calling approach was that the man and woman got to see one another in more natural settings—family life, church life, and community life. The evaluation of character and comprehensive attraction had time to develop. Modern dating and hook-ups get sexual quickly, and when that happens a romantic obsession can arise immediately. As we argued earlier in this book, that sort of experience tends to preclude a realistic assessment of who the person really is. The kind of love that lasts a lifetime is not only a matter of the emotions. It has to be a commitment strong enough to move us to glad, non-begrudging, sacrificial service of another person even during the inevitable seasons when the emotions are dry or cold. That kind of love grows out of this comprehensive attraction to the person's character, future, and mission in life. Sometimes in the early stages of dating we can be swept up with powerful emotions that seem on the surface to be deep love. Lauren Winner says it well:

> When we are "in love" with someone we often appear to attend to our beloved when in fact we are doing the very opposite. Instead of being attentive we are acquisitive. We use the other for our own glorification, we bask in the presence of our beloved because we enjoy the image of ourselves that is reflected back. . . . This is the opposite of Christian love. The opposite is all about me. Even idolizing my beloved—certainly a danger for the newly infatuated—is all about me, though it pretends to be all about the other, it is all about me because it does not take my beloved seriously as a person

created and redeemed by God but rather imagines him
to be perfect, heroic, sublime, and customized to meet
my needs.[22]

The fact that these infatuations can pass and become hostile
and bitter so quickly shows that the comprehensive attraction and
love was never really there. So often today's relationships careen
from each person being blind to one another's serious flaws to
being angry, disillusioned, and blind to one another's strengths.

What can you do? In counseling with many young adults
today, I often hear them insist that it is unwise to marry someone
before you have lived with them for a couple of years. They are
incredulous when I point out what we saw in earlier chapters—
namely, that statistics show that people who have lived together
before marriage are more likely to get a divorce. But "dating"
today is basically nothing but a round of entertainment venues
and sexual encounters. I have come to realize that many turn to
cohabitation because they have no other way to get into the other
person's everyday life enough to assess their character.

When two Christians participate together in the same Christian community, however, there are plenty of opportunities to
enter the worlds of one another in the older way. By serving the
poor, or going to Bible study and fellowship groups, or attending
worship you can come into each other's "front porches" and
"parlors" in a way that is difficult outside a community of faith.

One of the ways you can judge whether you have moved past
the infatuation stage is to ask a set of questions. Have you been
through and solved a few sharp conflicts? Have you been through
a cycle of repenting and forgiving? Have each of you shown the
other that you can make changes out of love for the other? Two
kinds of couples answer no. The first kind are those who never

have any conflicts. It may be they are not past infatuation. The second kind of couple has had a stormy relationship and has the same unresolved fights over and over again. They haven't learned even the rudimentary skills of repentance, forgiveness, and change. Neither of these couples may be ready for marriage.

One crucial way for you to avoid the blindness and mood swings of becoming too passionate too quickly is to refuse to have sex before you are married. The next chapter is devoted to the Christian reasoning and Biblical basis for this ancient sex ethic. But the practical fact is that sexual activity triggers deep passions in you for the other person before you have gotten a good look at him or her. Put friendship development before romantic development.[23]

However, also don't become a faux spouse for someone who won't commit to you. While some couples may get too serious too quickly, there are other couples in which one member in particular has a deep reluctance to move forward and commit to marriage. If a relationship has dragged on for years with no signs of deepening or progressing toward marriage, it may be that one person has found a level of relationship (short of marriage) in which he or she is receiving all that is wanted and feels no need to take it to the final stage of commitment.

Kathy and I observed this phenomenon while still in college. We dubbed it the "cheap girlfriend syndrome," because it most often was the woman who was interested in marriage while the man was not. Sometimes a man and a woman would spend a great deal of time together. This meant the man had a female companion to accompany him to events (when he wanted one), a woman to talk to (if he felt like talking), and a supportive listener (to his troubles, should he need to unburden himself). If the relationship did not involve sex, the man would insist to others that he and the girl weren't even dating, that they weren't "involved."

If she ever chanced to question this, he might protest: "I never said we were more than friends!" But this is unfair, because they *were* more than friends. He was getting much more than he would out of a male buddy relationship. He was getting many of the perks of marriage without the cost of commitment, while the woman was slowly curling up and dying inside.

While congratulating ourselves on this insight, we never thought it would apply to us.

However, there came a time in our relationship, after we had known each other for several years, when Kathy saw that this was exactly what had happened, and so she gave me what has come to be known in our family as the "pearls before swine" speech. Though we were best friends and kindred spirits, I was still hurting from a previous relationship that had ended badly. Kathy was patient and understanding, up to a point, but the day came when she said, "Look, I can't take this anymore. I have been expecting to be promoted from friend to girlfriend. I know you don't mean to be saying this, but every day you don't choose me to be more than a friend, it feels as if I've been weighed and found wanting—I feel it as a rejection. So I just can't keep going on the same way, hoping that someday you'll want me to be more than a friend. I'm not calling myself a pearl, and I'm not calling you a pig, but one of the reasons Jesus told his disciples not to cast pearls before swine was because a pig can't recognize the value of a pearl. It would seem like just a pebble. If you can't see me as valuable to you, then I'm not going to keep throwing myself into your company, hoping and hoping. I can't do it. The rejection that I perceive, whether you intend it or not, is just too painful."

That's exactly what she said. It got my attention. It sent me into a time of deep self-examination. A couple of weeks later, I made the choice.

Get and submit to lots of community input. Older patterns of calling and courtship assumed that friends and relatives would give you major input in the selection of a spouse. Some in newly formed Christian communities are seeking to return to practices that require so much input from families, especially fathers, that they are almost arranged marriages. But even orthodox Jewish communities know that it is not practicable, especially for single adults who have been away from home for years. In addition, many single Christians have parents who have little understanding of their Christian faith and therefore would be unhelpful guides. Nevertheless, the basic principle is right and important. Marriage should not be a strictly individual, unilateral decision. It is too important, and our personal perspective is too easily skewed. The community has many married people in it who have much wisdom for single people to hear. Singles should get community input at every step of the way when seeking marriage.

In fact, I would suggest something further. The Christian community has a deep investment in you and a deep interest in healthy and happy marriages. Christian marriage should be communal. That is, married Christians should look for ways to share their marriages with the singles and other married couples in their community. Christians are directed to invite one another into their homes (1 Peter 4:9), and that doesn't simply mean into their *houses.* We are to treat one another as members of the same family, according to Romans 12:10, and that means to let people see into our lives. We are called to be transparent before one another. "One particular way married people can do that is by displaying the real work of their marriages—not just the sweet, light parts . . . but the hard, embattled parts—to the unmarried."[24] Think of what an impact that would have! Singles must see how hard *and* how glorious marriage is, not just how satisfying it is. The only way that happens is if married couples share their lives with singles so they can understand what marriage is really like.

Marriage is God's gift to the church. Through Christian marriages, the story of the gospel—of sin, grace, and restoration—can be seen and heard both inside the church and out in the world. Christian marriages proclaim the gospel. That is how important they are. The Christian community has a deep interest in the development of strong, great marriages and therefore a vested interest in the community's singles marrying well. Singles must not act as if who they marry is a decision belonging just to them as individuals.

EIGHT

SEX AND MARRIAGE

*For this reason a man will leave his father and mother
and be united to his wife, and the two shall become one
flesh.*

Ephesians 5:31

We cannot talk about marriage without talking about sex,
but the subject of how sex relates to marriage has two
levels to it. At the foundational level, we need to understand
the basic principle of the Biblical sex ethic—why does God confine sexual activity exclusively to married couples? Then, once we
understand and receive the Biblical reasoning, how do we live
practically in accordance with it as Christians—whether as
single persons or as married couples?

Sex Is Just an Appetite; No, It's Not

Historically, there have been countless attitudes about sex. First,
there is sex as a natural appetite. This view goes something like
this: Sex, it is said, was once surrounded by taboos, but now we
realize that sex is indeed like eating or like any other good and
natural appetite. That means we should feel free to fulfill the
appetite when we feel the need. And there is no reason why we

shouldn't sample a variety of cuisines and continually look for "new taste sensations." Forbidding the satisfaction of a natural appetite or limiting it for years is as unhealthy (and, really, as impossible) as trying to stop eating for years.

Another view of sex is more negative, and it has deep roots in some forms of ancient thought. Sex is seen as part of our lower, physical nature, distinct from our higher, rational, more "spiritual" nature. In this view, sex is a degrading, dirty thing, a necessary evil for the propagation of the human race. This view is still very influential in the world.

Today, a third view is also prominent. While the first view sees sex as an unavoidable drive and the second as a necessary evil, this last view sees sex as a critical form of self-expression, a way to "be yourself" and "find yourself." In this view, the individual *may* wish to use sex within marriage and to build a family, but that is up to the individual. Sex is primarily for an individual's fulfillment and self-realization, however he or she wishes to pursue it.

The Biblical attitude toward sex is popularly thought to be the second view—sex as demeaning and dirty. But it is most definitely not. It differs quite radically from each of these other understandings.

Is sex just an appetite? Yes, it is an appetite, but it is not in the same category as our needs for food and sleep. Indeed, even those desires cannot simply be gratified, whatever their level of intensity. Most people struggle to discipline their eating because their appetite for food is seriously out of line with what their bodies really need. The sex drive, however, needs even more guidance. Sex affects our heart, our inward being, not just our body. Sin, which is first and foremost a disorder of the heart, therefore has a big impact on sex. Our passions and desires for sex now are very distorted. Sex is for whole-life self-giving. However, the sinful heart wants to use sex for selfish reasons, not self-giving, and therefore the Bible puts many rules around it to direct us to use it in the right way.[1]

The Christian sex ethic can be summarized like this: Sex is for use within marriage between a man and woman.

Sex Is Dirty; No, It's Not

Is sex dirty and demeaning, as others have said? No. Biblical Christianity may be the most body-positive religion in the world. It teaches that God made matter and physical bodies and saw that it was all good (Genesis 1:31). It says that in Jesus Christ God himself actually took on a human body (which he still has in glorified form), and that someday he is going to give us all perfect, resurrected bodies. It says that God created sexuality and gave a woman and man to each other in the beginning. The Bible contains great love poetry that celebrates sexual passion and pleasure. If anyone says that sex is bad or dirty in itself, we have the entire Bible to contradict him.

God not only allows sex within marriage but strongly commands it (1 Corinthians 7:3–5). In the book of Proverbs, husbands are encouraged to let their wives' breasts fill them with delight and be intoxicated by their sexual love (Proverbs 5:19; cf. Deuteronomy 24:5). The book Song of Solomon does much barefaced rejoicing in the delights of sexual love in marriage. Old Testament scholar Tremper Longman writes:

> The role of the woman throughout the Song of Solomon is truly astounding, especially in light of its ancient origins. It is the woman, not the man, who is the dominant voice throughout the poems that make up the Song. She is the one who seeks, pursues, initiates. In Song 5:10–16 she boldly exclaims her physical attraction

["His abdomen is like a polished ivory tusk, decorated with sapphires . . ." (14)]. . . . Most English translations hesitate in this verse. The Hebrew is quite erotic, and most translators cannot bring themselves to bring out the obvious meaning. . . . This is a prelude to their love-making. There is no shy, shamed, mechanical movement under the sheets. Rather, the two stand before each other, aroused, feeling no shame, but only joy in each other's sexuality. . . .[2]

The Bible is a very uncomfortable book for the prudish!

Sex Is Strictly a Private Matter; No, It's Not

Is sex, however, primarily a means of individual happiness and fulfillment? No, but that doesn't mean that sex is not about joy or that it is only about duty. The Christian teaching is that sex is primarily a way to know God and build community, and, if you use it for those things *rather* than for your own personal satisfaction, it will lead to greater fulfillment than you can imagine.[3]

The first explicit mention of sex in the Bible is in the famous passage Genesis 2:24, quoted also by Paul in Ephesians 5. Male and female are to be "united" to become "one flesh." When first reading this phrase in English, it appears to be talking only about physical, sexual union. But while the words do not mean less than that, they mean much more. When the Bible says that "all flesh" had corrupted their way on the earth (Genesis 6:12) or that God would pour out his spirit on "all flesh" (Joel 2:28), it did not mean that only bodies were sinning or that God was giving his spirit to all bodies. Rather, he was giving his Spirit to all people. "Flesh" is a synecdoche, a figure of speech in which a part of a thing is used to represent the whole (as in our phrase "counting noses").

In other words, marriage is a union between two people so profound that they virtually become a new, single person. The word "united" (in older translations, "to cleave") means "to make a binding covenant or contract." This covenant brings every aspect of two persons' lives together. They essentially merge into a single legal, social, economic unit. They lose much of their independence. In love they donate themselves, wholly, to the other.

To call the marriage "one flesh," then, means that sex is understood as both a sign of that personal, legal union and a means to accomplish it. The Bible says don't unite with someone physically unless you are also willing to unite with the person emotionally, personally, socially, economically, and legally. Don't become physically naked and vulnerable to the other person without becoming vulnerable in every other way, because you have given up your freedom and bound yourself in marriage.

Then, once you have given yourself in marriage, sex is a way of maintaining and deepening that union as the years go by. In the Old Testament, there were often "covenant renewal ceremonies." When God entered into a covenant relationship with his people, he directed that periodically there be an opportunity to have them remember the terms of the covenant by first reading it together, and then recommitting themselves to it. This was crucial if the people were to sustain a life of faithfulness.

It is the same with the marriage covenant. When you get married, you make a solemn covenant with your spouse—the Bible calls your spouse your "covenant partner" (Proverbs 2:17). That day is a great day, and your hearts are full. But as time goes on, there is a need to rekindle the heart and renew the commitment. There must be an opportunity to recall all that the other person means to you and to give yourself anew. Sex between a husband and a wife is the unique way to do that.

Indeed, sex is perhaps the most powerful God-created way to

help you give your entire self to another human being. Sex is God's appointed way for two people to reciprocally say to one another, "I belong completely, permanently, and exclusively to you." You must not use sex to say anything less.

So, according to the Bible, a covenant is necessary for sex. It creates a place of security for vulnerability and intimacy. But though a marriage covenant is necessary for sex, sex is also necessary for the maintenance of the covenant. It is your covenant renewal service.

Sex as a Uniting Act

One Biblical author who is popularly thought to have a negative view of sex is St. Paul. Yet a closer look at what Paul actually says makes that hard to support.

In 1 Corinthians 6:17ff, Paul forbids Christians from having sex with a prostitute. But the reasoning he gives is remarkable:

> *Do you not know that a person who is united in intimacy with a prostitute is one body with her? For as it is said, "The two shall become one flesh." . . . Keep away from sexual immorality . . . for you do not belong to yourselves. You were bought with a price. Show forth God's glory, then, in how you live your bodily life.*
>
> (1 Corinthians 6:17, 18, 20)

What does this mean? Clearly "one flesh" means something different to Paul than mere sexual union, or Paul would be reciting a mere tautology: "Don't you know that when you have physical union with a prostitute you are having physical union with a prostitute?" Obviously, Paul also understands becoming "one flesh" here to mean becoming one person. One flesh refers to the personal union of a man and woman at *all* levels of their lives. Paul, then, is decrying the monstrosity of physical oneness without all the other kinds of oneness that every sex act should mirror.[4]

D. S. Bailey, who wrote the magisterial *The Man-Woman Relation in Christian Thought*, argues how groundbreaking and unprecedented the New Testament and Pauline view of sex was in the history of human thought:

> Here [Paul's] thought owes nothing to any antecedent notions, and displays a psychological insight into human sexuality which is altogether exceptional by first-century standards. The apostle denies that coitus is . . . no more than an appropriate exercise of the genital organs. On the contrary he insists that it is an act which . . . engages and expresses the whole personality in such a way as to constitute a unique mode of self-disclosure and self-commitment.[5]

In short, according to Paul, sex with a prostitute is wrong because *every* sex act is supposed to be a *uniting act*. Paul insists it is radically dissonant to give your body to someone to whom you will not also commit your whole life. C. S. Lewis likened sex without marriage to tasting food without swallowing and digesting. The analogy is apt.

Sex as a Commitment Apparatus

The modern sexual revolution finds the idea of abstinence from sex till marriage to be so unrealistic as to be ludicrous.[6] In fact, many people believe it is psychologically unhealthy and harmful. Yet despite the contemporary incredulity, this has been the unquestioned, uniform teaching of not only one but all of the Christian churches—Orthodox, Catholic, and Protestant.

The Bible does not counsel sexual abstinence before marriage because it has such a low view of sex but because it has such a lofty one. The Biblical view implies that sex outside of marriage is not just morally wrong but also personally harmful. If sex is designed to be part of making a covenant and experiencing that covenant's renewal, then we should think of sex as an emotional "commitment apparatus."

If sex is a method that God invented to do "whole life entrustment" and self-giving, it should not surprise us that sex makes us feel deeply connected to the other person, even when used wrongly. Unless you deliberately disable it, or through practice you numb the original impulse, sex makes you feel personally interwoven and joined to another human being, as you are literally physically joined. In the midst of sexual passion, you naturally want to say extravagant things such as, "I'll *always* love you." Even if you are not legally married, you may find yourself very quickly feeling marriage-like ties, feeling that the other person has obligations to you. But that other person has no legal, social, or moral responsibility even to call you back in the morning. This incongruity leads to jealousy and hurt feelings and obsessiveness if two people are having sex but are not married. It makes breaking up vastly harder than it should be. It leads many people to stay trapped in relationships that are not good because of a feeling of having (somehow) connected themselves.

Therefore, if you have sex outside marriage, you will have to steel yourself against sex's power to soften your heart toward another person and make you more trusting. The problem is that, eventually, sex will lose its covenant-making power for you, even if you one day do get married. Ironically, then, sex outside of marriage eventually works backwards, making you *less* able to commit and trust another person.

Practical Chastity

What if you decide that, as a single person, you are going to adopt the Christian ethic and practice chastity? Certainly that will be difficult, especially in a culture that gives you no support for your conviction. But you can be successful if you rely on the following resources.

First, you need the "spousal love" of Jesus in your life. Sex is for fully committed relationships because it is a foretaste of the joy that comes from being in complete union with God through Christ. The most rapturous love between a man and woman on earth is only a hint of what that is like (Romans 7:1-6; Ephesians 5:22ff). Knowing this helps a lot. One reason we can burn with seemingly uncontrollable sexual passion is because, at the moment, our hearts believe the lie that if we have a great, romantic, sexual experience, we will finally feel deeply fulfilled.

To resist temptation, we have to speak the truth to our hearts. We must remind them that sex simply cannot fill the cosmic need for closure that our souls seek in romance. Only meeting Christ face-to-face will fill the emptiness in our hearts that sin created when we lost our unbroken fellowship with him. But we are not simply called to wait for an experience of Christ's full love in the future. The Bible tells us that we can have not just intellectual belief in his love but actual experience of it now (Romans 5:5; Ephesians 3:17ff). This is available through prayer.

Also, to walk this path, single people need a Christian community.

They should live in community with other singles who are

neither too hungry to be married nor too fearful of it. They should be in a community with singles who don't use the world's standards—physical beauty and wealth—as a basis for making partner choices. It would additionally be important for singles to live in community with Christian families who do not make family an idol nor make singles feel superfluous.

Another mark of this community should be free and open discussion about how the Bible's perspective on sex plays out in life and relationships. The more often singles and married Christians reflect on the Biblical teaching about this, the more support singles will feel for abiding by it. Most of all, singles who want romantic involvement without mandatory sexual intercourse will need a sufficiently large community of single people who are all pursuing the same goal.

Some will survey the last two paragraphs and exclaim: "But there aren't any churches like that!" That is largely true, and as a pastor I freely confess that my own church goes through cycles in which it serves singles well, but it has more often failed to provide the kind of community described. I want to challenge readers to take it upon themselves to create those conditions in their churches, or start some new churches that make such community a priority.

Finally, strike a balance with regard to your sexual thoughts and desires. Some Christians feel deeply stained and defiled by any strong sexual thoughts or daydreams. Others indulge in them. The gospel is neither legalism, nor antinomianism. Christians are not saved by obeying God, and yet true salvation will lead to obeying God, out of gratitude. This should lead to a very balanced approach to thoughts and temptations. Martin Luther, for example, was reputed to say about sexual desires, "You can't stop birds from flying over your head, but you can stop them from making nests in your hair." By that he meant that we can't stop sexual thoughts from occurring to us—they are natural and unavoidable. However, we are responsible for what we do with those thoughts. We must not entertain and dwell on them.

And if we do something sexually that is wrong, we should use the gospel of grace on our consciences. That gospel will neither take the sin lightly nor lead you to flagellate yourself and wallow in guilt indefinitely. It is important to get the gospel's pardon and cleansing for wrongdoing. Often it is unresolved shame for past offenses that stir up present, obsessive fantasies.

The Inner Dialogue

Ultimately, it is not techniques that will enable single Christians to practice the Christian sex ethic. It will take conviction. In the classic novel *Jane Eyre*, Jane has fallen in love with Mr. Rochester, but she has also learned that he is married and that his mentally ill wife lives in an upper room in his estate. Nevertheless, he urges her to live with him as his mistress. This touches off an inner storm, an enormous conflict in her heart:

> . . . . while he spoke my very conscience and reason turned traitors against me, and charged me with crime in resisting him. They spoke almost as loud as Feeling: and that clamoured wildly. "Oh, comply!" it said. "Think of his misery; think of his danger—look at his state when left alone; remember his headlong nature; consider the recklessness following on despair—soothe him; save him; love him; tell him you love him and will be his. Who in the world cares for YOU? or who will be injured by what you do?"

Jane discerns different rooms or faculties in her soul. There is conscience, there is reason, and there is feeling, and they all rise up and argue that they should do what Mr. Rochester asks. He is lonely and miserable—she could comfort him. He is rich and adores her—after a life of hardship, surely she deserves this. But she resists what they all say.

> Still indomitable was the reply: "I care for myself. The more solitary, the more friendless, the more unsustained I am, the more I will respect myself. I will keep the law given by God; sanctioned by man. I will hold to the principles received by me when I was sane, and not mad—as I am now. Laws and principles are not for the times when there is no temptation: they are for such moments as this, when body and soul rise in mutiny against their rigour; stringent are they; inviolate they shall be. If at my individual convenience I might break them, what would be their worth? They have a worth— so I have always believed; and if I cannot believe it now, it is because I am insane—quite insane: with my veins running fire, and my heart beating faster than I can count its throbs. Preconceived opinions, foregone determinations, are all I have at this hour to stand by: there I plant my foot."
>
> I did.

Jane Eyre has been made into a movie or TV show many times, and as far as I know, when this scene comes and Mr. Rochester makes his powerful plea, none of this inner dialogue is ever depicted. We hear Jane resisting only by saying things like, "I will respect myself." Modern viewers are therefore likely left with the illusion that Jane was able to resist temptation simply out of an effort to keep high self-esteem. She appears to be saying not that being Mr. Rochester's mistress would be immoral, but that it would be demeaning. All the movie versions I have seen give the impression that she looks inside and finds the inner self-assurance and self-respect to refuse a second-class position.

But see how she actually does resist. She does not look into her heart for strength—there's nothing there but clamorous conflict. She *ignores* what her heart says and looks to what God says. The moral laws of God at that very moment made no sense to her heart and mind at all. They did not appear reasonable, and they did not appear fair. But, she says, if she could break them when they appear inconvenient to her, of what would be their worth? If you only obey God's word when it seems reasonable or profitable to you—well, that isn't really obedience at all. Obedience means you cede someone an authority over you that is there even when you don't agree with him. God's law is *for* times of temptation, when "body and soul rise in mutiny against their rigour."

On God's Word then, not her feelings and passions, she plants her foot. I've never seen anywhere a more clear or eloquent example of what a Christian single person's inner dialogue should be with regard to temptation. Learn how to plant your foot.

The Importance of Erotic Love in Marriage

Since the Bible confines sex to marriage, we should not be surprised to find that various passages instruct married couples to enjoy sex and to do so frequently. We have already mentioned the eye-opening passages from the Song of Solomon and Proverbs 5:19, which exhort husbands to be delighted with their wives' bodies. In 1 Corinthians 7:3–5, Paul speaks with surprising candor about the importance and realities of marital sexual relations:

> The husband should fulfill his marital duty to his wife,
> and likewise the wife to her husband. The wife's body

does not belong to her alone but also to her husband. In the same way, the husband's body does not belong to him alone but also to his wife. Do not deprive each other except by mutual consent and for a time. . . .

Here, at a time in which women were legally considered the possession of their husbands, Paul makes the revolutionary claim that "the husband's body does not belong to him alone but also to his wife." "It communicates, negatively, his obligation to refrain from engaging in sexual relations with anyone other than his wife and, positively, his obligation to fulfill his marital duty to provide her with sexual pleasure and satisfaction."[7] This was a major blow to the traditional double standard—namely, that men were expected and allowed to have multiple sexual partners but if a woman did she was despised. Paired with the previous statement, that the wife's body also belongs to her husband, Paul was teaching that each partner, male and female, had the right to mutual sexual relations. Nothing like this had ever been said before.

Modern readers will find this text satisfying because of our contemporary Western view of human rights, but that is not Paul's main point at all. He is giving us a remarkably positive view of sexual satisfaction within marriage. The view of the Roman culture in which the Corinthian Christians lived was that "men were to take wives in order to have legal heirs, while sexual pleasure, if it was to be sought at all, would typically be found outside the marriage." Historians point out, however, that, "Paul, in effect, redefines marriage as a context for the mutual satisfying of erotic desires in contrast to the pagan philosophical idea that the purpose of marriage was the procreation of legitimate heirs who would inherit and continue the name, property and sacred rites of the family."[8] In other words, Paul is telling married Christians that mutual, satisfying sexual relations must be an important part their life together. In fact, this passage indicates that sex should be frequent and reciprocal. One spouse was not allowed to deny sex to the other.

The Erotic Marriage

I believe this particular part of 1 Corinthians 7 is an important practical resource. Each partner in marriage is to be most concerned not with getting sexual pleasure but with *giving* it. In short, the greatest sexual pleasure should be the pleasure of seeing your spouse getting pleasure. When you get to the place where giving arousal is the most arousing thing, you are practicing this principle.

When I was doing research for this chapter, I found some old talks that Kathy and I did together. I had forgotten some of the struggles we had in our early days, and some of the notes reminded me that in those years we started to dread having sex. Kathy, in those remarks, said that if she didn't experience an orgasm during lovemaking, we both felt like failures. If I asked her, "How was that?" and she said, "It just hurt," I felt devastated, and she did, too. We had a great deal of trouble until we started to see something. As Kathy said in her notes:

> We came to realize that orgasm is great, especially climaxing together. But the awe, the wonder, the safety, and the joy of just being one is stirring and stunning even without that. And when we stopped trying to perform and just started trying to simply love one another in sex, things started to move ahead. We stopped worrying about our performance. And we stopped worrying about what we were getting and started to say, "Well, what can we do just to give something to the other?"

This concept also has implications for a typical problem that many couples experience in their marital relationship—namely, that one person wants sex more often than the other. If your main purpose in sex is giving pleasure, not getting pleasure, then a person who doesn't have as much of a sex drive physically can give to the other person as a gift. This is a legitimate act of love, and it shouldn't be denigrated by saying, "Oh, no, no. Unless you're going to be all passionate, don't do it." Do it as a gift.

Related to this are the differences that many spouses experience over what is the most satisfying context for sex. While I am not saying this is universal, I will share that, as a male, context means very little to me. That means, to be blunt, pretty much anytime, anywhere. However, I came to see that that meant I was being oblivious to something that was very important to my wife. Context? Oh, you mean candles or something? And, of course, Kathy, like so many women, did *not* mean "candles or something." She meant preparing for sex emotionally. She meant warmth and conversation and things like that. I learned this, but slowly. And so we learned to be very patient with each other when it came to sex. It took years for us to be good at sexually satisfying one another. But the patience paid off.

Sex as a Test

The Bible gives us a high view of sex. It is a sign and seal of our oneness with each other and with God. We should not, then, be surprised to discover that you may find problems "showing up in bed," which, if it wasn't for sex, you might never have seen. There may be guilt, fear, or anger over past relationships. There may be growing mistrust or disrespect, or unresolved differences in your present relationship. Sex is such a great and sensitive thing that you will not be able to sweep these problems under the rug.

Unless your marital relationship is in a good condition, sex doesn't work. So be very careful to look beneath the surface. A lack of "sexual compatibility" might not really be a lack of lovemaking skill at all. It may be a sign of deeper problems in the relationship. It is often the case that, if those problems are addressed, the sexual intimacy improves.

A fundamental rule of marriage is that time marches on, and as Lewis Smedes said, you don't marry one woman or one man but many. Time, children, illness, and age all bring changes that may require creative, disciplined responses to rebuild a sexual intimacy that was easier at an earlier time. If you don't confront and adapt to these changes, they'll erode your sex life. Kathy and I often liken sex in a marriage to oil in an engine—without it, the friction between all the moving parts will burn out the motor. Without joyful, loving sex, the friction in a marriage will bring about anger, resentment, hardness, and disappointment. Rather than being the commitment glue that holds you together, it can become a force to divide you. Never give up working on your sex life.

The Glory of Sex

Sex is glorious. We would know that even if we didn't have the Bible. Sex leads us to words of adoration—it literally evokes shouts of joy and praise. Through the Bible, we know why this is true. John 17 tells us that from all eternity, the Father, Son, and Holy Spirit have been adoring and glorifying each other, living in high devotion to each other, pouring love and joy into one another's hearts continually (cf. John 1:18; 17:5, 21,24–25). Sex between a man and a woman points to the love between the Father and the Son (1 Corinthians 11:3). It is a reflection of the joyous self-giving and pleasure of love within the very life of the triune God.

Sex is glorious not only because it reflects the joy of the Trinity but also because it points to the eternal delight of soul that we will have in heaven, in our loving relationships with God and one another. Romans 7:1ff tells us that the best marriages are pointers to the deep, infinitely fulfilling, and final union we will have with Christ in love.

No wonder, as some have said, that sex between a man and a woman can be a sort of embodied out-of-body experience. It's the most ecstatic, breathtaking, daring, scarcely-to-be-imagined look at the glory that is our future.

EPILOGUE

Marriage does not consist of just one form of human love. It is not merely romantic passion or friendship, or acts of duty and service. It is all of these things and more. It is overwhelming. Where do we get the power to meet the seemingly impossible demands of marriage?

Seventeenth-century Christian poet George Herbert wrote three poems about love, but the most famous was the last, entitled, simply, "Love (III)."

> Love bade me welcome, yet my soul drew back,
> Guilty of dust and sin.
> But quick-ey'd Love, observing me grow slack
> From my first entrance in,
> Drew nearer to me, sweetly questioning
> If I lack'd anything.
> "A guest," I answer'd, "worthy to be here";
> Love said, "You shall be he."
> "I, the unkind, the ungrateful? ah my dear,
> I cannot look on thee."
> Love took my hand and smiling did reply,
> "Who made the eyes but I?"

"Truth, Lord, but I have marr'd them; let my shame
Go where it doth deserve."
"And know you not," says Love, "who bore the blame?"
"My dear, then I will serve."
"You must sit down," says Love, "and taste my meat."
So I did sit and eat.

Love welcomes him in, but because of the poet's sense of guilt and sin, he "grows slack" and shrinks back just inside the doorway. Love notices everything, however. He sees the hesitation and approaches with sweet words, like an innkeeper of old asking, "What d'ye lack?" The guest answers that he does indeed lack something important—the very worthiness to be loved. His host replies, with realism but confidence, that he intends to bring that worthiness about. He doesn't love the guest because he is lovely but to make him lovely.

Unconvinced, the guest answers back that he can't even look upon Love.

The mysterious figure reveals then who he is. "I'm the One who made your eyes, you know, and I made them to look upon me." The guest now knows who Love is, because he calls him Lord, but he is still without hope.

"Just let this wretch depart in shame."
"But don't you know, I bore your blame?"
For this, even the guest's deepest fears and doubts have no answer. And so the Lord lovingly but firmly tells him to sit down. And now the Lord of the universe, who humbly washed his disciples' feet, serves the loved, unworthy man at the table.

"You must taste my meat."
"So I did sit—and eat."[1]
French philosopher, writer, and activist Simone Weil was a

Jewish agnostic. But one day in 1938, she was meditating on this poem of George Herbert, and, as she did so, she had an overwhelming, powerful experience of Christ's love. "Christ came down," she wrote about that moment, "and took possession of me."[2] From that time forward, she became a professing Christian. She had not been expecting or seeking such an experience. She had never read any books on mystical experience, and as a Jewish agnostic she certainly was not looking to Christ for anything like this. And yet, through this poem, Christ's sacrifice on the Cross became a reality to her. "In this sudden possession of me by Christ . . . I felt in the midst of my suffering the presence of a love, like that which one can read on the smile of a beloved face."[3]

When we looked at the conversion of Louis Zamperini and saw how the flood of Christ's love gave him the immediate ability to forgive people who had tortured him for years, we cautioned that spiritual growth doesn't always work like that. We must say the same thing about Simone Weil's experience. Herbert's poem is a masterpiece of spiritual art. It will yield endless insights, and I have personally found that it has worked on my heart powerfully, but if you turn to it for a once-and-for-all spiritual encounter that removes all your doubts and fears, you will probably be disappointed.

Nevertheless, at the end of the day, Christ's love is the great foundation for building a marriage that sings. Some who turn to Christ find that his love comes in like a wave that instantly floods the hard ground of their hearts. Others find that his love comes in gently and gradually, like soft rain or even a mist. But in any case, the heart becomes like ground watered by Christ's love, which enables all the forms of human love to grow.

Dear friends, let us love one another, for love comes from God. . . . Whoever does not love does not know God,

*because God is love. . . . This is love: not that we loved
God, but that he loved us and sent his son as an atoning
sacrifice for our sins. Dear friends, since God so loved us,
we also ought to love one another. No one has ever seen
God; but if we love one another, God lives in us and his
love is made complete in us."*

(1 John 4:7,8,10–11)

APPENDIX:
DECISION MAKING AND GENDER ROLES

Tim and I (Kathy) have used the following principles to guide us in our everyday decisions as well as our more complicated decisions. These five guidelines have proved useful to us, and so I hope they will for you.

The husband's authority (like the Son's over us) is never used to please himself but only to serve the interests of his wife. Headship does not mean a husband simply "makes all the decisions," nor does it mean he gets his way in every disagreement. Why? Jesus never did anything to please himself (Romans 15:2–3). A servant-leader must sacrifice his wants and needs to please and build up his partner (Ephesians 5:21ff).

A wife is never to be merely compliant but is to use her resources to empower. She is to be her husband's most trusted friend and counselor, as he is hers (Proverbs 2:17). The "completion" that embracing the Other entails involves a lot of give and take. To complement each other means husband and wife need to hear each other out, make their arguments. Completion is hard work and involves loving contention

(Proverbs 27:17), with affection (1 Peter 3:3–5), until you sharpen, enrich, and enhance each other. She must bring every gift and resource that she has to the discussion, and he must, as any wise manager, know when to allow her expertise to trump his own, less well-informed opinion.

A wife is not to give her husband unconditional obedience. No human being should give any other human being unconditional obedience. As Peter said, "We must obey God rather than men" (Acts 5:29). In other words, a wife should not obey or aid a husband in doing things that God forbids, such as selling drugs or physically abusing her. If, for example, he beats her, the "strong help" that a wife should exercise is to love and forgive him in her heart but have him arrested. It is never kind or loving to anyone to make it easy for him or her to do wrong.

Assuming the role of headship is only done for purposes of ministering to your wife and family. Some say, "In the Biblical view, both husband and wife are to minister to each other unselfishly, so then what is the difference?" It is clear that the Son *obeys* his head, the Father, and that we *obey* our head, the Christ.[1] But how does this authority work out in the context of mutually serving persons equal in dignity and being? The answer is that a head can only overrule his spouse if he is sure that her choice would be destructive to her or to the family. He does not use his headship selfishly, to get his own way about the color of the car they buy, who gets to hold the remote control, and whether he has a "night out with the boys" or stays home to help with the kids when his wife asks him.

This is the area in which the most misunderstanding, on the part of both men and women, has occurred. Some men, unaware or unwilling to assume their servant-leader roles, believe that simply being male brings entitlement with it. And women, often the victims of such mistaken understanding, want no part of any teaching that would demote them to inferior status.

But in a marriage, where there are only two "votes," how can a stalemate be broken without someone having to give way? In the vast majority of cases, the stalemate is broken because each will try to give the other his or her pleasure. The wife will try to respect the husband's leadership, and the husband will in turn try to please his wife. If this dynamic is in place, in the course of a healthy Biblical marriage, "overruling" will be rare.

But what of a case where both parties cannot agree, but some kind of decision must be made? Someone must have the right to cast the deciding vote and (thus) take the greater responsibility for the decision.

This should be the place where the one the Bible calls "head" takes the accountability. When it happens, both people "submit" to their role. Often, an intelligent husband doesn't want this role, and the intelligent wife does! The situation could be chaotic, but here we are called to act out the drama of redemption, where the Son voluntarily gives the headship to the Father, saying, "Not my will, but thine be done."

In the late 1980s, our family was comfortably situated in a very livable suburb of Philadelphia where Tim held a full-time position as a professor. Then he got an offer to move to New York City to plant a new church. He was excited by the idea, but I was appalled. Raising our three wild boys in Manhattan was unthinkable! Not only that, but almost no one who knew anything about Manhattan thought that the project would be successful. I also knew that this would not be something that Tim would be able to do as a nine-to-five job. It would absorb the whole family and nearly all of our time.

It was clear to me that Tim wanted to take the call, but I had serious doubts that it was the right choice. I expressed my strong doubts to Tim, who responded, "Well, if you don't want to go, then we won't go." However, I replied, "Oh, no, you don't! You aren't putting this decision on me. That's abdication. If you think this is the right thing to do, then exercise your leadership and made the choice. It's your job to break this logjam. It's my job to wrestle with God until I can joyfully support your call."

Tim made the decision to come to New York City and plant Redeemer Presbyterian Church. The whole family, my sons included, consider it one of the most truly "manly" things he ever did, because he was quite scared, but he felt a call from God. At that point, Tim and I were both submitting to roles that we were not perfectly comfortable with, but it is clear that God worked in us and through us when we accepted our gender roles as a gift from the designer of our hearts.

Why should the woman submit at times like these? We must reject the "traditionalist" answer—namely, that "women are not decisive enough." The fact is that many wives are more decisive than their husbands. So why are women called to this position? As I said, the answer to that question is another question: "Why did Christ become the one to give up the authority to the Father?" We don't know, but it is a mark of his greatness, not his indecisiveness! Women are called to follow him here. But remember, taking authority properly is just as hard as granting it.

NOTES

INTRODUCTION

1. I, Tim, am writing in my own voice because most of this volume is based on a series of nine sermons I preached in the fall of 1991, during the early days of the ministry of Redeemer Presbyterian Church in New York City. Nevertheless, this book is very much the product of *two* people's mutual experience, conversation, reflection, formal study, teaching, and counseling over thirty-seven years. Kathy and I have come to our understanding of marriage together. Even those nine sermons were mainly the fruit of our common effort to understand marriage in Christ. I just did the reporting.

2. As a girl of twelve, Kathy wrote to C. S. Lewis and received answers from him, which she taped to the inside covers of her copies of the *Narnia Chronicles*. His four letters to her (to "Kathy Kristy") can be found in his *Letters to Children* and the third volume of *Letters of C. S. Lewis*.

3. C. S. Lewis, *The Problem of Pain* (HarperOne, 2001), 150. Ironically, Lewis himself was a major component in the "thread" we shared.

4. "How Firm a Foundation" was written by John Rippon, 1787.

5. This book necessarily will deal with two of the most contentious issues in our church and society today—gender roles and sexuality. The main Biblical passages we will look at—Ephesians 5 and Genesis 2—are theological battlegrounds. Within those texts, there are terms like

"head" and "helper" that are the objects of enormous and lengthy debates as to their meaning and significance. The specific questions are: Are there distinct gender roles for a man and a woman within marriage, and should a woman give her husband final authority within a marriage? A second issue has to do with same-sex marriage. Here the Biblical texts are much less debatable. The Bible strongly endorses heterosexuality and prohibits homosexuality. Indeed, as we will see, one of the main purposes of marriage according of the Bible is to create deep cross-gender companionship. However, in our society, the argument that persons of the same sex should have the right to marry is growing in power and force.

It is impossible to write a book on marriage without coming to some working assumptions about these issues. There is no way to remain neutral. Our position is that of a carefully expressed but traditional Christian understanding of male leadership, gender roles, and homosexuality. We will take the time, in the footnotes, to outline the Biblical arguments for the positions we take. However, they cannot be extensive. This is not a book written to provide a full case for these views, including responses to all the best counterarguments. Rather, our purpose is to state these views as well as possible within the book and to *use* them—to show how they work themselves out practically in marriage. And so we urge readers to grant and "try on" on these views as they consider the vision for married life we are laying out in this volume.

6. We will discuss the issues in this paragraph later, mainly in chapters 7 and 8.

7. I am aware that the belief I have just articulated—that the Bible's teaching on sex and marriage is coherent and profoundly wise—has been under major assault in popular culture. Jennifer Knust's *Unprotected Texts: The Bible's Surprising Contradictions About Sex and Desire* (HarperOne, 2011) is an example. Knust argues that the Bible accepts polygamy and prostitution (in certain parts of the Old Testament) but then forbids it (in parts of the New Testament). She concludes that, therefore, taken as whole, the Bible provides no coherent and unified guidance on sex and marriage.

For example, in her introduction, she writes, "the Bible does not object to prostitution, at least not consistently. The biblical patriarch Judah, for example, was quite content to solicit a prostitute while out on a business trip . . . It was only later, when he learned that this 'prostitute' was actually his daughter-in-law Tamar, that he became angry. . . . Does the Bible have a problem with prostitutes or prostitution? Not necessarily . . ." (p. 3). But just because Biblical writers report that behavior occurred does not mean they are promoting it. Knust should know that Hebrew literature scholar Robert Alter, in his classic *The Art of Biblical Narrative* (Perseus Books, 1981), makes a very detailed case that Genesis 38 is tightly connected to the next chapter, about Joseph refusing to sleep with his master's wife. Alter concludes, "When we return from Judah to the Joseph story (Gen 39) we move in pointed contrast from a tale of exposure through sexual incontinence to a tale of seeming defeat and ultimate triumph through sexual continence—Joseph and Potiphar's wife" (pp. 9–10). Alter, perhaps the dean of Hebrew narrative experts, in no way thinks the author of Genesis "has no problem with prostitutes." The narrator is deliberately contrasting Judah's behavior to Joseph's in the next chapter, where he calls sex outside of marriage "this wicked thing" and a "sin against God" (Genesis 39:9). To say that Genesis condones prostitution, or polygamy for that matter—when the prostitution and polygamy in the narrative bring untold misery to all participants—shows, I think, an elementary failure to learn how to read narrative.

I have personally studied and publicly taught for four decades on all the texts Knust treats, and there are mountains of good scholarship, as well as common sense, opposed to her reading of every one. Strangely, Knust doesn't give readers much hint of that, and even in places (like her Genesis 38 interpretation) where almost the entire body of Biblical scholarship, from liberal to conservative, is against her, she offers not even a footnote to mention it. I find this to be the case with most all the speakers, books, and articles assailing the Bible's wisdom on sexuality.

CHAPTER ONE – THE SECRET OF MARRIAGE

1. When Adam sees Eve, he breaks into poetry, a very striking move designed to signal the significance of the event and the power of Adam's inner response to Eve. His first words are hard to translate. Literally he says, "This—this time!" The New International translation simply renders it, "Now!" The New Revised Standard Version does a better job, translating it to be, "This *at last*—is bone of my bones and flesh of my flesh!"

2. The figures in this paragraph are taken from W. Bradford Wilcox, ed., The State of Our Unions: Marriage in America, 2009 (The National Marriage Project, University of Virginia), and The Marriage Index: A Proposal to Establish Leading Marriage Indicators (Institute for American Values and the National Center on African American Marriages and Parenting, 2009). Both of these reports can be found in PDF form online at, respectively, www.stateofourunions.org and www.americanvalues.org (Wilcox) and www.hamptonu.edu/ncaamp (American Values).

3. While 77 percent of first marriages were intact in the year 1970, today only 61 percent are (*The Marriage Index*, 5). Put another way, today about 45 percent of all marriages end in separation or divorce (*The State of Our Unions*, 78).

4. *The Marriage Index*, 5.

5. "The Decline of Marriage and the Rise of New Families" (Pew Research Center Report, November 18, 2010). Accessed at http://pewsocialtrends.org/2010/11/18/the-decline-of-marriage-and-rise-of-new-families/2/

6. Wilcox, *The State of Our Unions*, 84.

7. Mindy E. Scott, et al., "Young Adult Attitudes about Relationships and Marriage: Times May Have Changed, but Expectations Remain High," in *Child Trends: Research Brief* (Publication #2009-30, July 2009). See front page. Accessed at www.childtrends.org/Files/Child_Trends-2009_07_08_RB_YoungAdultAttitudes.pdf.

8. David Popenoe and Barbara Dafoe Whitehead, *The State of Our Unions: 2002—Why Men Won't Commit* (National Marriage Project), 11.

9. Ibid., 85.

10. Ibid. People who cohabit before marriage end up getting divorced at higher rates than those who do not cohabit before the wedding. However, there is no agreement on why this is true. Some believe that the experience of cohabitation teaches people bad habits that later serve the couple poorly when they are married. Others theorize that people who choose to cohabit before marriage have different characteristics than those who do not, and it is these preexisting characteristics, not the cohabitation itself, that causes the marriages to later break up. These theories do not make much difference to the ultimate finding. The willingness to cohabit is associated with future marital weakness. Regardless of the causes, a desire and choice to cohabit weakens your chances for a strong future marriage.

11. "Your Chances of Divorce May Be Much Lower than You Think," in Wilcox, *The State of Our Unions, 2009,* 80.

12. Popenoe, *The State of Our Unions,* p. 7. One of the ten reasons men give for living together rather than marrying is "They want to own a house before they get a wife" (number 9).

13. "The Surprising Economic Benefits of Marriage," in Wilcox, *The State of Our Unions,* 86.

14. Ibid., 87.

15. http://answers.yahoo.com/question/index?qid=20090823-064213AAoKwvq

16. Adam Sternburgh, "A Brutally Candid Oral History of Breaking Up," *New York Times Magazine,* March 11, 2011.

17. Ibid.

18. Linda Waite, et al., *Does Divorce Make People Happy? Findings from a Study of Unhappy Marriages* (American Values Institute, 2002). See www.americanvalues.org/UnhappyMarriages.pdf.

19. "The study found that on average unhappily married adults who divorced were no happier than unhappily married adults who stayed married when rated on any of the 12 separate measures of psychological well-being. Divorce did not typically reduce symptoms of depression, raise self-esteem, or increase a sense of mastery. This was even true after controlling for race, age, gender and income. . . .

[R]esults like these suggest the benefits of divorce have been over-sold," says Linda J. Waite. From the press release for *Does Divorce Make People Happy?*, which can be found at www.americanvalues .org/html/r-unhappy_ii.html.

20. "The Decline of Marriage" (2010 Pew Center report). This report concludes that 84 percent of married people are very satisfied with their family lives, compared to 71 percent of those living with a part-ner, 66 percent of those who are single, and 50 percent of those who are divorced or separated.

21. Wilcox, *The State of Our Unions*, 101.

22. See "Teen Attitudes about Marriage and Family" in Wilcox, *The State of Our Unions,* 113. Yet surprisingly, after years of increasing, the number of teens who think that cohabiting before marriage is a "good idea" has begun to decline. The report concludes, "Both boys and girls have become more accepting of lifestyles that are alterna-tives to marriage, especially unwed childbearing, although the latest data show a surprising drop in acceptance of premarital cohabitation" (p. 112).

23. John Witte, Jr., *From Sacrament to Contract: Marriage, Religion, and Law in the Western Tradition* (Louisville: John Knox Press, 1997), 209.

24. See his article "God's Joust, God's Justice: An Illustration from the History of Marriage Law" in *Christian Perspectives on Legal Thought*, ed. M. McConnell (New Haven: Yale University Press, 2001), 406ff.

25. See W. Bradford Wilcox. *Why Marriage Matters: Twenty-six Conclu-sions from the Social Sciences*, 3rd ed. (Institute for American Values, 2011). One of the findings of this volume is that "marriage seems to be particularly important in civilizing men, turning their attention away from dangerous, antisocial, or self-centered activities and towards the needs of a family." See www.americanvalues.org/html/ r-wmm.html.

26. *New York Times*, December 31, 2010, www.nytimes.com/2011/01/ 02/weekinreview/02parkerpope.html.

27. Popenoe and Whitehead, *The State of Our Unions.* Accessed at www .virginia.edu/marriageproject/pdfs/SOOU2002.pdf.

28. Sternburgh, "A Brutally Candid Oral History."

29. Ibid., 13.

30. Ibid., 15.

31. Ibid., 17.

32. Ibid., 17.

33. Sara Lipton, "Those Manly Men of Yore," *New York Times*, June 17, 2011.

34. Popenoe and Whitehead, *The State of Our Unions*, 14. Accessed at www.virginia.edu/marriageproject/pdfs/SOOU2004.pdf.

35. Ibid.

36. John Tierney, "The Big City: Picky, Picky, Picky," *New York Times*, February 12, 1995.

37. *Haven in a Heartless World: The Family Besieged* (New York, Basic Books, 1977). Lasch was one of the first to contrast the traditional understanding of marriage as the creation of character and community with the "therapeutic" view of marriage as the fulfillment of autonomous individuals' personal needs.

38. Tierney, "Picky, Picky, Picky."

39. C. S. Lewis, *The Four Loves* (New York: Harcourt, 1960), 123.

40. Stanley Hauerwas, "Sex and Politics: Bertrand Russell and 'Human Sexuality,'" *Christian Century*, April 19, 1978, 417–422. Available online at www.religion-online.org/showarticle.asp?title=1797.

41. A Latin term meaning "to be curved inward on oneself" used by Martin Luther to describe sinful human nature. See his lectures on Romans where he uses this term several times to describe the original sin and ordinary sinfulness. For much more on the subject of self-centeredness as the main problem in marriage, see chapter 2, The Power for Marriage.

42. *Love in the Western World* (New York: Harper and Row, 1956), 300. Quoted in Diogenes Allen, *Love: Christian Romance, Marriage, Friendship* (Eugene, OR, Wipf and Stock, 2006). 96.

43. Ernest Becker, *The Denial of Death* (New York: Free Press, 1973), 160.

44. Ibid., 167. In the book *Counterfeit Gods* (Dutton, 2009), I apply Becker's analysis to a close reading of the Biblical story of Jacob, Rachel, and Leah. See chapter 2, Love Is Not All You Need.

45. Examples of married couples such as this one, as they appear throughout the book, are taken from my personal life experience but are not
cases taken from my ministry of pastoral counseling within my con-
gregations.

46. See, for example, Sharon Jayson, "Many Say Marriage is Becoming
Obsolete" *USA Today,* November 11, 2010.

47. Rashida Jones, speaking to E! Reported at http://ohnotheydidnt
.livejournal.com/57296861.html.

48. There is not only no evidence that "open marriages" are better for
most people, but there is plenty of anecdotal evidence that the opposite is the case. That was the message when Nena O'Neill died.
O'Neill was one of the two authors of the landmark book *Open Marriage: A New Life Style for Couples* (M. Evans and Company, 1972),
which has sold over 35 million copies in fourteen languages. The
book ever so tentatively proposed: "We are not recommending outside sex, but we are not saying it should be avoided, either. The choice
is up to you." That statement, along with the famous line, "Sexual
fidelity is the false god of a closed marriage," backed up with lots of
seventies-era popular psychology, provided many married readers
with a warrant for sex with partners beside their spouses. In O'Neill's
New York Times obituary, it was said that the book's "bolder sugges-
tions [now] seem not so much daring as painfully naïve." Some years
after the publication of *Open Marriage*, O'Neill told the *New York
Times*, "The whole area of extramarital sex is touchy. I don't think we
ever saw it as a concept for the majority, and certainly it has not
proved to be." She is referring to the fact that so many couples who
have tried it have found it devastating, bringing in feelings of jealousy
and betrayal that destroy intimacy. (These quotes are taken from
Margalit Fox, "Nena O'Neill, 82, an Author of 'Open Marriage,' Is
Dead" *New York Times,* March 26, 2006.) In other words, despite
the popularity of the idea of non-monogamous marriages, there is no
empirical or anecdotal evidence that it works at all.

49. Elissa Strauss, "Is Non-Monogamy the Secret to a Lasting Marriage?" Posted June 1, 2011, at slate.com/blogs/xx_factor/2011.

50. For example, in Mark Oppenheimer's *New York Times Magazine* June 30, 2011, article "Married, with Infidelities," he quotes sex-advice columnist Dan Savage as saying, "I acknowledge the advantages of monogamy . . . when it comes to sexual safety, infections, emotional safety, paternity assurances. But people in monogamous relationships have to be willing to meet me a quarter of the way and acknowledge the drawbacks of monogamy . . ."

51. For example, see Dr. Neil Clark Warren, "On Second Thought, Don't Get Married," at huffingtonpost.com/dr-neil-clark-warren/ on-second-thought-dont-ge_b_888874.html.

52. This sounds like a controversial statement, but it is not. As all social history books will tell you, marriage had its origins in "prehistory"—in other words, the human race cannot remember a time in which marriage did not exist. There have been some efforts to make the case that this or that remote culture or small ethnic group has existed without marriage, but none of these efforts are widely regarded as successful. One example is the argument some have made regarding the Mosuo (or the "Na people"), a small ethnic population in southern China. In this society, marriage partners do not live together in the same home. Brothers and sisters live together in households and raise the children of the sisters. Men are held most responsible to support and raise their sisters' children—their nieces and nephews, not their biological children. This family arrangement is highly unusual, but that does not mean that marriage and family mores are not in existence and, indeed, they are strongly enforced. Fathers are definitely part of their children's lives even though they do not live in the same household. Women form long-term relationships with their partners. Some married couples practice cohabitation as well. See Tami Blumenthal's 2009 report, *The Na of Southwest China: Debunking the Myths*, at web.pdx.edu/~tblu2/Na/myths.pdf.

53. P. T. O'Brien, *The Letter to the Ephesians* (Grand Rapids, MI: Eerdmans, 1999), 109–10. I follow closely O'Brien's exegesis of the Ephesians 5 passage throughout this book. In particular, I believe he is right in his belief that in Paul, "there are not many mysteries but

several aspects of one mystery"(pp. 433–4). "The mystery [secret] is not . . . marriage itself; it is the union of Christ and the church that is reflected in Christian marriage. . . . [Marriage] reproduces in miniature the beauty shared between the Bridegroom and the Bride. And through it all the mystery of the gospel is unveiled"(p. 434).

54. G. W. Knight, "Husbands and Wives as Analogues of Christ and the Church: Ephesians 5:21–33 and Colossians 3:18–19," in *Recovering Biblical Manhood and Womanhood: A Response to Evangelical Feminism,* eds. J. Piper and W. Grudem (Wheaton, IL: Crossway, 1991), 176. Quoted in O'Brien, *Ephesians,* 434n.

55. Robert Letham, *The Holy Trinity: In Scripture, History, Theology, and Worship* (Phillipsburg, NJ: Presbyterian and Reformed, 2004), 456.

56. O'Brien, *Ephesians,* 434.

CHAPTER TWO – THE POWER FOR MARRIAGE

1. Does Ephesians 5:21 mean that each and every believer is to submit to each and every other believer? Or is this a "programmatic" statement introducing what follows and therefore a general statement that all Christians should submit to those in authority over them in their varied roles and social arrangements? P. T. O'Brien (*The Letter to the Ephesians* [Grand Rapids, MI: Eerdmans, 1999], 436) and others make a good case for the latter interpretation of the term in this particular context. Verse 21 is an opening summary statement that Paul then unpacks by giving specific directions for relationships between spouses, parents and children, and masters and servants. For example, verse 21 not only introduces the section on husbands and wives (verses 22–32) but also the section on the relationship of parents and children. It is clear that parents are not to submit to children in the same way that children submit to their parents. The point here is that we should not use verse 21 to "flatten" the distinctions between the duties of wives and husbands, arguing that they are identical. Husbands do not submit to their wives in exactly the same way wives submit to their husbands. (See chapter 6.)

On the other hand, we must not make the opposite mistake and fail to see the mutuality and reciprocity in the duties of husbands and wives to each other. Philippians 2:1–3 tells all Christians to look not to their own interests but to the interests of others. They should always submit their own desires for the good of others and the community. Many other Biblical texts talk about all Christians serving and deferring to one another. See Galatians 5:13, where Paul boldly tells all Christians to be *douloi* of one another—literally bond-servants Extending the metaphor, Paul says that we owe one another love as a kind of "debt" (Romans 13:8). In light of these exhortations, it would be a mistake to think that, though wives are not called to love their husbands nor husbands to serve and defer to his wife in Ephesians 5:22–31, some kind of mutual love and service is not implied. In the end, both husband *and* wife are to "give themselves up" and make sacrifices for one another.

2. Strictly speaking, it is the apostles themselves who are the primary beneficiaries of this ministry of the Spirit to which Jesus is referring. In the "Upper Room Discourse" of John 13–17 Jesus was preparing his apostles for their ministry as his representatives after his death and resurrection. Jesus assures them that the Spirit will enable them in particular to remember the things that he said to them during his earthly ministry with them (John 14:26), since they had been with him since the beginning of that ministry (John 15:27). The apostles' eyewitness testimony and teaching was the basis for the New Testament. Nevertheless, "derivatively, we may speak of the Spirit's continued work in the disciples of Jesus today." (D. A. Carson, *The Gospel According to John* [Leicester, England: Inter-Varsity Press], 541). Other texts in the Bible confirm that the Holy Spirit's work in all believers is to make Jesus glorious to their hearts and minds, as described in John 14–17. See Ephesians 1:17, 18–20; 3:14–19; 1 Thessalonians 1:5.

   We should remember that in John 14–17, Jesus is promising this Spirit ministry primarily to the apostles, so we do not lose sight of the main vehicle for the Spirit's ministry to *us*—namely, the Scriptures. Ordinarily, the Spirit glorifies Jesus in our hearts as we read, study, or hear taught the apostolic word, the gospel that has come to us in the documents of the New Testament, and which illumines the

Old Testament. In conclusion, the Spirit's illumination of the Word to us is the ordinary way that the fullness of the Spirit comes.

3. The subject of a husband's headship is taken up and given more extensive treatment in chapter 6.

4. A classic treatment of self-centeredness is C. S. Lewis's chapter "The Great Sin" in *Mere Christianity* (Macmillan, 1960). The chapter is short and can be found many places online, such as at www.btinter net.com/~a.ghinn/greatsin.htm.

5. This does not mean, by the way, that those who aren't Christians cannot have a good marriage. But it does mean that anyone who is living unselfishly and having an increasingly satisfying marriage is getting some help from God, whether they know it or not (James 1:17). I am referring here to what Christian theologians have called "common grace." It refers to the understanding that God generously gives gifts of truth, moral character, wisdom, and beauty to all kinds of people, including those who do not acknowledge him, as a merciful way to restrain and moderate the effects of human sin and selfishness on human life. Biblical texts that indicate this include James 1:17 and Romans 2:14–15. The Bible regularly describes the deeds and works of nonbelieving men and women as good and right (2 Kings 10:29–30; Luke 6:33) but insists that such goodness always has its source in God.

6. C. S. Lewis, *The Problem of Pain* (HarperOne, 2001), 157. Lewis is quoting George MacDonald.

7. C. S. Lewis, *Mere Christianity* (Macmillan, 1960), 190.

8. This does not mean there are not situations in which divorce is not allowed and wise. See chapter 3 and endnote 79.

9. Derek Kidner, *Psalms 73–150: An Introduction and Commentary* (Leicester, UK: IVP, 1973), 446.

10. The quotes and this account are taken from the last three chapters of Laura Hillenbrand, *Unbroken: A World War II Story of Survival, Resilience, and Redemption* (Random House, 2010). The chapters are 37, Twisted Ropes; 38, A Beckoning Whistle; and 39, Daybreak.

11. "The fear of the Lord" is the main way the Old Testament speaks of spiritual experience, while it is used more seldom in the New. On the

other hand, the fullness of the Spirit is a phrase used extensively in the New Testament and much less in the Old. For a good overview of the first concept, see John Murray's chapter "The Fear of God" in *Principles of Conduct: Aspects of Biblical Ethics* (Grand Rapids, MI: Eerdmans, 1957). Murray demonstrates that, according to the Old Testament, mere external belief and observance without this inward spiritual experience and motivation is considered false religion. There is far more written on the ministry of the Holy Spirit. Because the Holy Spirit was given in a heightened way through Christ, it would be an overgeneralization to say that the fear of God in the Old Testament was identical to the fullness of the Spirit in the New. Nevertheless, they are describing the same basic reality.

CHAPTER THREE – THE ESSENCE OF MARRIAGE

1. Deuteronomy 10:20, 11:22; Joshua 22:5; 23:8. See especially Deut 10:20: "Fear the Lord your God and serve him. Cleave to him and take your oaths in his name."

2. From Russell, *Marriage and Morals*, 1957, quoted in Stanley Hauerwas, "Sex and Politics: Bertrand Russell and 'Human Sexuality'" in the *Christian Century*, April 19, 1978, 417–22.

3. What I heard is increasingly typical. The Wikipedia entry on "Wedding Vows" (http://en.wikipedia.org/wiki/Wedding_vows) included the following on February 3, 2011: "Many couples today opt to write their own vows. Inspirations are often taken from poems, movies, or music. Vows usually consist of what characteristics each bring out in each other, what they look forward to in life, how their lives changed once they met. Vows tend to last 2–3 minutes in length and are a public expression of love." Notice that the emphasis is on a declaration of present love, not the promise of future love.

4. Linda Waite, et al., *Does Divorce Make People Happy? Findings from a Study of Unhappy Marriages* (American Values Institute, 2002). Available at www.americanvalues.org/UnhappyMarriages.pdf.

5. The subject of marriage, divorce, and remarriage is an enormous subject, and those who want to lay out the Biblical guidelines must do a great deal of detailed exegetical work. That is beyond the scope of

this book. Nevertheless, here is a summary of my own conclusions after years of reflection and research.

I believe that, for a Christian, there are two Biblical grounds for divorce: (a) If your spouse has committed adultery, the believer may sue for divorce. Matthew 19:3–9 indicates this. (b) If your spouse deserts you and refuses to return. In such a case, the believer may acquiesce in the divorce (1 Corinthians 7:15). In this second case, the text speaks about the deserting spouse being an "unbeliever." (The man or woman conducting this behavior may profess to be a non-believer or may be designated so through church discipline. That is, if the person is not acting as a Christian and is refusing to repent, a church body can censure the party in line with Matthew 18:15–17.) In either case, the spouse who has been wronged and now divorced is, according to Paul, "not bound" (1 Corinthians 7:15). This would be a pointless tautology unless he were saying the divorced person is free to remarry.

A fair question is, What is meant by "desertion"? The Biblical text says the spouse must be "willing to live with her" (1 Corinthians 7:13). What about physical abuse? Could it not be argued that a man who is beating a woman has essentially deserted her, has given up his willingness to be *with* his wife? Yes, I personally think so. But this very question leads to an important conclusion. Christians who are weighing divorce, if they want to live with their consciences and their God for the rest of their lives, should not make these decisions all by themselves. Matthew 18:15ff says that when someone sins against you—and adultery, desertion, and abuse are grievous sins—you should "tell it to the church." Most commentators read this as, at least, consulting with your church's leaders.

A final question is this: Can the person who did not get a divorce on Biblical grounds ever remarry? There is little agreement among pastors and Biblical scholars here, and this question is complex, but I think the short answer is yes, in some cases—when there has been both inner repentance and public admissions of wrongdoing. In the end, the answer is yes because, as Jay Adams has asked, why should divorce be the only unpardonable sin? (See Jay E. Adams,

Marriage, Divorce, and Remarriage Grand Rapids, MI: Zondervan, 1980], 92ff.)

6. This passage is a discourse in which God expresses his grief and anger that Israel had turned to worship other gods. This was, spiritually speaking, adultery. The people were giving themselves to a new covenant partner, a new lover. God responds by saying, "Then I saw that for all the causes for which backsliding Israel had committed adultery, I had put her away and *given her a certificate of divorce....*" According to this text, God knows the pain of betrayal and divorce. This has been a comfort to many who have had the same experience.

7. Quoted in Gary Thomas, *Sacred Marriage* (Grand Rapids, MI Zondervan, 2000), 11.

8. Published in *Christianity Today,* January 21, 1983.

9. Peter Baehr, *The Portable Hannah Arendt* (New York: Penguin Classics, 2003), 181. Also quoted in Smedes's article.

10. Wendy Plump, "A Roomful of Yearning and Regret," *New York Times,* December 9, 2010. Available at www.nytimes.com/2010/12/12/fashion/12Modern.html.

11. J. R. R. Tolkien, *The Lord of the Rings: The Return of the King* (New York: Houghton-Mifflin, 2005) p. 146 chapter 8, The Houses of Healing.

12. Kierkegaard discusses the nature of romantic love and marriage in a number of works. See "The Aesthetic Validity of Marriage" in *Either/Or, Concluding Scientific Postscript,* and "On the Occasion of a Wedding" in *Three Discourses on Imagined Occasions.* I am relying on the distillation of Kierkegaard's thought in these works by Diogenes Allen, in *Love: Christian Romance,* 68ff.

13. Allen, 69.

14. Ibid., 15.

15. Lewis, *Mere Christianity.* (Harper San Francisco, 2001). p. 130–131.

16. Ibid, pg 131–132.

17. It should be said here that the "arranged marriages" of traditional cultures can still fit the Biblical pattern, indeed they can fit it quite well. My grandmother was born to Italian immigrants in the United States just before the turn of the century, and her marriage to my grandfather was arranged by her parents. She didn't choose her

husband. But, she told me, "I knew he was a good man. I wasn't in love with him at first, but I learned to love him. That's how it worked in the old days." Actions of love led to feelings of love.

18. From Lewis, *Mere Christianity*, Book III, chater 6, Christian Marriage.

19. Ibid.

20. Ibid.

Chapter Four – The Mission of Marriage

1. The repeated expression "it was good" in Genesis 1 shows that the material world/physical reality is intrinsically good. The Greeks believed that the creation of the physical world was an accident or even a rebellious action of some lower deities. They taught that matter was the prison house of the soul. It was intrinsically bad, dirty, and stultifying to soul/spirit. In this view, the body was something to be transcended in order to reach spiritual heights. As a result, many in Greco-Roman society believed that sexual pleasure was either demeaning or just unimportant. In contrast to this view, Genesis 1–2 shows us a God with his hands dirty, creating the world and deliberately putting a spirit in a body. In addition, the incarnation of Christ and the resurrection of the body make Christianity perhaps the most pro-physical faith. Even our future is a physical one! No other religion envisions matter and spirit living together in integrity forever. It can be argued that Jews and Christians were stricter about sexual ethics than pagan society because they saw the body as more important and therefore sex as a greater good.

2. For standard treatments in systematic theologies, I suggest looking at Louis Berkhof, *Systematic Theology* (Grand Rapids, MI: Eerdmans, 1949), Part Two, chapter III, Man: The Image of God; Herman Bavinck, *Reformed Dogmatics: God and Creation*, Volume 2 (Grand Rapids, MI: Baker, 2004), Part V, The Image of God; Michael Horton, *The Christian Faith: A Systematic Theology for Pilgrims on the Way* (Grand Rapids, MI Zondervan, 2011), Part Three, chapter 12, Being Human; G. C. Berkouwer, *Man: The Image of God* (Grand Rapids, MI: Eerdmans, 1962).

3. The word *'ezer* comes from a verb that means "to surround and protect." Most of the debate about the meaning of this word has to do with its implications for the concept of gender and gender roles. We will say more about this elsewhere in this book. Here and now we are merely pointing out that the first spouse was not just a lover but a friend.

4. Dinah Maria Mulock Craik, *A Life for a Life* (New York: Harper and Brothers, 1877, pg 169.

5. Ralph Waldo Emerson, in his essay on friendship, argued that the best friendships are between people who are profoundly like *and* unlike each other but who nevertheless have a common vision and travel together toward it: "Friendship requires that rare mean betwixt likeness and unlikeness. Better be a nettle in the side of your friend than his echo. There must be very two, before there can be very one. Let it be an alliance of two large, formidable natures, mutually beheld, mutually feared, before yet they recognize the deep identity which beneath these disparities unites them."Accessed at www.emersoncentral.com/friendship.htm.

6. C. S. Lewis, *The Four Loves*, first paperback ed. (New York: Mariner Books, 1971), chapter 4.

7. Peter O'Brien argues that the "cleansing" Jesus performs on the church is not a long process of gradual sanctification but a single act of what theologians call "definitive sanctification." In the Bible, the word "sanctification" can sometimes refer to the gradual, progressive process by which a man or woman is renewed into glory and Christlikeness, but more often it is used for the one time "setting apart" that occurs when a man or woman puts faith in Christ. O'Brien argues that the word Paul uses for *cleanse* is in an aorist form, which means a single past action, not a long procedure (P. T. O'Brien, *Letter to the Ephesians* [Grand Rapids, MI: Eerdmans], 1999, 422). Nevertheless, as O'Brien says in his commentary on Philippians 1:6, there is indeed a gradual process of sanctification that Jesus oversees in us, and the goal of Jesus as our spiritual husband in Ephesians is to make us "glorious" (verse 27, Greek *endoxan*). This clearly refers to future "spiritual and ethical perfection" (O'Brien,

Ephesians, 425). See also on Philippians 1:6 Peter T. O'Brien, *The Epistle to the Philippians: The New International Greek Testament Commentary* [Grand Rapids, MI: Eerdmans, 1991], 64–5).

8. We should again observe that in Ephesians 5:22ff, Paul only tells husbands to sacrificially commit to the spiritual growth of their wives and see them through to her future glory-selves. He doesn't give this duty to wives, and this has caused some readers to be confused. But as we have made clear, *all* Christians are to confess sins to each other, hold each other accountable for growth, serve and exhort each other. Ephesians 5 can't mean wives can do this for every other Christian except their husbands. Though this is only speculation, I propose that Paul singles out the husbands here, (a) because they are less likely to do this duty than their wives, and/or because (b) Paul holds them more responsible if the marriage fails to enhance the spiritual growth of both partners.

9. Lewis, *Mere Christianity,* 174–5.

10. "His love for the church is the model for husbands in its purpose and goal, as well as in its self-sacrifice (v. 25). In the light of Christ's complete giving of himself to make the church holy and cleanse her, husbands should be utterly committed to the total well-being, especially the spiritual welfare, of their wives" (O'Brien, *Ephesians,* 423).

11. This truth is excellently illustrated in the 1996 film *The Truth about Cats & Dogs,* starring Uma Thurman, Janeane Garofalo, Jamie Foxx, and Ben Chaplin. Ben Chaplin's character falls in love with Garofolo's mind (over the phone) but Thurman's body (in person).

12. C. S. Lewis, *The Problem of Pain* (New York: HarperOne, 2001), 47.

CHAPTER FIVE – LOVING THE STRANGER

1. Stanley Hauerwas, "Sex and Politics: Bertrand Russell and 'Human Sexuality'" in the *Christian Century,* April 19, 1978, 417–22.

2. Gary Chapman, *The Five Love Languages: The Secret to Love that Lasts* (Chicago: Northfield Publishing, 2010), from chapter 3, Falling in Love.

3. The quote in full: "Do you not know that there comes a midnight hour when every one has to throw off his mask? Do you believe that life will always let itself be mocked? Do you think you can slip away a little before midnight in order to avoid this? Or are you not terrified by it?" Soren Kierkegaard, *Either/Or*, II, Princeton: Princeton University Press, 1988, p 160.

4. This is too short an answer to the question, "How do I know if I should marry this person?" We give more extended treatment to it in chapter 7.

5. As ingenious as this plate-smashing incident was, it isn't the ordinary way that spouses handle conflict and send and receive difficult messages from each other. Kathy has often said about her wedding china strategy, "It only works once."

6. For many of the ideas in this part of the chapter, I am indebted to Arvin Engelson: "Marriage as a vehicle for sanctification." (From his unpublished paper, Gordon-Conwell Theological Seminary.) "In the context of marriage, one encounters the possible redemption of the full life, the retrospective healing of your personal history. The third conversion of one's biography is a divine work begun in this life, and it would seem that God has invested the marriage relationship with sufficient emotional power to challenge the authority of accumulated biographical verdicts and to thereby redeem the past."

7. Readers of this illustration should observe that this not only demonstrates the importance of "love currency" or "love language." It also demonstrates the importance of what we covered in chapter 4, of "leaving and cleaving." Each marriage is a new community, and we must not insist on imposing patterns from the family you grew up in on your spouse. Kathy and I were failing to examine how our previous family's patterns of life were influencing us. Each of us was unconsciously assuming that our marriage had to operate on the same bases our former families had. We had to make a deliberate, consensual decision about how to live out our lives together. That was one very significant way in which we "left" our families to better "cleave" to one another.

8. This account is taken from chapter 10, Love Is a Choice" in Chapman's *The Five Love Languages: Secrets to Love That Lasts* (Chicago: Northfield Publishing, 2010, p 134–138.

9. Ibid.

10. In this section I will group love expressions under three categories: affection, friendship, and service. For the category of love expressed though romance and sex, see chapter 8.

CHAPTER SIX – EMBRACING THE OTHER

1. We confine ourselves here to how gender roles operate within marriage, since that is the subject of this book. Naturally, the subject cannot be completely separated from the subject of gender in general, including how that affects the relationship of men and women in the church and in the world, but it is beyond our present scope to explore every aspect of those issues.

2. "So God created man in his own image, in the image of God he created him; male and female he created them. God blessed them and said to them, 'Be fruitful and increase in number; fill the earth and subdue it. Rule over the fish of the sea and the birds of the air and over every living creature that moves on the ground'" (Genesis 1:26–28).

3. It is no mere linguistic curiosity that God says, "Let us make man in OUR image" (Genesis 1:26). The only time in Genesis where God refers to himself as "we" or "us" is when he is about to create male and female. This is a hint that the relationship between male and female is a reflection of the relationships within the Godhead itself—the Trinity. Gender relations tell us something of the relationships between the Father, the Son, and the Holy Spirit. If God is tripersonal—Father, Son, and Holy Spirit—it would take at least two people (with the potential for a loving, serving, honoring, glorifying-one-another relationship) to capture the full image of God. More significantly, it would take two people who performed different roles, as the Father, Son, and Holy Spirit have all taken different roles in the accomplishment of Creation and Redemption. See the Nicene Creed, which from the early years of Christianity has

spelled out the differing roles that the Father, Son, and Holy Spirit played in Creation and Redemption, while affirming their identical essence. Although all people, men and women, are bearers of God's image, resembling him as his children, reflecting his glory, and representing him as stewards over nature, it requires the unique union of male and female within the one flesh of marriage to reflect the relationship of love within the triune God.

4. "The LORD God said, 'It is not good for the man to be alone. I will make a helper suitable for him.' So the LORD God caused the man to fall into a deep sleep; and while he was sleeping, he took one of the man's ribs and then closed up the place with flesh" (Genesis 2:18, 21). The significance of this lies in that, up until now, every object and situation brought about by the creative activity of God is given the verdict "it was good." Here we have the first thing said to be *not* good, and this occurs before the Fall, the sin in the garden. One reason for this "not-goodness" is that human beings were made for community with other human beings. But this also means that maleness will not do without femaleness. This strongly implies the complementary nature of the sexes.

5. Genesis 2:20; 3:20: "Adam named his wife Eve, because she would become the mother of all the living." The significance of "naming" cannot be ignored. It is evidence of headship and authority. We have the right to name someone only if we have some responsibility and authority over the person. Compare this with Adam naming the animals, God naming John the Baptist and Jesus rather than allowing their parents to do it, God renaming Abram, Sarai, and Jacob, and so on. For this traditional understanding of naming, see Bruce Waltke, *Genesis: A Commentary* (Grand Rapids, MI: Zondervan, 2001), 89. However, others deny that Adam's naming entails any authority, but only indicates discernment. See Victor Hamilton, *The Book of Genesis: Chapters 1–17* (Grand Rapids, MI: Eerdmans, 1990), 176. Gerhard Von Rad probably does best when he combines these two ideas and argues that naming is "an act of appropriative ordering." That is, when Adam names, he discerns a being's nature, and the name puts it in a proper relationship to himself. However,

the namer is the one doing the ordering, not the named. See Gerhard Von Rad, *Genesis* (Philadelphia Westminster, 1961), 81.

6. See Gordon J. Wenham, *Genesis 1–15* (Waco, TX: Word, 1987), 68. "Elsewhere *'ezer* usually refers to divine assistance, but it is used in three prophetic passages to denote military aid (Isaiah 30:5; Ezekiel 12:14; Hosea 13:9). To help someone does not imply that the helper is stronger [or weaker] than the helped: simply that the latter's strength is inadequate by itself."

7. Gordon Wenham says the phrase expresses "the notion of complementarity rather than identity." See Wehnam, *Genesis*, 68.

8. There are some obvious and less obvious observations to make. An obvious one is that this whole passage explains why later in the Bible homosexuality is always forbidden. A less obvious one is that we all need, even apart from marriage, "cross-gender" discipling. That is, we need the friendship and fellowship of persons of the opposite sex—whether they are siblings and relatives, or Christian brothers and sisters, or friends, or spouses. There are always ways in which we need the "stretching" and enriching experience of cross-gender interaction. There are things you will only be able to learn (either through counsel or example) from people of the other sex. We must not think that we have to be married for this enrichment to take place.

9. "Then the man and his wife heard the sound of the LORD God as he was walking in the garden in the cool of the day, and they hid from the LORD God among the trees of the garden. But the LORD God called to the man, 'Where are you?' He answered, 'I heard you in the garden, and I was afraid because I was naked; so I hid.' And he said, 'Who told you that you were naked? Have you eaten from the tree that I commanded you not to eat from?' The man said, 'The woman you put here with me—she gave me some fruit from the tree, and I ate it.' Then the LORD God said to the woman, 'What is this you have done?' The woman said, 'The serpent deceived me, and I ate'" (Genesis 3:8–13).

10. Throughout the gospels, every encounter that Jesus has with women is a positive one. The women understand him before the men do; women are excused their housewifely duties in order to sit and learn

with the men (Luke 10:38 ff.). Women stay with him at the Cross when his male disciples have mostly hidden; it is to women that Jesus shows himself first after his resurrection, and it is a woman, Mary Magdalene, who is for a few moments the entire church: She is charged by Jesus to tell his disciples of his resurrection and his commands—the first Christian, the first evangelist. (John 20:1 ff.) Jesus's every interaction with women elevates their status in a culture that very much considered them second-class beings. The early church, having seen the Holy Spirit fall on women the same as on men at Pentecost, adopted such a radical attitude toward women that Paul had to remind women not to adopt a unisex approach to ministry. Even when engaged in the identical ministry as men, they should do it in a way that affirms their female role, rather than denies it. See 1 Corinthians 11, 14.

11. "Your attitude should be the same as that of Christ Jesus: Who, being in very nature God did not consider equality with God something to be grasped, but made himself nothing, taking the very nature of a servant, being made in human likeness. And being found in appearance as a man, he humbled himself and became obedient to death—even death on a cross! Therefore God exalted him to the highest place and gave him the name that is above every name, that at the name of Jesus every knee should bow, in heaven and on earth and under the earth, and every tongue confess that Jesus Christ is Lord, to the glory of God the Father" (Philippians 2:5–11).

12. 1 Corinthians 11:3: "The head of the woman is man, and the head of Christ is God." Like all texts having to do with gender, this passage is debated and argued over. There are three kinds of "headship" mentioned in the verse, and they are clearly not identical in quality. Nevertheless, the submission of the Son to the Father in Philippians 2 is here linked to the relationship between male and female.

13. From "Notes on the Way," *Time and Tide,* Volume XXIX (August 14, 1948).

14. When I announced to Pittsburgh Presbytery my decision to pull out of the ordination track that I had been on in my seminary education

and instead pursue an unordained status "because I believe that is what the Bible teaches," I was booed and hissed by a majority of the 350 ministers and elders attending the meeting!

15. Mark 10:32–45; see also Matthew 20:17–28: "Whoever wants to become great among you must be your servant, and whoever wants to be first must be slave of all. For even the Son of Man did not come to be served, but to serve, and to give his life as a ransom for many."

16. Marietta Cheng, "When Women Make Music," *New York Times*, April 19, 1997.

17. See Carol Gilligan, *In a Different Voice: Psychological Theory and Women's Development* (Cambridge, MA: Harvard University Press, 1993). Gilligan's book took on the highly influential work of Laurence Kohlberg, who outlined "stages of moral development." Kohlberg concluded that males generally reached a higher level of moral development than females, but Gilligan argued that Kohlberg's definitions privileged the kind of moral reasoning done by males rather than females. For Kohlberg, the highest level of moral development is a "personal moral system based on abstract principles." This will leave women out, Gilligan argued, because men indeed do tend to inform their judgment of "right" and "wrong" by reasoning from abstract principles, while women tend to judge them on the basis of personal relationships, on the basis of compassion and empathy. This has been called "difference feminism" by some.

18. Gilligan calls for a new definition of adult development she calls a "maturity of interdependence" (p.155). Like Marietta Cheng, Gilligan sees the female path of adult development to be superior, and many have argued against that. Indeed, to use Christian categories, this would imply that women are less "fallen" than men, and that does not fit in with Biblical teaching. However, Gilligan does a good job arguing that women are profoundly different than men in their psychological and psychosocial makeup and development.

19. "A given man may make a very bad husband; you cannot mend matters by trying to reverse the roles. He may make a bad male partner in a dance. The cure for that is that men should more diligently attend dancing classes; not that the ballroom should henceforward

ignore distinctions of sex and treat all dancers as neuter. That would, of course, be eminently sensible, civilized, and enlightened, but, once more, 'not near so much like a Ball.'" C. S. Lewis, "Notes on the Way," in *Time and Tide,* Volume XXIX (August 14, 1948).

20. Continental philosophers Jacques Lacan and Emmanuel Levinas popularized the term "the Other" and "Difference" as opposed to "the Same." For an accessible Christian account of the discussion and a Christian response, see Miroslav Volf, *Exclusion and Embrace: A Theological Exploration of Identity, Otherness, and Reconciliation* (Nashville: Abingdon, 1996).

21. "Let every creature rise and bring Peculiar honors to the king." (Isaac Watts, *Jesus Shall Reign,* 1719)

22. Refer to the brief discussion of homosexuality in the introduction.

23. Volf, *Exclusion and Embrace*, quoting Jurgen Moltmann, 23.

24. "The husband is the head of the wife just in so far as he is to her what Christ is to the Church. He is to love her as Christ loved the Church—*and give his life for her* (Ephesians 5:25). This headship, then, is most fully embodied not in the husband we should all wish to be but in him whose marriage is most like a crucifixion; whose wife receives most and gives least . . . [and who is] in her own mere nature—least lovable." C. S. Lewis, *The Four Loves*, p. 148

25. When Adam and Eve fall into sin, God lays out the consequences and says to Eve, "Your desire will be for your husband, but he shall rule over you" (Genesis 3:16). As Derek Kidner says, "To 'love and cherish' has become to 'desire and dominate.'" (*Genesis: An Introduction and Commentary* [Leicester, England: Tyndale, 1967], 71.)

26. Apparently this has been necessary ever since the first child pinned a red bath towel to his shoulders and tried to emulate Superman by flying off the porch, roof, or tree branch.

27. In 1 Timothy 3:15, Paul refers to the church as "the household of God." However, the deployment of gender roles within the life of the church is, as I have said, for another book. We are confining ourselves to a discussion of how divinely created gender roles operate within a marriage.

28. I was so enamored of the idea of my marriage being a revelation of God's redemption in this area that I originally planned for my bridesmaids each to wear one of the colors of the liturgical church year and for Tim and I to mime the roles of Christ and his bride, the Church. Arguing that many guests would not perceive the symbolism and that the truths I wished to convey were best exhibited over the course of day-to-day living as a married couple, my mother persuaded me to go with the more usual one-style-flatters-no-one bridesmaids dresses, and Tim and his groomsmen were all attired in matching brown tuxedos. I am still not convinced that mine would not have been at least as good a choice.

29. Elisabeth Elliot, from whom I first learned to understand gender roles as a gift rather than a curse or an embarrassment, spoke from experience with several different cultures. When she lived among the Auca Indians of Equador, after they murdered her husband and four other missionaries, she noted that the idea of the "masculine" in Auca culture included the writing of poetry and a dedication to the decorative arts. Women, as the ones responsible for the nurture of the family, oversaw the gathering of roots and berries and rudimentary agriculture.

CHAPTER SEVEN – SINGLENESS AND MARRIAGE

1. This chapter 1 Corinthians 7 quote is often referenced in Christian discussions of marriage and singleness. However, it poses many exegetical challenges. Here I follow the lead of two commentaries— Roy Ciampa and Brian Rosner, *The First Letter to the Corinthians* (Grand Rapids, MI: Eerdmans, 2010); and Anthony Thistelton, *The First Epistle to the Corinthians* (Grand Rapids, MI: Eerdmans, 2000). In verses 25–38, Paul gives extended counsel for single adults in "complex urban settings" (Ciampa and Rosner, 328). The basic argument is this: Paul says that singleness is a good state, even a better state in some circumstances. Those circumstances are these:

    1) In verses 25–28, he teaches that singleness is especially good if there is a temporary time of crisis. Paul says that many people are wise to refrain from marriage during the "present distress" (26).

Thistelton, Ciampa, and Rosner all argue that this phrase is most often employed to refer to temporary periods of crisis, such as famine or war or other times of social upheaval. This explains why in Paul's pastoral guidance for the Corinthians he seems somewhat less supportive of marriage than he does in his other writings.

2) In verses 29–31, he argues that singleness is good because "the time is short" and "this world is passing away." Paul's meaning here is that because this present world will someday give way to God's new heavens and new earth, we do not need to cling to worldly sources of security like money, family, and heirs. Many people are driven into marriage out of a deep need for security that should only be found in God. Because this world will pass away, we should not marry out of such desperation. Therefore, he hints, singleness can help you refrain from putting too much spiritual hope in the things of this world, such as money, investments, homes, and social status.

3) In verses 32–35, Paul teaches that there are advantages that singles have in spreading the gospel and doing God's work of ministry. Family life necessarily absorbs us and directs large amounts of our time and attention onto a small number of people. Single life can free you to serve and minister to more people. And, Paul argues, that is one more reason to remain single if you can.

2. There is now such an overwhelming consensus about this Biblical teaching that it is hard to give any one or two bibliographic sources. Some of the most prominent works include Oscar Cullman, *Christ and Time: The Primitive Christian Conception of Time and History* (Philadelphia: Westminster, 1962); and Herman Ridderbos, *The Coming of the Kingdom* (Philadelphia: Presbyterian and Reformed, 1962) and *Paul: An Outline of His Theology* (Grand Rapids, MI: Eerdmans, 1997).

3. A related passage is Colossians 3:1–3, where Paul writes, "Since, then, you have been raised with Christ, set your hearts on things above, where Christ is seated at the right hand of God. Set your minds on things above, not on earthly things. For you died, and your life is now hidden with Christ in God. When Christ, who is

your life, appears, then you also will appear with him in glory."
Here Paul says that nothing on earth is "your life." You may have
wealth, success, family—but your safety, hope, and identity are now
"hidden in Christ" because you are united with him by faith. Therefore, our minds are "not set on earthly things." It cannot mean that
we take no thought to savings, family life, marriage, and ordinary
life of eating, playing, working. It means that our hearts and minds
don't find their ultimate rest and hope in those things.

4. Stanley Hauerwas, *A Community of Character* (South Bend, IN:
   University of Notre Dame Press, 1991), 174.

5. Rodney Stark, *The Rise of Christianity: A Sociologist Reconsiders
   History* (Princeton, NJ: Princeton University Press, 1996), 104.

6. "We must remember that the 'sacrifice' made by singles was not
   [just in] 'giving up sex' but in giving up heirs. There could be no
   more radical act than that! This was a clear expression that one's
   future is not guaranteed by the family, but by the [kingdom of God
   and the] church. . . ." (Hauerwas, *A Community of Character*, 190).
   "[Now] *both* singleness and marriage are symbolic institutions for
   the constitution of the church's witness of the kingdom. Neither
   can be valid without the other. If singleness is a symbol of the
   church's confidence in God's power to convert lives for the growth
   of the church, marriage, and procreation is the symbol of the
   church's hope for the world." (Hauerwas, 191)

7. Paige Benton Brown, "Singled Out by God for Good." Available
   several places on the Internet, including www.pcpc.org/ministries/
   singles/singledout.php.

8. It would be natural to ask, if (as we laid out in chapter 6) we believe
   in the principle of male headship in Christian marriage, how does
   headship play out in relationships in the church between men and
   women? The answer is twofold. First, if a church has only male
   elders and pastors, that expresses the male headship principle, and
   both men and women corporately live out the principles of servant-
   leadership in community. Second, however, I think we must guard
   against the possible assertion that in the church every individual
   man should express leadership over every individual woman in some

way. C. S. Lewis points out in a little essay called "Equality" why it is so important *not* to expect or encourage every women to submit/defer to every man in general in society. He says we have to take seriously the reality of the Fall. In a sinful, broken world, authority is constantly abused. Genesis 3 says specifically that men will tend to tyrannize women due to sin (cf. 3:16). So Lewis argues that we must support the concept of equal rights and justice for every citizen, every person, regardless of sex, as a hedge against the abuse of power that would otherwise run rampant. (C. S. Lewis, "Equality" in *Present Concerns* [London: Fount, 1986].) This is a very Biblical, Christian perspective that takes seriously the Fall in Genesis 3. We should discourage Christian men from implying or expecting that as a man in any situation, formal or informal, he should just be given the leadership—whether it is a committee or a group of friends deciding where to go next.

9. This refers to an extensive number of passages in the New Testament that describe the kind of mutual ministry that all Christians are to have with all other Christians. The categories are these: affirming one another's strengths, abilities and gifts (Romans 12:10; James 5:9; Romans 12:3–6); affirming one another's equal importance in Christ (Romans 15:7:1 Corinthians 12:25; 1 Peter 5:5); affirming one another through visible affection (Romans 16:16; James 1:19; 1 Thessalonians 3:12); sharing one another's space, goods, and time (Romans 12:10; 1 Thessalonians 5:15; 1 Peter 4:9); and sharing one another's needs and problems (Galatians 6:2; 1 Thessalonians 5:11).

Also: sharing one another's beliefs, thinking, and spirituality (Romans 12:16; Colossions 3:16; 1 Corinthians 11:33; Ephesians 5:19); serving one another through accountability (James 5:16; Romans 15:14; Hebrews 3:13; Ephesians 4:25); serving one another through forgiveness and reconciliation (Ephesians 4:2,32; Galatians 5:26; Romans 14:19; James 4:11; Matthew 5:23ff; 18:15ff); and serving one another's interests rather than our own (Romans 14:9; Hebrews 10:24; Galatians 5:13; Romans 15:1–2).

10. I am often asked why it is that in big cities, where there are churches filled with singles, there isn't more success in seeking and finding marriage. I think there are at least three answers. The first reason is the power of the culture. The contemporary approach to hooking up or dating is 1) dating is simply for fun, sex, and maybe social status, while 2) seeking marriage is optional, only for the brave, and when it is done it is only for risk-free personal fulfillment, sex, and career. Christians may realize that their dating relationships should be different, but the culture is powerful and tends to shape our behavior. These cultural influences have led to fewer marriages in society and, if adopted, will lead to fewer marriages in the church. Second, some people simply have temperaments that highly value individual freedom and autonomy. Disproportionate numbers of these people are attracted to big cities. There they can construct their own lives and lifestyles free from the constraints and expectations put on them in most of the rest of the world. They feel stifled by the loss of freedom that marriage will bring. Third, dating and marriage have always been frightening prospects for a significant percentage of every generation. In more traditional settings, singles get significant support and guidance (and some pressure to marry!) from the surrounding community—which consists mainly of married couples—and the general culture. But most of that communal and cultural support in big cities is lacking.

11. Paige Benton Brown, *op. cit.*

12. Lauren Winner, "The Countercultural Path" in *Five Paths to the Love of Your Life*, ed. A. Chediak (Colorado Springs, CO: NavPress, 2005). Winner gives us a brief social history of dating based largely on Beth L. Bailey, *From Front Porch to Back Seat: Courtship in Twentieth Century America* (Baltimore: Johns Hopkins University Press, 1989).

13. Bailey, *Front Porch*, 15–20, cited in Winner, "Countercultural Path," 22.

14. Bailey, *Front Porch*, 16.

15. Benoit Denizet-Lewis, "Friends, Friends with Benefits and the Benefits of the Local Mall," *New York Times Magazine,* May 30, 2004.

This article has been reprinted with slight changes as a chapter called "Whatever Happened to Teen Romance?," *American Voyeur: Dispatches from the Far Reaches of Modern Life*, ed. Denizet-Lewis (New York: Simon and Schuster, 2010).

16. See Lauren Winner's interesting take on modern *shidduch* dating ("Countercultural Path," 17–9). Or see a generic description of the practice at http://en.wikipedia.org/wiki/Shidduch.

17. Winner, "Countercultural Path," 25.

18. Ibid., 17ff. Winner is speaking of a fictional couple from a novel *The Outside World* by Tova Mirvis (New York: Knopf, 2004).

19. "The issue is not whether an individual has some elusive gift of celibacy, but whether he or she can concentrate on living a life worthy of the gospel to the glory of God without being distracted by sexual desires" (Ciampa and Rosner, *Corinthians*, 285).

20. Winner, "Counterculture Path," 45.

21. Ciampa and Rosner, *Corinthians*, 289

22. Winner, "Counterculture Path," 38.

23. The concept of not having sex before marriage is unthinkable to most young adults. However, once the Christian concept (see chapter 8) is grasped and accepted, the natural questions are, "Are we able to express physical intimacy even though we are not going to have intercourse? What ways of expressing intimacy are appropriate?" Lauren Winner tells how she and her future husband asked their campus minister that question, and he quipped, "Don't do anything sexual that you wouldn't be comfortable doing on the steps of the Rotunda" (the building at the heart of the University of Virginia's campus). The couple decided that this practical guidance made a lot of sense. Indeed, one time they went up onto the steps of the Rotunda and kissed passionately to their hearts content, but, they noted, they didn't feel comfortable taking their clothes off. That was their answer (Winner, "Counterculture Path," 30).

24. Winner, "Counterculture Path," 32–3.

Chapter Eight – Sex and Marriage

1. In the 1940s, C. S. Lewis wrote that in sophisticated British and European circles, the thinking about sex was this: "Sexual desire is in the same state as any of our other natural desires and if only we abandon the silly old Victorian idea of hushing it up, everything in the garden will be lovely" (*Mere Christianity*, 97–8). Lewis, however, retorts: "It is not true." He argues that sex may be an appetite, but it is not in the same vein as our appetite for food.

   "You can get a large audience together for a strip-tease act—that is, to watch a girl undress on the stage. Now suppose you come to a country where you could fill a theater by simply bringing a covered plate onto the stage and then slowly lifting the cover so as to let every one see, just before the lights when out, that it contained a mutton chop or a bit of bacon. Would you not think that in that country something had gone wrong with the appetite for food? One critic said that if he found a country in which such strip-tease acts were popular, he would conclude that the people of that country were starving." (*Mere Christianity*, 96).

2. Dan B. Allender and Tremper Longman, *Intimate Allies: Rediscovering God's Design for Marriage and Becoming Soulmates for Life* (Wheaton, IL: Tyndale, 1999), 254.

3. Essayist and critic Wendell Berry, in his book *Sex, Economy, Freedom, and Community* (New York: Pantheon, 1994), takes aim at a premise beneath much of today's hostility to the Christian ethic—namely, the assumption that sex is private, and what I do in the privacy of my bedroom with another consenting adult is strictly my own business. Thinkers like Berry retort that this claim appears on the surface to be broad minded but is actually very dogmatic. That is, it is based on a set of philosophical assumptions that are not neutral at all but semi-religious and have major political implications. In particular, it is based on a highly individualistic understanding of human nature. Berry writes, "Sex is not, nor can it be any individual's 'own business,' nor is it merely the private concern of any couple.

Sex, like any other necessary, precious, and volatile power that is commonly held, is everybody's business . . ." (p. 119).

Communities occur only when individuals voluntarily out of love bind themselves to each other, curtailing their own freedom. In the past, sexual intimacy between a man and a woman was understood as a powerful way for two people to bind themselves to stay together and build a family. Sex, Berry insists, is the ultimate "nurturing discipline." It is a "relational glue" that creates the deep oneness and therefore stability in the relationship that not only is necessary for children to flourish but is crucial for local communities to thrive. The most obvious social cost to sex outside marriage is the enormous spread of disease and the burden of children without sufficient parental support. The less obvious but much greater cost is the exploding number of developmental and psychological problems among children who do not live in stable family environments for most of their lives. Most subtle of all is the sociological fact that what you do in private shapes your character, and that affects how you relate to others in society. When people use sex for individual recreation and fulfillment, it weakens the entire body politic's ability to live for others. You learn to commodify people and think of them as a means to satisfy your own passing pleasure. It turns out that sex is not just your business; it's everybody's business.

4. We might paraphrase Paul's statement this way: "Don't you know that the purpose of sex is always 'one flesh'—to become united to another person in every area of life? Is that what you are seeking with the prostitute? Of course not—so don't have sex with her."

5. D. S. Bailey, *The Man-Woman Relation in Christian Thought* (London: Longmans, Green, 1959), 9–10.

6. An important new book by Mark Regnerus and Jeremy Uecker, *Premarital Sex in America: How Young Americans Meet, Mate, and Think about Marrying* (Oxford, 2011) provides a wealth of empirical research that supports many of the contentions and claims we have been making (especially in chapters 1, 7, and 8) about the

mistaken beliefs of young adults regarding sex and marriages. The book's last chapter makes a list of "Ten Myths about Sex and Relationships" that are commonly believed by young adults in America, despite the fact that the "evidence supporting them just isn't there" (p. 240). These myths include: (1) "The Introduction of sex is necessary to sustain a fledgling or struggling relationship" (p. 242). On the contrary, the authors point to the empirical fact that the sooner a relationship becomes sexual, the greater the chances for a breakup. (2) "Porn won't affect your relationships" (p. 246). The authors argue that pornography "now affects virtually everyone's relationships." People who use it can experience crushingly unrealistic expectations regarding physical appearance and sexual performance. But Regnerus and Uecker go further and demonstrate how pornography is now affecting everyone's relationships whether they use it personally or not. A significant number of male porn-users experience a diminished desire for the difficulties of real relationships and marriage, and this shrinks the marriage pool for women. And all women, they argue, are increasingly being forced to accommodate their sex behavior to the images and style of porn. (3) "Sex need not mean anything" (p. 247). [It's possible to have sex without making a big deal about it.] The writers say that a certain percentage of men can have sex without much emotional involved and commitment. And increasing numbers of women, in the name of equality, have sought to have sex as many men have, but in chapter 5 the authors make the case that few women can or want to achieve this level of detachment. (4) "Moving in together is definitely a step toward marriage" (p. 249). In general, people who cohabit before marriage are *more* likely to divorce, and the authors show, cohabitation does not usually lead to marriage. Despite these statistics, young adults persist in the belief that living together helps relationships develop well. "Those [cohabitations] that conclude with marriage lend credibility to the popular narrative about its wisdom, while those that simply end become ignored or forgotten."

7. "The marked mutuality of Paul's comments (the husband has authority over his wife's body, and she has authority over his), was,

however, revolutionary in the ancient world where patriarchy was the norm. . . . [it] clearly pointed to a radical and unprecedented restriction on the husband's sexual freedom. To our knowledge, the only other place a similar thought is recorded prior to Paul is in the poetic notes of mutual belonging in the Song of Solomon (2:16a; 6:3a; 7:10a): 'I am my beloved's and he is mine.' " (Ciampa and Rosner, *Corinthians*, 280–1).

8. Quotes in this paragraph are from Ciampa and Rosner, *Corinthians*, 278–9.

Epilogue

1. Many have pointed out that this passage looks back to Jesus girding himself to serve his disciples and wash their feet (John 13), but it may have a clearer connection to the astonishing promise of Jesus that at the Final Banquet at the end of history, he will gird himself to serve us and meet our deepest longings with his infinite power (Luke 12:37).

2. Simone Weil, *Waiting for God* (New York: Harper, 2009), 27.

3. Ibid. This subjective experience changed Weil's understanding of the world. In her "Spiritual Autobiography" (contained in the volume *Waiting for God*) she recounted how in her youth she had considered the existence of God an unsolvable philosophical problem. She could not find enough hard evidence or arguments to either prove that there was a God or prove that there was not. But, she wrote, "I had never foreseen the possibility of that, of a real contact, person to person, here below, between a human being and God . . ." (p. 27).

Appendix

1. 1 Corinthians 11:3.

ACKNOWLEDGMENTS

As always, I am grateful to David McCormick and Brian Tart, whose editorial and literary skills continue to make my writing possible. I also thank Janice Worth as well as Tim and Mary Courtney Brooks, who made it possible for Kathy and me to get away to finish the book. A thank-you also goes to Jennifer Chan, Michael Keller, Martin Bashir, Scott Kauffmann, and John and Sarah Nicholls, who read and commented on the manuscript before it was published.

A huge thanks to Laurie Collins, who first transcribed the tapes into hard copy; also to Marion Gengler Melton, who did another version—and anyone else who gave us hard copy in the hopes it would result in a book.

Thanks also to Susie Case and Dianne Garda, who funded/worked on Laurie's transcriptions. Though my rambling expository style defeated the attempt, it was a noble sally.

Over the years, we have been encouraged by many people who have listened to the 1991 sermons that used to be called simply "The Marriage Tapes." For a long time, listeners have written us or called us and urged us to put the substance of those recordings into a book. Thanks to all of you who nagged us so lovingly toward getting this thing written. Here it is!

Acknowledgments

Finally, we are so grateful for those named in the book's dedication, whose years of friendship and of navigating our marriages together have borne fruit in all our lives. Much of that hard-won wisdom appears in various forms in this volume. Thanks for all you mean to Kathy and me, friends.

ABOUT THE AUTHORS

Timothy Keller was born and raised in Pennsylvania and educated in Bucknell University, Gordon-Conwell Theological Seminary, and Westminster Theological Seminary. He was first a pastor in Hopewell, Virginia. In 1989 he started the Redeemer Presbyterian Church, in New York City, with his wife, Kathy, and their three sons. Today, Redeemer has more than five thousand regular Sundy attendees and has helped to start nearly two hundred new churches around the world. Also the author of *Generous Justice, Counterfeit Gods, The Prodigal God, King's Cross,* and *The Reason for God.* Timothy Keller lives in New York City with his family.

Kathy Keller grew up outside Pittsburgh, Pennsylvania, and attended Allegheny College, where she led Christian fellowship groups, before attending Gordon-Conwell Theological Seminary. She met Timothy Keller while studying there, and they were married at the beginning of their final semester. She received her MA in Theological Studies at Gordon-Conwell in 1975. Kathy and Tim then moved to Virginia, where Tim started at his first church, West Hopewell Presbyterian Church, and their three sons were born. After nine years. Kathy and her family moved to New York City to start the Redeemer Presbyterian Church.

REDEEMER

The Redeemer imprint is dedicated to books that address pressing spiritual and social issues of the day in a way that speaks to both the core Christian audience and to seekers and skeptics alike. The mission for the Redeemer imprint is to bring the power of the Christian gospel to every part of life. The name comes from Redeemer Presbyterian Church in New York City, which Tim Keller started in 1989 with his wife, Kathy, and their three sons. Redeemer has begun a movement of contextualized urban ministry, thoughtful preaching, and church planting across America and throughout major world cities.